MARY WOLLSTONECRAFT

(From a picture by Opie)

Frontispiece Portrait of Mary Wollstonecraft (engraved from a
picture by John Opie) accompanying Eliza Lynn Linton's
essay on Wollstonecraft in *The English Republic* (1854).
By permission of The British Library (8008c27 p419).

A Routledge Literary Sourcebook on

Mary Wollstonecraft's
A Vindication of the
Rights of Woman

This sourcebook provides the first interdisciplinary guide to the founding text of
modern feminism, Mary Wollstonecraft's *A Vindication of the Rights of Woman*
(1792). The sourcebook covers the evolving reception of this landmark work over
the last two hundred years, while tracing the development of the modern wom-
en's movement and exploring the full historical significance of Wollstonecraft's
argument in her context.

In addition to closely annotated key passages of the *Rights of Woman*, this
sourcebook includes a wealth of primary and secondary material in three areas:
Contexts, including key letters by Wollstonecraft and her most important influ-
ences; Nineteenth-Century Responses, tracing the reception of the text from the
Romantic through to the Victorian period; Twentieth-Century Responses, which
are essays by leading political, feminist, and literary theorists, and historians, on
specific aspects of the text, such as slavery, sexuality, religion, and sensibility.
Additional features such as a contextual chronology of Wollstonecraft and her
times, as well as an annotated reading list and substantial introductory materials,
make this the most up-to-date and thorough guide available.

This essential guide not only contributes to the understanding of Wollstonecraft's role in the development of the women's movement, but also allows readers
to gain a deeper understanding of British literature and politics at the turn of the
nineteenth century, of the Romantic movement, and of the origins of feminism.

Adriana Craciun directs the Centre for Byron Studies at the University of
Nottingham. She has published on Wollstonecraft, Mary Robinson, Mary Lamb,
and Charlotte Dacre and has edited Dacre's *Zofloya, or The Moor* (1997) and
co-edited *Rebellious Hearts: British Women Writers and the French Revolution*
(2001). Her book *Fatal Women of Romanticism* is forthcoming (2002).

Routledge Literary Sourcebooks

Series Editor: Duncan Wu, St Catherine's College, Oxford University

Also available are Routledge Literary Sourcebooks on:
E. M. Forster's *A Passage to India* edited by Peter Childs
Mary Shelley's *Frankenstein* edited by Timothy Morton

Forthcoming titles are:
The Poems of John Keats edited by John Strachan
William Shakespeare's *Othello* edited by Andrew Hadfield
William Shakespeare's *The Merchant of Venice* edited by Susan Cerasano
William Shakespeare's *King Lear* edited by Grace Ioppolo
The Poems of W. B. Yeats edited by Michael O'Neill

A Routledge Literary Sourcebook on

Mary Wollstonecraft's *A Vindication of the Rights of Woman*

Edited by Adriana Craciun

London and New York

First published 2002
by Routledge
11 New Fetter Lane, London EC4P 4EE

Simultaneously published in the USA and Canada
by Routledge
29 West 35th Street, New York, NY 10001

Routledge is an imprint of the Taylor & Francis Group

Typeset in Sabon by RefineCatch Limited, Bungay, Suffolk
Printed and bound in Great Britain by
TJ International, Padstow, Cornwall

British Library Cataloguing in Publication Data
A catalogue record for this book is available from the British Library

Library of Congress Cataloging in Publication Data
A Routledge literary sourcebook on Mary Wollstonecraft's *A vindication
of the rights of woman* / edited by Adriana Craciun.
     p.   cm.—(Routledge literary sourcebooks)
   Includes bibliographical references and index.
     ISBN 0–415–22735–6—ISBN 0–415–22736–4 (pbk.)
       1. Wollstonecraft, Mary, 1759–1797. Vindication of the rights of
woman. 2. Wollstonecraft, Mary, 1759–1797—Criticism and interpretation.
3. Women's rights—Great Britain.   4. Women—Education—Great Britain.
5. Women's rights in literature.   I. Craciun, Adriana, 1967–   .   II. Series.

HQ1596.R68   2002
305.42′0941—dc21   2001048678

ISBN 0–415–22735–6 (hbk)
ISBN 0–415–22736–4 (pbk)

for Kari Lokke

Poetry will no longer give rhythm to action; it *will be in advance*.
And there will be poets like this! When the eternal slavery of
Women is destroyed, when she lives for herself and through
herself, when man – up till now abominable – will have set her free,
she will be a poet as well! Woman will discover the unknown!
                    –Arthur Rimbaud, letter to Paul Demeny, 1871

Contents

Series Editor's Preface   xii
Acknowledgments   xiii

Introduction   I

I : Contexts

Contextual Overview   7

Chronology   12

Contemporary Documents   17

Sources of *A Vindication of the Rights of Woman*   17

Jean-Jacques Rousseau, from *Emile, or On Education* (1762)   17
Catharine Macaulay, *Letters on Education* (1790)   22

Letters by Wollstonecraft   23

To Catharine Macaulay Graham, 1790, on women   23
To Mary Hays, 1792, on publishing   24
To Gilbert Imlay, 1794, on imagination   25
To Gilbert Imlay, 1795, on sex and sentiment   27
To William Godwin, 1796, on her writing   28
To Amelia Alderson (Opie), 1797, on marriage   29

2: Interpretations

Critical History   33

Nineteenth-Century Responses   39

Romantic-Period Responses and Reviews   39

Review of *Rights of Woman* in *Monthly Review* (1792)   39
Thomas Taylor, *A Vindication of the Rights of Brutes* (1792)   40
Anna Laetitia Barbauld, "The Rights of Woman" (comp. *c*.1792, pub. 1825) 41
William Godwin, *Memoirs of the Author of A Vindication of the Rights of
Woman* (1798)   42
Richard Polwhele, *The Unsex'd Females* (1798)   44
Robert Bisset, Review of Godwin's *Memoirs, Anti-Jacobin Review* (1798) 46
Mary Robinson, *A Letter to the Women of England on the Injustice of Mental
Subordination* (1799)   47
Anne Grant, *Letters from the Mountains* (1807)   48
Mary Hays, "Memoirs of Mary Wollstonecraft" (1800)   49
William Blake, "Mary" (1801–5)   50
Anonymous, *A Defence of the Character and Conduct of the Late Mary
Wollstonecraft Godwin* (1803)   52
William Beloe, "Mary Wollstonecraft," *The Sexagenarian* (1818)   53

Victorian and Early Twentieth-Century Responses   54

Elizabeth Barrett Browning, "Fragment of an 'Essay on Woman'" (*c*.1821) 54
Eliza Lynn Linton, "Mary Wollstonecraft," *The English Republic* (1854) 55
Harriet Martineau, *Harriet Martineau's Autobiography* (1877)   56
Mathilde Blind, "Mary Wollstonecraft," *New Quarterly Magazine* (1878)   57
Millicent Garrett Fawcett, "Introduction to the New Edition" of *Rights of
Woman* (1890)   58
Emma Goldman, "Mary Wollstonecraft: Her Tragic Life and Her Passionate
Struggle for Freedom" (1911)   59
Virginia Woolf, "Mary Wollstonecraft," *The Second Common Reader* (1932) 60

Twentieth-Century Responses   62

Wollstonecraft's Political and Social Arguments   62

Wollstonecraft's Dilemma: Equality vs. Difference, Carole Pateman   62
Wollstonecraft and Liberal Individualism, Virginia Sapiro   63
Wollstonecraft and Separate-Spheres Ideology, Linda Colley   65
Wollstonecraft and Sensibility, G.J. Barker-Benfield   67
Wollstonecraft and Slavery, Moira Ferguson   69

Wollstonecraft and Religion, Daniel Robinson   71
Wollstonecraft and Nationalism, Jan Wellington   73

Wollstonecraft on the Body and Sexuality   **75**

Wollstonecraft and Self-Control, Mary Poovey   75
Wollstonecraft and Sexuality, Cora Kaplan   76
Wollstonecraft and (Anti)Commercialism, Harriet Guest   77
Wollstonecraft and Sexual Distinction, Claudia Johnson   79
Wollstonecraft and Physical Abuse, Carol Poston   80
Wollstonecraft and Physical Strength, Adriana Craciun   82

Wollstonecraft and Literary Traditions   **84**

Wollstonecraft's Early Reception, Regina Janes   84
Wollstonecraft as Literary Critic, Mitzi Myers   86
Wollstonecraft's Discourse, Gary Kelly   88
Wollstonecraft and Imagination, John Whale   90

3: Key Passages

Introduction   **95**

Key Passages of *A Vindication of the Rights of Woman*   **101**

Hints   **161**

4: Further Reading

Recommended Editions of Wollstonecraft   **167**

Recommended Book-Length Studies of Wollstonecraft   **168**

Further Reading   **169**

Index   173

Series Editor's Preface

The Routledge Literary Sourcebook series has been designed to provide students with the materials required to begin serious study of individual literary works, all in a single volume. This includes an overview of the critical history of the work, including extracts from important critical debates of recent decades, and a selection of key passages from the text itself. Volume editors provide introductory commentaries and annotation for the reader's guidance. These handy books provide almost everything most students will need for the contextual and critical overview of literature expected in schools and universities today.

This aim is reflected in the structure of each Sourcebook. Section 1, "Contexts," provides biographical data in the form of an author chronology and contemporary documents relating to the author and his or her work. In Section 2, "Interpretations," the editor assembles extracts from the most influential and important criticism throughout the history of the work. In some cases this includes materials relating to performances or adaptations. The third section, "Key Passages," gathers together the essential episodes from the literary text connected by editorial commentary and annotation so as to relate them to ideas raised earlier in the volume. The final section offers suggestions for further reading, including recommended editions and critical volumes.

Annotation is a key feature of this series. Both the original notes from the reprinted texts and new annotations by the editor appear at the bottom of the relevant page. The reprinted notes are prefaced by their author's name in square brackets, e.g. [Robinson's note].

Routledge Literary Sourcebooks offer the ideal introduction to single literary works, combining primary and secondary materials, chosen by experts, in accessible form.

Duncan Wu

Acknowledgments

To Duncan Wu I am particularly grateful, for his enthusiasm, intellectual openness, and bracing confidence while seeing this book through to completion. While working on this project, I benefitted from the insights and conversation of many friends and colleagues, including James Chandler, Janette Dillon, Markman Ellis, Emma Francis, Dana Frank, Michael Gamer, Madelyn Gutwirth, Tracy Hargreaves, Ian Haywood, Anne Janowitz, Steve Jones, Anne Mellor, Máire ní Fhlathúin, Mary Peace, Rebecca Sammel, and Angela Smallwood. I particularly appreciate Jerome McGann's generosity and imagination. Like all those who work on Wollstonecraft, I am indebted to previous editors and scholars, notably Marilyn Butler, Gary Kelly, David Lorne Macdonald, Carol Poston, Virginia Sapiro, Kathleen Scherf, Ashley Tauchert, Claire Tomalin, Janet Todd, Ralph Wardle, and to all who agreed to allow their work to be excerpted for this sourcebook. To David Lorne Macdonald, Kevin Binfield, and Seth Schein I owe special thanks for their help in clarifying some of my annotations.

The amount and quality of editorial assistance from Routledge, I fear, may have spoiled me for future efforts. Liz Thompson in particular, Rosie Waters, and their staff worked patiently and thoroughly to improve the manuscript. Joanna Dodd provided helpful research and proofreading assistance at key stages. Closer to home, John Logan's seemingly endless store of patience, affection, and intellectual engagement simply made this book possible, and its editor happy. I remain grateful also for the affectionate support of Magdalena Craciun, Rodica and Aurel Dragut, and Nan and Bruce Parker. To Kari Lokke I owe the greatest debt, for the example of her feminist scholarship and practice, for her ongoing support and friendship, and for showing me how to find a wealth of new possibilities in Wollstonecraft and women writers of the Romantic period as a whole.

The following publishers, institutions, and individuals have kindly given permission to reprint materials.

ASSOCIATED UNIVERSITY PRESSES, for Adriana Craciun, "Violence Against Difference: Mary Wollstonecraft and Mary Robinson" in *Making History: Textuality and the Forms of 18th Century Culture*, ed. Greg Clingham (Bucknell Review 42.1), Bucknell University Press/Associated University Presses, 1997;

Mitzi Myers, "Sensibility and the Walk of Reason: Mary Wollstonecraft's Literary Review as Cultural Critique" in *Sensibility in Transformation*, ed. Syndy Conger. Associated University Presses, 1990.

BODLEIAN LIBRARY, for letters of Mary Wollstonecraft held in the Abinger Collection.

THE BRITISH LIBRARY, for engraving of Mary Wollstonecraft from a picture by Opie in *The English Republic* (1854), 8008c27, p. 419. Reprinted by permission of The British Library.

COLUMBIA UNIVERSITY PRESS, for Moira Ferguson, *Colonialism and Gender Relations from Mary Wollstonecraft to Jamaica Kincaid*. Copyright © 1993 Columbia University Press. Reprinted by permission of the publisher.

EIGHTEENTH-CENTURY FICTION, for Daniel Robinson, "Theodicy versus Feminist Strategy in Mary Wollstonecraft's Fiction". In *ECF* 9:2, January 1997.

FEMINIST STUDIES INC., for Alice Wexler, "Emma Goldman on Mary Wollstonecraft". In *Feminist Studies*, Volume 7, No. 1 (Spring 1981). Reproduced by permission of the publisher.

JOHNS HOPKINS UNIVERSITY PRESS, for R.M. Janes, "On the Reception of Mary Wollstonecraft's *A Vindication of the Rights of Woman*". In *Journal of the History of Ideas* 39 (1978), 293–302. Copyright © *Journal of the History of Ideas*, Inc. Reprinted by permission of the Johns Hopkins University Press.

MACMILLAN LTD., for Gary Kelly, *Revolutionary Feminism: The Mind and Career of Mary Wollstonecraft*. Published by Macmillan, 1982.

NATIONAL MUSEUMS AND GALLERIES ON MERSEYSIDE, for a British School image of Mary Wollstonecraft, WAG 1541. Reprinted by permission of the Board of Trustees of the National Museums and Galleries on Merseyside (Walker Art Gallery).

NEW YORK PUBLIC LIBRARY, for quotations from "Mary Wollstonecraft to Mary Hays" November 12, 1792 and "Mary Wollstonecraft to Mrs. Macaulay" December 1790. Reproduced with permission of Carl H. Pforzheimer Collection of Shelley and His Circle, The New York Public Library, Astor, Lenox, and Tilden Foundations.

PENN STATE UNIVERSITY PRESS, for Carol Poston, "Mary Wollstonecraft and the Body Politic" in *Feminist Interpretations of Mary Wollstonecraft*, ed. Maria Falco. Published by Penn State University Press, 1996. Reproduced by permission of the publisher.

ST MARTIN'S PRESS, for John Whale, "Preparations for Happiness: Mary Wollstonecraft and Imagination" in *Reviewing Romanticism*, ed. Philip Martin and Robin Jarvis. Copyright © 1992. Reprinted by permission of St Martin's Press, LLC.

SOCIETY OF AUTHORS, for Virginia Woolf, "Mary Wollstonecraft" in *The*

Second Common Reader. Published by Hogarth Press, 1965. Reproduced by permission of The Society of Authors as the Literary Representative of the Estate of Virginia Woolf, and in the United States of America by Harcourt Brace Inc., copyright © 1932 by Harcourt Brace Inc., and renewed 1960 by Leonard Woolf.

STATE UNIVERSITY OF NEW YORK PRESS, for Jan Wellington, "Blurring the Borders of Nation and Gender: Mary Wollstonecraft's Character Evolution" in *Rebellious Hearts: British Women Writers and the French Revolution*, ed. Adriana Craciun and Kari Lokke. Published by SUNY Press, 2001.

TAYLOR AND FRANCIS, for Harriet Guest, "The Dream of Common Language: Hannah More and Mary Wollstonecraft" in *Textual Practice* (1995), 9:2.

UNIVERSITY OF CHICAGO PRESS, for Mary Poovey, *The Proper Lady and the Woman Writer*, University of Chicago Press, 1984; Claudia Johnson, *Equivocal Beings: Politics, Gender & Sentimentality in the 1790s*, University of Chicago Press, 1995; G.J. Barker-Benfield, *The Culture of Sensibility: Sex and Society in Eighteenth Century Britain*, University of Chicago Press, 1992; Virginia Sapiro, *A Vindication of Political Virtue: the Political Theory of Mary Wollstonecraft*, University of Chicago Press, 1992.

UNIVERSITY OF PENNSYLVANIA, for Elizabeth Barrett Browning, "Fragment of 'An Essay on Woman'" (*c.*1821). Unpublished MS poem. Reproduced by permission of Elizabeth Barrett Browning Miscellaneous Manuscripts, Annenberg Rare Book and Manuscript Library, University of Pennsylvania.

VERSO, for Cora Kaplan, *Sea Changes: Essays in Culture and Feminism*. Published by Verso, 1986.

YALE UNIVERSITY PRESS, for Linda Colley, *Britons: Forging the Nation 1707–1837*. Yale University Press, 1992.

Figure 1 Portrait of Mary Wollstonecraft commissioned in 1791 by the abolitionist William Roscoe (artist unknown, British School). By permission of the Board of Trustees of the National Museums and Galleries on Merseyside (Walker Art Gallery, Liverpool).

Introduction

⌐Mary Wollstonecraft was "in advance of her age," ⌐"the herald of the demand not⌐
yet wholly conceded by all," according to one Victorian biographer.[1] Wollstonecraft's life and writings found their most appreciative audience in the future,
toward which her intellectual and political efforts were consistently directed.
Given her commitment to social reform, it is no surprise that for more than two
hundred years, feminists and radicals have seen Wollstonecraft as a formidable
precursor.

The turn of the nineteenth century witnessed an unprecedented number of
experiments in politics, science, and literature, in which revolutionary changes
were debated, enacted, or suppressed. William Wordsworth and Samuel T.
Coleridge's *Lyrical Ballads* (1798) announced that their poems were to be "considered as experiments," and, despite Robert Southey's damning review that "The
'experiment,' we think, has failed,"[2] *Lyrical Ballads* has long been regarded as
representative of the originality valued by Romanticism. Perhaps the most imaginative (and certainly the most famous) Romantic-period exploration of the dangers
to which this passion for experiment could lead is *Frankenstein* (1818), written by
the daughter of Mary Wollstonecraft and William Godwin, Mary Shelley.

In her memorial of Wollstonecraft, fellow feminist Mary Hays found much to
praise in Wollstonecraft's "passion for experiment," and the anonymous author
of the *Defence of the Character and Conduct of the Late Mary Wollstonecraft
Godwin* (1803) similarly lamented "the failure of her experiment." The boldness
of writings such as Wollstonecraft's *A Vindication of the Rights of Men* (1790) and
A Vindication of the Rights of Woman (1792), as well as her scandalous rejection
of the institution of marriage, drew about Wollstonecraft this aura of dangerous
philosophical and sexual experimentation, which many of her contemporaries

---

1 Charles Kegan Paul, *William Godwin, His Friends and Contemporaries*, 2 vols. (London, 1876), in
   *Lives of the Great Romantics III: Godwin, Wollstonecraft and Mary Shelley by their Con-
   temporaries*, vol. 2: *Wollstonecraft*, ed. Harriet Jump (London: Pickering & Chatto, 1999) 290,
   289.
2 Wordsworth, Advertisement to *Lyrical Ballads*, in Duncan Wu, ed., *Romanticism: An Anthology*,
   2nd edn (Oxford: Blackwell, 2000) 191; Southey, rev. of *Lyrical Ballads*, *Critical Review* 24 (1798),
   in Wu, *Romanticism*, 565.

feared in the repressive domestic climate of 1790s Britain. Even as late as the 1930s, Virginia Woolf praised Wollstonecraft's boldness but nevertheless remained subtly critical of her "last experiment," her use of a female midwife instead of a male doctor. In retrospect, it seems Wollstonecraft's choice of a female midwife for her second pregnancy, while not typical, was not unusually "experimental" for 1797 London, and was not directly responsible for her death.[3] Yet these dual connotations of experiment – suggesting both bold innovation and foolhardy disregard for common sense – would shape Wollstonecraft's posthumous reputation for two centuries.

This Routledge Literary Sourcebook traces *A Vindication of the Rights of Woman*'s reception over these two centuries, revealing its central role in the development of Anglo-American feminism. First published in 1792 by the radical publisher Joseph Johnson (who also published Thomas Paine and William Godwin), *Rights of Woman* went through three British editions in Wollstonecraft's lifetime, and numerous editions throughout the nineteenth century. The version used for the Key Passages of *Rights of Woman* here is the second edition published in Wollstonecraft's lifetime, in 1792. All modern editions follow the second edition as it seems most likely that the emendations made therein are Wollstonecraft's.[4]

This Sourcebook's four sections – Contexts, Interpretations, Key Passages, and Further Reading – are designed to introduce readers to the *Rights of Woman*'s significance both in its historical moment and as a central text in ongoing feminist and political traditions. The Contexts section supplements the *Rights of Woman*'s argument with Wollstonecraft's own letters on issues like marriage, sexuality, and the profession of writing. Her two main inspirations for writing the *Rights of Woman* are also excerpted here – Catharine Macaulay and Jean-Jacques Rousseau. While a number of early responses to the *Rights of Woman* are well known (such as Richard Polwhele's *The Unsex'd Females* (1798)), most of the Romantic-period responses included in the Interpretations section are not readily available to general readers (for example, the contrasting critiques of Anne Grant and William Beloe). Victorian responses to Wollstonecraft are also understudied and rarely discussed, thus the Victorian and early twentieth-century responses (including an unpublished poem by Elizabeth Barrett Browning and excerpts from leading feminists) offer a rare opportunity to follow Wollstonecraft's role in the development of the nineteenth century's diverse approaches to the "Woman Question."

Twentieth-century interpretations of the *Rights of Woman* have until recently

---

3   Vivien Jones, "The Death of Mary Wollstonecraft," *British Journal for Eighteenth-Century Studies* 20 (1997) 187–205.

4   The vast majority of the second edition's emendations are corrections of printer's errors and accidentals in the first. A number of substantive emendations are noted in footnotes to this Sourcebook. The changes made in the 1796 edition may or may not have been made by Wollstonecraft; Ulrich Hardt in his Critical Edition of the *Rights of Woman* argues that they are not hers (*A Critical Edition of Mary Wollstonecraft's A Vindication of the Rights of Woman*, ed. Ulrich Hardt (Troy, NY: Whitston, 1982)). The overall effect of the second edition's revisions is to convey Wollstonecraft's increased confidence as a writer and feminist; see Carol Poston and Janet Todd, "Some Textual Variations in the First Two Editions of *A Vindication of the Rights of Woman*," *Mary Wollstonecraft Journal* 2.2 (May 1974) 27–9.

been dominated by the 1970s and 1980s Anglo-American Marxist readings that also helped revive interest in Wollstonecraft's work as a whole. Yet this Sourcebook goes beyond the tradition established by these early readings by Cora Kaplan and Mary Poovey, which emphasized the perceived limitations of the *Rights of Woman*'s treatment of sexuality and reason. In addition to this early focus on the politics of sexuality in Wollstonecraft, this Sourcebook includes a broader range of interdisciplinary criticism, including writings by historians, philosophers, and feminist and literary theorists. Together, these modern interpretations place the *Rights of Woman* at the center of late eighteenth-century debates on citizenship, slavery, education, economics, religion, imagination, and sensibility, in addition to reaffirming its role in debates on sexual and republican politics.

When considered in these multiple dimensions, the *Rights of Woman*'s radicalness emerges clearly, as Jennifer Lorch has argued: "Wollstonecraft's feminism envisaged a reordering of society that would go well beyond the provision of equal opportunities to women and men within the existing structures."[5] In 1797, the year of her death, Wollstonecraft wrote to a friend about the consequences of such a radical experiment:

> Those who are bold enough to advance before the age they live in, and to throw off, by the force of their own minds, the prejudices which the maturing reason of the world will in time disavow, must learn to brave censure. We ought not to be too anxious respecting the opinions of others. – I am not fond of vindications. – Those who know me will suppose that I acted from principle.[6]

What a fitting self-evaluation for a woman (and author of two vindications) who believed in the perfectibility of reason, the immortality of the soul, the power of the mind, and the value of strong, persevering passion. In many ways, Wollstonecraft's daughter Mary Shelley[7] (whose birth caused Wollstonecraft's death) imagined the mother she never knew according to Wollstonecraft's own self-representations in quotations like that above. Like Wollstonecraft, Mary and Percy Shelley sought to "[think] and [to love] on a comprehensive scale," with what William Blake in his poem "Mary" called "conscious delight."[8] Wollstonecraft saw herself as "bold enough to advance before the age" in which she lived. In this respect she is thoroughly of her age (that is, Romantic), one reason that this vision of her persists in so many subsequent accounts, including this one.

---

5 Jennifer Lorch, *Mary Wollstonecraft: The Making of a Radical Feminist* (New York: St Martin's Press, 1990) 109.
6 *Collected Letters of Mary Wollstonecraft*, ed. Ralph Wardle (Ithaca: Cornell University Press, 1979) 413.
7 See Mary Shelley's "Life of Godwin" excerpted in *Lives of the Great Romantics III*, ed. Jump, 247–50.
8 See Mary Hays, "Mary Wollstonecraft," in *Lives of the Great Romantics III* vol. 2: 186, and William Blake (pp. 50–2).

1

Contexts

Contextual Overview

Throughout the nineteenth and twentieth centuries, Wollstonecraft's "life came to serve as a text for analysis by those who felt compelled to comment on the situation of women,"[1] from fellow travelers and conservative critics at the end of the eighteenth century, to Victorian suffragists and twentieth-century feminist theorists. Because Wollstonecraft's unusual life has remained central to the interpretation and reception of her writings, particularly the *Rights of Woman*, the circumstances of Wollstonecraft's life are relevant to any initial reading of her text. *Rights of Woman* was shaped by the author's experiences as daughter, pupil, teacher, governess, servant, writer, radical, philosopher, lover, wife, and mother – a larger range of experiences than typically available to middle-class women of that time, and one which helps account for the unprecedented political and philosophical ambitions of her polemic.

On 27 April 1759, Mary Wollstonecraft was born in Spitalfields, east London, into a prosperous middle-class family. Wollstonecraft's grandfather had been an upwardly mobile weaver and, when he died in 1765, he left one third of his estate to Mary's father, one third to her elder brother Ned, aged seven, and one third to a grown daughter from a previous marriage. Mary and her other three siblings received nothing, an early encounter with the system of primogeniture that she and fellow radicals would challenge in the 1790s. The family moved often, as Mary's father tried to live the life of the gentleman farmer with little success, first in Epping, then Barking, and finally in Beverley, Yorkshire, where she developed her love for the natural world that would inspire her spirituality, aesthetics, and politics. In Beverley she also met Jane Arden, with whom she shared a passionate friendship, more passionate on Mary's side than Jane's – her first of several disappointments with people who did not match the intensity of her attachment. Her letters to Jane revealed her father's drunkenness and physical abuse: Mary would sometimes sleep on her mother's doorstep to intervene in her father's drunken attacks.

Back in London in 1775, Mary fell in love with Fanny Blood. Godwin later

---

1   Virginia Sapiro, *A Vindication of Political Virtue: The Political Theory of Mary Wollstonecraft* (Chicago: University of Chicago Press, 1992) 277.

wrote that this meeting "bore a resemblance to the first encounter of Werther and Charlotte," with Mary playing the role of the desperate lover in Goethe's novel. As had happened with Jane Arden, and as would happen with Henry Fuseli and Gilbert Imlay, Wollstonecraft idealized the object of her affection, and dreamed of setting up scenes of domestic tranquility to compensate for the abuse and dis-harmony at home. She also demonstrated her characteristic resourcefulness by helping support Fanny's large and poor family.

The years 1784 and 1785 brought two crises: her sister Eliza, recently married, had a breakdown following the birth of her child, and Mary helped her flee from her husband. Fanny Blood also married at this time and left for Lisbon, where Mary followed to help with the birth of her child; she arrived in time to nurse Fanny on her deathbed, a loss from which she never fully recovered. Fanny's death, along with Eliza's flight and her own mother's unhappy marriage and death, deeply impressed upon Wollstonecraft the dangers and injustices resulting from women's economic dependence on men, and from the burden of repro-duction that they disproportionately bore. She developed a firm commitment to independence, one articulated most fully in *A Vindication of the Rights of Woman*: "Independence I have long considered as the grand blessing of life, the basis of every virtue" (**p. 102**).

Central to *Rights of Woman* are Wollstonecraft's views on education, which she developed from first-hand experience as a governess and while running her own school. Wollstonecraft had established two schools for girls in order to sup-port her sisters and Fanny Blood – the first in Islington in 1783, the second in Newington Green the following year. At Newington Green she met Rev. Richard Price, a leading Dissenter whose doctrines of perfectibility and reform shaped her thinking, and the radical publisher Joseph Johnson, who gave Wollstonecraft her first literary commission, publishing her *Thoughts on the Education of Daughters* in 1787. When the school failed, Wollstonecraft became a governess to one of the wealthiest families in Ireland, that of Lord and Lady Kingsborough. As a governess she gained valuable insight into the frivolous dissipation of the aristocracy, particularly its women, insight that she channeled into her occasion-ally unforgiving critique of women of leisure in *Rights of Woman*. Lady Kings-borough dismissed Wollstonecraft abruptly in 1787, setting the stage for Wollstonecraft's next transformation, and confirming her views on the aris-tocracy: "Thank heaven that I was not so unfortunate as to be born a Lady of quality," she wrote to her sister.[2]

Having failed at two of the few professions available to middle-class women at that time, Wollstonecraft now launched into her most successful attempt at self-sufficiency – as a professional woman of letters, "the first of a new genus" as she described herself.[3] Wollstonecraft had found in Joseph Johnson a seemingly

2   Mary Wollstonecraft to Everina Wollstonecraft, 24 March 1787, in *Collected Letters of Mary Wollstonecraft*, ed. Ralph Wardle (Ithaca: Cornell University Press, 1979) 145; hereafter *Letters*.
3   Mary Wollstonecraft, letter to Everina Wollstonecraft, 7 November 1787 (*Letters* 164). Her use of "genus," a term of biological classification, reveals Wollstonecraft's (and the eighteenth century's) interdisciplinary outlook, and specifically her keen interest in natural history.

indefatigable source of intellectual and financial support. He gave her a position editing and writing for his radical *Analytical Review*, and published all of her subsequent books and translations. The book that put Wollstonecraft on the political map was her reply to Edmund Burke's conservative *Reflections on the Revolution in France* (1790). She fired off her anonymous *Vindication of the Rights of Men* in November 1790, then published a second edition under her own name the following month. She was now a public intellectual, boldly entering the political fray alongside more seasoned radicals like Thomas Paine and the feminist historian Catharine Macaulay.

In 1790 Macaulay had published her feminist *Letters on Education*, arguing for co-education of boys and girls and maintaining that there is "no characteristic difference" between women's and men's intelligence, only differences in their education (excerpted **pp. 22–3**). By September 1791 Wollstonecraft was at work on her own manifesto on women's rights, which she claimed to have written in just six weeks. Taking on the leading male authorities on the nature and limitations of women, for example Rousseau and conduct-book writers like James Fordyce and John Gregory, Wollstonecraft launched into an impassioned critique of gender-based and class-based privilege. Expanding the revolutionary *Rights of Man* argument to include women, Wollstonecraft produced an original and timely manifesto that helped shape the evolving discourse on human rights. The portrait commissioned by William Roscoe (Figure 1) at this time gives us a glimpse of Wollstonecraft as Enlightenment philosopher, formal, serious, and deliberately unfeminine.

The most immediate catalyst for her argument was Jean-Jacques Rousseau, whose *Emile, or On Education* (1762) argued that men and women are essentially different, and thus require different educations:

> the whole education of women ought to relate to men. To please men, to be useful to them, to make herself loved and honored by them, to raise them when young, to care for them when grown, to counsel them, to console them, to make their lives agreeable and sweet – these are the duties of women at all times, and they ought to be taught from childhood.[4]

Macaulay had attacked precisely this model of female (mis)education in her *Letters on Education*, and an admiring Wollstonecraft wrote to Macaulay that "You are the only female writer who I coincide in opinion with respecting the rank our sex ought to endeavour to attain in the world" (**p. 24**). Rousseau's idea that women's lives should revolve around men was extremely influential, as evidenced by the conduct books of Fordyce and Gregory, which Wollstonecraft also singled out for criticism in chapter 5. Yet Rousseau was arguably the most important touchstone throughout her intellectual development, particularly on

---

4   Jean-Jacques Rousseau, *Emile, or On Education* (1762), trans. Allan Bloom (NY: Basic, 1979); see excerpt (**pp. 18–22**).

education; Wollstonecraft famously wrote to Imlay that "I have always been half in love with" Rousseau (p. 26). The vehemence of her critique in *Rights of Woman* reveals her disappointment over Rousseau's views on women, given her admiration for his earlier political writings, especially the *Social Contract* (1762) and *Discourse on Inequality* (1755).

Immersing herself in the leading philosophical debates of the day, Wollstonecraft thrived in Johnson's eclectic circle of artists, poets, and revolutionaries, which included William Blake, who illustrated two of her books, and William Godwin, who would become her husband. At Johnson's she also met and fell in love with the radical Swiss painter Henry Fuseli, whose painting "The Nightmare" (1782) captured the dark side of the Romantic period. Like Blake, whose poem "Mary" seems to reflect on the costs of Wollstonecraft's revolutionary life, Wollstonecraft believed that love and virtue should not be shackled by convention and hypocrisy. She proposed to Fuseli her radical experiment, that she should move in with him and his wife. When they declined, a heartbroken Wollstonecraft departed alone for revolutionary France on the eve of war with Britain.

Like most British at this time, Wollstonecraft associated the French with the superficial and dissipated sensibility of the aristocracy in general. Yet as Jan Wellington argues in her essay on Wollstonecraft and French character, in France Wollstonecraft began to appreciate more fully the importance of sensuality, sexuality, and pleasure. She attended Helen Maria Williams's famed Paris salons; Williams, whose many volumes of *Letters from France* were an important source of information on French politics for British readers, lived openly with the married republican Dissenter John Hurford Stone, and Wollstonecraft must have felt some affinity for this open-minded approach to sexuality and marriage. She fell in love with an American businessman, Gilbert Imlay, and by May 1794 had given birth to her first child, named Fanny after her deceased friend.

Wollstonecraft's volatile relationship with Imlay, and her resulting two suicide attempts in 1795 when he had moved in with another woman, dominated the reception of her works throughout the nineteenth century. Yet out of this deep unhappiness came Wollstonecraft's best works: her beautifully written *Letters Written During a Short Residence in Norway, Denmark, and Sweden* (1796), and the semi-autobiographical unfinished novel *The Wrongs of Woman, or Maria* (published posthumously in 1798). Wollstonecraft's letters to Imlay (excerpted **pp. 26–8**) were also published posthumously by Godwin, and reveal the passion and imagination that lie beneath the surface of the *Rights of Woman*.

Putting Imlay behind her, Wollstonecraft found happiness with the most notorious radical of the day, the author of the *Enquiry Concerning Political Justice* (1793), William Godwin. Agreed in their opposition to marriage as an oppressive institution, they only married in March 1797 when Wollstonecraft learned she was pregnant. During the day, they worked independently in nearby apartments, and corresponded through a constant stream of domestic and often flirtatious notes. Wollstonecraft enjoyed renewed productivity during this time, writing a new novel, several educational works, and an autobiographical comedic play, which Godwin afterwards destroyed. The marriage ironically led to Wollstonecraft's abandonment by friends and acquaintances because it signaled that she had not been married to Imlay as most people had assumed. Wollstonecraft's letter to Opie (**pp. 29–30**) reveals her awareness of the consequences of such unconventional actions; that Opie later published a novel (*Adeline Mowbray*, 1805) condemning Wollstonecraft and Godwin's relationship reveals the force of sexual propriety among erstwhile liberal thinkers like Opie.[5]

Ten days after she gave birth to Mary Wollstonecraft Godwin (later Shelley), Mary Wollstonecraft died of puerperal fever. A grief-stricken Godwin published his account of her life in 1798, the *Memoirs of the Author of a Vindication of the Rights of Woman*, revealing the details of her affair with Imlay (to whom most people had assumed she had been married) and of the suicide attempts, as a testament to the intensity of Wollstonecraft's capacity for love and of her commitment to her ideals. The gesture backfired disastrously, resulting in an antifeminist backlash that would engulf fellow feminists like Mary Hays and Mary Robinson, associating all those who spoke on behalf of the "Rights of Woman" with sexual and moral transgression.

---

5   Amelia Alderson Opie, *Adeline Mowbray*, ed. Shelley King and John Pierce (Oxford: Oxford University Press, 1999); on Wollstonecraft and Opie see Roxanne Eberle, "Amelia Opie's *Adeline Mowbray*: Diverting the Libertine Gaze; or, The Vindication of a Fallen Woman," *Studies in the Novel* 26.2 (1994) 121–52. For a modern novel about Wollstonecraft, see Frances Sherwood, *Vindication* (London: Phoenix, 1993).

Chronology

Bullet points are used to denote events in Wollstonecraft's life, and asterisks to denote historical and literary events.

1759
- MW born (27 Apr.) in Spitalfields, London
* Smith, *Theory of Moral Sentiments*; Burns born

1765
- Death of MW's grandfather; leaves estate to MW's father and brother

1768
- Family moves to Beverley, Yorkshire, where MW meets Jane Arden, and begins passionate friendship
* Sterne, *A Sentimental Journey*

1774
* Goethe, *The Sorrows of Young Werther* (translated into English 1779); Gregory, *A Father's Legacy to His Daughters*

1775
- Family moves to Hoxton, London; MW meets Fanny Blood, begins passionate friendship

1776
* 1776 American Revolutionary War begins; Smith, *Wealth of Nations*; Paine, *Common Sense*

1777
- Family moves to Walworth, London, so that MW can be close to Fanny Blood

1778
- MW works as lady's companion to Mrs Dawson, in Bath and Windsor
* Burney, *Evelina*

1780
- MW returns home to nurse her mother
* London Gordon Riots against Catholic rights

1782
- Death of MW's mother (19 Apr.); MW's younger sister Eliza marries Meredith Bishop (Oct.); MW moves in with Blood family; MW's father remarries
* Treaty of Paris ends American Revolutionary War; Burney, *Cecilia*; Fuseli, "The Nightmare"; Laclos, *Les Liasons dangereuses*

1783
- Birth of Eliza's daughter (Aug.); MW establishes school in Islington
* 1783 William Pitt becomes Prime Minister; Lee, *The Recess*; Godwin leaves Christian ministry

1784
- Eliza's post-partum depression (Jan.); MW moves in with Eliza, and then takes her out of Bishop household; MW, with Eliza, Everina, and Fanny Blood, move school to Newington Green; MW meets Richard Price; death of Eliza's daughter
* Samuel Johnson dies; Rousseau, *Julie; ou La Nouvelle Héloïse* (London translation); Smith, *Elegiac Sonnets*; Williams, *Peru*; Merry founds Society della Crusca in Florence

1785
- Fanny Blood marries Hugh Skeys in Lisbon (Feb.); MW goes to Portugal to help with birth of Fanny's child (Nov.); Fanny Blood Skeys dies
* Boswell, *Life of Johnson*; Warren Hastings resigns as Governor-General of India; Cowper, *The Task*

1786
- MW returns to London and closes failed school at Newington Green; meets radical publisher Joseph Johnson; hired as governess by Lord and Lady Kingsborough at Mitchelstown, County Cork, Ireland
* Beckford, *Vathek*; Burns, *Poems, Chiefly in the Scottish Dialect*

1787
- *Thoughts on the Education of Daughters* published by Johnson; MW dismissed by Kingsboroughs (Aug.) and returns to London. Begins work for Johnson and Christie's *Analytical Review*
* 1787 Committee for the Abolition of the Slave Trade founded

1788

- MW's first novel *Mary*, her children's book *Original Stories from Real Life* (illus. by Blake), and a translation from the French of *Of the Importance of Religious Opinions* (by Necker) are published by Johnson
* Parliamentary motion to abolish British slave trade; Estates General summoned in France; London Revolutionary Society formed; Saint-Pierre, *Paul and Virginia*; Kant, *Critique of Practical Reason*; More, *Slavery, A Poem*

1789

- MW's *The Female Reader*, an anthology, is published by Johnson; MW works on translations and reviews for *Analytical Review*
* Fall of Bastille (14 July); French Revolution begins; Richard Price, *Discourse on the Love of Our Country* (Nov.); mutiny on the HMS *Bounty*; slave trade resolutions introduced by Wilberforce; Blake, *Songs of Innocence*

1790

- MW translates (from the German) Salzmann's *Elements of Morality* (illus. by Blake) and (from the Dutch) de Cambon's *Young Grandison*; publishes *A Vindication of the Rights of Men*, anonymously (Nov.); second edition of *A Vindication of the Rights of Men* published under MW's name (Dec.)
* French Jews granted civil rights; first steam-powered mill; Burke, *Reflections on the Revolution in France* (Nov.); Macaulay, *Letters on Education*; Radcliffe, *A Sicilian Romance*; Williams, *Letters Written in France*; Wordsworth's first visit to France

1791

- MW begins writing *A Vindication of the Rights of Woman* (Sept.); meets William Godwin at Johnson's (Nov.); second edition of *Original Stories*; William Roscoe meets MW and commissions portrait (Figure 1)
* Legislative Assembly convenes in Paris; slave revolt in Santo Domingo (Haiti); Birmingham "Church and King" riots destroy Priestley's library; death of Richard Price; Paine, *Rights of Man* Part 1; Olympe de Gouges, *Déclaration des droits de la femme et de la citoyenne*

1792

- *A Vindication of the Rights of Woman* published by Johnson (January); meets Talleyrand (Feb.) and Mary Hays; crisis with Fuseli; leaves for Paris alone (Dec.); second edition of *Rights of Woman*
* Storming of Tuilleries in Paris; September Massacre in Paris turns British public opinion against Revolution; Etta Palm D'aers addresses French Legislative Assembly regarding women's rights; French divorce laws passed; Paine, *Rights of Man* Part 2

1793

- MW meets Gilbert Imlay in Paris and begins affair; MW becomes pregnant

(Aug.) and registers as Imlay's wife with American embassy to prevent being arrested (Sept.); MW meets Helen Maria Williams at her Paris salon

* Execution of Louis XVI (Jan.); France declares war on England (Feb.); Girondin faction in Paris purged (May); Charlotte Corday assassinates Marat and is executed (July); Reign of Terror begins; English in France are arrested; execution of Marie Antoinette, Olympe de Gouges and Madame Roland; women's political clubs in France banned; Godwin, *Enquiry Concerning Political Justice*

1794

• MW moves to Le Havre; birth of first child, Fanny Imlay (14 May); *An Historical and Moral View of the Origin and Progress of the French Revolution* published by Johnson

* Treason Trials of Hardy, Tooke, and Thelwall in London; death of Robespierre and end of Reign of Terror in France (July); *habeus corpus* suspended in Britain; Godwin, *Caleb Williams*; Paine, *The Age of Reason*; Radcliffe, *The Mysteries of Udolpho*

1795

• MW returns to London (April); first suicide attempt (May); in June goes to Scandinavia with Fanny and maid on secret business for Imlay; MW returns to London (Sept.) and finds Imlay living with another woman; second suicide attempt (Oct.); MW writes autobiographical comedy

* Two Acts in Britain passed prohibiting public meetings and "seditious" publications; first English horse-drawn railroad; the Directory comes to power in France; Sade, *Philosophy in the Bedroom*

1796

• *Letters Written During a Short Residence in Norway, Denmark and Sweden* published by Johnson (Jan.); MW calls on Godwin (14 Apr.); Godwin proposes to Amelia Alderson (Opie) and is refused; MW begins affair with Godwin (summer)

* Napoleon begins Italian campaign; Jenner develops smallpox vaccine; Robinson, *Sappho and Phaon*; Hays, *Memoirs of Emma Courtney*; Lewis, *The Monk*; Yearsley, *The Rural Lyre*

1797

• MW pregnant (Feb.); marries Godwin (29 Mar.); writes *The Wrongs of Woman; or Maria*; birth of second child, Mary Wollstonecraft Godwin (30 Aug.); MW dies of puerperal fever (10 Sept.)

* Radcliffe, *The Italian*; *Anti-Jacobin* journal started; Coleridge visits the Wordsworths

1798

• Godwin publishes *Memoirs of the Author of a Vindication of the Rights of Woman* and Wollstonecraft's *Posthumous Works*

*   Irish rebellion; France invades Switzerland; Nelson defeats French in Battle of the Nile; Malthus, *First Essay on the Principle of Population*; Polwhele, *The Unsex'd Females*; Wordsworth and Coleridge, *Lyrical Ballads*

Contemporary
Documents

Sources of *A Vindication of the Rights of Woman*

Jean-Jacques Rousseau, from *Emile, or On Education* (1762),
trans. and introduced by Allan Bloom (NY: Basic Books, 1979) 167–74.
From Book 5, "Sophie"

Wollstonecraft once described the French philosopher Rousseau (1712–78) as "a strange inconsistent unhappy clever creature" (*Letters* 145) and later in her life wrote to Imlay that "I have always been half in love with him" (*Letters* 263; included **p. 26**). He was arguably the most important touchstone throughout her intellectual development, particularly on education. The vehemence of her critique in *Rights of Woman* reveals her disappointment over his views on women, given her admiration for his political writings, especially the *Social Contract* (1762) and *Discourse on Inequality* (1755), and the Romantic *Confessions* (1781–8) and *Reveries of the Solitary Walker* (see her reviews in *Works of Mary Wollstonecraft* 7: 228–34, 362–3, 409). Wollstonecraft clearly felt an affinity with the French philosopher and his candid revelations of his struggle to balance passion and reason.

Yet the immediate and most significant object of attack in *Rights of Woman* is Rousseau's educational philosophy, as described in his immensely influential *Emile*. Rousseau asserted that men and women are essentially different, physically and intellectually, and that women are the inferior, passive, weak counterparts of men, whose pleasure and comfort they should study and aim to promote. Accordingly, women can only develop their influence over men, since they cannot aspire to power or representation as citizens of the public sphere; this influence they pursue through their physical beauty, charm, sexuality, and sensibility. This complementary and essentialist view of women increasingly dominated middle-class notions of "natural" female behavior throughout the late eighteenth century, as echoed in James Fordyce and John Gregory's conduct books (which Wollstonecraft also critiqued, **pp. 141** and **142**).

Sophie OR THE WOMAN

In everything not connected with sex, woman is man. She has the same organs, the same needs, the same faculties. The machine is constructed in the same way; its parts are the same; the one functions as does the other; the form is similar; and in whatever respect one considers them, the difference between them is only one of more or less.

In everything connected with sex, woman and man are in every respect related and in every respect different. The difficulty of comparing them comes from the difficulty of determining what in their constitutions is due to sex and what is not. On the basis of comparative anatomy and even just by inspection, one finds general differences between them that do not appear connected with sex. They are, nevertheless, connected with sex, but by relations which we are not in a position to perceive. We do not know the extent of these relations. The only thing we know with certainty is that everything man and woman have in common belongs to the species, and that everything which distinguishes them belongs to the sex. From this double perspective, we find them related in so many ways and opposed in so many other ways that it is perhaps one of the marvels of nature to have been able to construct two such similar beings who are constituted so differently.

These relations and these differences must have a moral influence. This conclusion is evident to the senses; it is in agreement with our experience; and it shows how vain are the disputes as to whether one of the two sexes is superior or whether they are equal – as though each, in fulfilling nature's ends according to its own particular purpose, were thereby less perfect than if it resembled the other more! In what they have in common, they are equal. Where they differ, they are not comparable. A perfect woman and a perfect man ought not to resemble each other in mind any more than in looks, and perfection is not susceptible of more or less.

In the union of the sexes each contributes equally to the common aim, but not in the same way. From this diversity arises the first assignable difference in the moral relations of the two sexes. One ought to be active and strong, the other passive and weak. One must necessarily will and be able; it suffices that the other put up little resistance.

Once this principle is established, it follows that woman is made specially to please man. If man ought to please her in turn, it is due to a less direct necessity. His merit is in his power; he pleases by the sole fact of his strength. This is not the law of love, I agree. But it is that of nature, prior to love itself.

If woman is made to please and to be subjugated, she ought to make herself agreeable to man instead of arousing him. Her own violence is in her charms. It is by these that she ought to constrain him to find his strength and make use of it. The surest art for animating that strength is to make it necessary by resistance. Then *amour-propre*[1] unites with desire, and the one triumphs in the victory that

---

[1]   Self-love, as distinguished from self-esteem (*l'amour de soi même*). See also note to **p. 152**.

the other has made him win. From this there arises attack and defense, the audacity of one sex and the timidity of the other, and finally the modesty and the shame with which nature armed the weak in order to enslave the strong.[2]

Who could think that nature has indiscriminately prescribed the same advances to both men and women, and that the first to form desires should also be the first to show them? What a strange depravity of judgment! Since the undertaking has such different consequences for the two sexes, is it natural that they should have the same audacity in abandoning themselves to it? With so great an inequality in what each risks in the union, how can one fail to see that if reserve did not impose on one sex the moderation which nature imposes on the other, the result would soon be the ruin of both and mankind would perish by the means established for preserving it? If there were some unfortunate region on earth where philosophy had introduced this practice – especially in hot countries, where more women are born than men – men would be tyrannized by women. For, given the ease with which women arouse men's senses and reawaken in the depths of their hearts the remains of ardors which are almost extinguished, men would finally be their victims and would see themselves dragged to death without ever being able to defend themselves. [. . .]

Whether the human female shares man's desires or not and wants to satisfy them or not, she repulses him and always defends herself – but not always with the same force or, consequently, with the same success. For the attacker to be victorious, the one who is attacked must permit or arrange it; for does she not have adroit means to force the aggressor to use force? The freest and sweetest of all acts does not admit of real violence. Nature and reason oppose it: nature, in that it has provided the weaker with as much strength as is needed to resist when it pleases her; reason, in that real rape is not only the most brutal of all acts but the one most contrary to its end – either because the man thus declares war on his companion and authorizes her to defend her person and her liberty even at the expense of the aggressor's life, or because the woman alone is the judge of the condition she is in; and a child would have no father if every man could usurp the father's rights.

Here, then, is a third conclusion drawn from the constitution of the sexes – that the stronger appears to be master but actually depends on the weaker. This is due not to a frivolous practice of gallantry or to the proud generosity of a protector, but to an invariable law of nature which gives woman more facility to excite the desires than man to satisfy them. This causes the latter, whether he likes it or not, to depend on the former's wish and constrains him to seek to please her in turn, so that she will consent to let him be the stronger. Then what is sweetest for man in his victory is the doubt whether it is weakness which yields to strength or the will which surrenders. And the woman's usual ruse is always to leave this doubt between her and him. In this the spirit of women corresponds perfectly to their constitution. Far from blushing at their weakness, they make it their glory. Their

---

2 In a section of chapter 3 of the *Rights of Woman* not included here, Wollstonecraft quoted the previous three paragraphs, adding: "I shall make no other comment on this ingenious passage, than just to observe, that it is the philosophy of lasciviousness."

tender muscles are without resistance. They pretend to be unable to lift the light-est burdens. They would be ashamed to be strong. Why is that? It is not only to appear delicate; it is due to a shrewder precaution. They prepare in advance excuses and the right to be weak in case of need. [. . .]

Observe how the physical leads us unawares to the moral, and how the sweetest laws of love are born little by little from the coarse union of the sexes. Women possess their empire not because men wanted it that way, but because nature wants it that way. It belonged to women before they appeared to have it. The same Hercules who believed he raped the fifty daughters of Thespitius was never-theless constrained to weave while he was with Omphale; and the strong Samson was not so strong as Delilah.[3] This empire belongs to women and cannot be taken from them, even when they abuse it. If they could ever lose it, they would have done so long ago.

There is no parity between the two sexes in regard to the consequences of sex. The male is male only at certain moments. The female is female her whole life or at least during her whole youth. Everything constantly recalls her sex to her; and, to fulfill its functions well, she needs a constitution which corresponds to it. She needs care during her pregnancy; she needs rest at the time of childbirth; she needs a soft and sedentary life to suckle her children; she needs patience and gentleness, a zeal and an affection that nothing can rebuff in order to raise her children. She serves as the link between them and their father; she alone makes him love them and gives him the confidence to call them his own. How much tenderness and care is required to maintain the union of the whole family![4] And, finally, all this must come not from virtues but from tastes, or else the human species would soon be extinguished.

The strictness of the relative duties of the two sexes is not and cannot be the same. When woman complains on this score about unjust man-made inequality, she is wrong. This inequality is not a human institution – or, at least, it is the work not of prejudice but of reason. It is up to the sex that nature has charged with the bearing of children to be responsible for them to the other sex. Doubtless it is not permitted to anyone to violate his faith, and every unfaithful husband who deprives his wife of the only reward of the austere duties of her sex is an unjust and barbarous man. But the unfaithful woman does more; she dissolves the fam-ily and breaks all the bonds of nature. In giving the man children which are not

3   Omphale and Delilah are two examples of how women's "empire of beauty," specifically their sexuality, can humiliate and overpower men who are physically stronger. The Greek hero Hercules, son of Zeus, was tricked into raping the fifty daughters of Thespitius. For a different transgression he was punished by the Delphic Oracle to serve Omphale, queen of Lydia, who dressed him as a woman and made him spin wool; he later became her lover. In the Bible, Delilah is paid by the Philistines to betray her lover Samson by finding out the source of his extraordinary strength (his hair); after she cuts Samson's hair, the Philistines take out his eyes, but before they can sacrifice him he brings down the entire house, killing everyone (Judges 16).
4   In his *Confessions*, Rousseau discussed giving his five children up to an orphanage after each was born: "in handing my children over for the State to educate, for lack of means to bring them up myself, by destining them to become workers and peasants instead of adventurers and fortune-hunters, I thought I was acting as a citizen and a father, and looked upon myself as a member of Plato's Republic" (*Rousseau's Political Writings*, ed. Alan Ritter and Julia Conaway Bondanella (NY: Norton, 1988) 183).

his, she betrays both. She joins perfidy to infidelity. I have difficulty seeing what disorders and what crimes do not flow from this one. If there is a frightful condition in the world, it is that of an unhappy father who, lacking confidence in his wife, does not dare to yield to the sweetest sentiments of his heart, who wonders, in embracing his child, whether he is embracing another's, the token of his dishonor, the plunderer of his own children's property. What does the family become in such a situation if not a society of secret enemies whom a guilty woman arms against one another in forcing them to feign mutual love?

It is important, then, not only that a woman be faithful, but that she be judged to be faithful by her husband, by those near her, by everyone. It is important that she be modest, attentive, reserved, and that she give evidence of her virtue to the eyes of others as well as to her own conscience. If it is important that a father love his children, it is important that he esteem their mother. These are the reasons which put even appearances among the duties of women, and make honor and reputation no less indispensable to them than chastity. There follows from these principles, along with the moral difference of the sexes, a new motive of duty and propriety which prescribes especially to women the most scrupulous attention to their conduct, their manners, and their bearing. To maintain vaguely that the two sexes are equal and that their duties are the same, is to lose oneself in vain declaiming; it is to say nothing so long as one does not respond to these considerations.

Is it not a sound way of reasoning to present exceptions in response to such well-grounded general laws? Women, you say, do not always produce children? No, but their proper purpose is to produce them. What! Because there are a hundred big cities in the universe where women living in license produce few children, you claim that it is proper to woman's status to produce few children! And what would become of your cities if women living more simply and more chastely far away in the country did not make up for the sterility of the city ladies? In how many provinces are women who have only produced four or five children taken to be infecund![5] Finally, what does it matter that this or that woman produces few children? Is woman's status any less that of motherhood, and is it not by general laws that nature and morals ought to provide for this status? [. . .]

Once it is demonstrated that man and woman are not and ought not to be constituted in the same way in either character or temperament, it follows that they ought not to have the same education. In following nature's directions, man and woman ought to act in concert, but they ought not to do the same things. The goal of their labors is common, but their labors themselves are different, and consequently so are the tastes directing them. After having tried to form the natural man, let us also see how the woman who suits this man ought to be formed so that our work will not be left imperfect.

---

5 [Rousseau's note.] Without that, the species would necessarily fade away. In order for it to be preserved, every woman must, everything considered, produce nearly four children; for nearly half the children who are born die before they can have others, and the two remaining ones are needed to represent the father and the mother. See if the cities will provide you with this population.

Do you wish always to be well guided? Then always follow nature's indications. Everything that characterizes the fair sex ought to be respected as established by nature. You constantly say, "Women have this or that failing which we do not have." Your pride deceives you. They would be failings for you; they are their good qualities. Everything would go less well if they did not have these qualities. Prevent these alleged failings from degenerating, but take care not to destroy them.

For their part, women do not cease to proclaim that we raise them to be vain and coquettish, that we constantly entertain them with puerilities in order to remain more easily their masters. They blame on us the failings for which we reproach them. What folly! And since when is it that men get involved in the education of girls? Who prevents their mothers from raising them as they please? They have no colleges. What a great misfortune! Would God that there were none for boys; they would be more sensibly and decently raised! Are your daughters forced to waste their time in silliness? Are they made in spite of themselves to spend half their lives getting dressed up, following the example you set them? Are you prevented from instructing them and having them instructed as you please? Is it our fault that they please us when they are pretty, that their mincing ways seduce us, that the art which they learn from you attracts us and pleases us, that we like to see them tastefully dressed, that we let them sharpen at their leisure the weapons with which they subjugate us? So, decide to raise them like men. The men will gladly consent to it! The more women want to resemble them, the less women will govern them, and then men will truly be the masters.

Catharine Macaulay, *Letters on Education* (1790), Facsimile edition, introduction by Gina Luria (NY: Garland, 1974) 204, 206–7, 208

Macaulay (1731–91) and Wollstonecraft had many things in common: they were well-known public figures among British radicals; both published pro-Revolution responses to Burke's *Reflections on the Revolution in France* and wrote widely on political matters and women's rights; both were objects of public scorn because of their unconventional private lives (in Macaulay's case, because as a widow she married a man twenty-six years younger than her). Macaulay wrote a multi-volume *History of England* (1763–83), but it is her feminist *Letters on Education* to which Wollstonecraft is deeply indebted. Macaulay's *Letters* anticipated many of Wollstonecraft's arguments, notably that women's intellectual and physical weakness are products of (mis)education, not nature, and that women and men should be educated together. Wollstonecraft's praise for Macaulay in *Rights of Woman* (she called her "the woman of the greatest abilities . . . that this country has ever produced" (**p. 142**)) echoes the letter she wrote to Macaulay in 1790 (**p. 24**) and acknowledges her debt to her feminist predecessor.

It must be confessed, that the virtues of the males among the human species, though mixed and blended with a variety of vices and errors, have displayed a bolder and a more confident picture of excellence than female nature has hitherto done. It is on these reasons that, when we compliment the appearance of a more than ordinary energy in the female mind, we can call it masculine; and hence it is, that Pope has elegantly said *a perfect woman's but a softer man*.[1] And if we take in the consideration, that there can be but one rule of moral excellence for beings made of the same materials, organized after the same manner, and subjected to similar laws of Nature, we must either agree with Mr. Pope, or we must reverse the proposition and say, that *a perfect man is a woman formed after a coarser mold*. [. . .]

But whatever might be the wise purpose intended by Providence [. . .], certain it is, that some degree of inferiority, in point of corporal strength, seems always to have existed between the two sexes; and this advantage, in the barbarous ages of mankind, was abused to such a degree, as to destroy all the natural rights of the female species, and reduce them to a state of abject slavery. What accidents have contributed in Europe to better their condition, would not be my purpose to relate; for I do not intend to give you a history of women; I mean only to trace the sources of their peculiar foibles and vices: and these I firmly believe to originate in situation and education only: for so little did a wise and just Providence intend to make the condition of slavery an unalterable law of female nature, that in the same proportion as the male sex have consulted the interest of their own happiness, they have relaxed in their tyranny over women; and such is their use in the system of mundane creation, and such their natural influence over the male mind, that were these advantages properly exerted, they might carry every point of any importance to their honour and happiness. However, till that period arrives in which women will act wisely, we will amuse ourselves in talking of their follies.

The situation and education of women [. . .] is precisely that which must necessarily tend to corrupt and debilitate both the powers of mind and body. From a false notion of beauty and delicacy, their system of nerves is depraved before they come out of their nursery; and this kind of depravity has more influence over the mind, and consequently over morals, than is commonly apprehended. [. . .] Whilst we still retain the absurd notion of a sexual excellence, it will militate against the perfecting a plan of education for either sex.

Letters by Wollstonecraft

To Catharine Macaulay Graham (December 1790), on women

Macaulay Graham was a well-known historian and radical political writer, whose feminist *Letters on Education* (1790) had inspired Wollstonecraft's *Rights of*

---

1   Alexander Pope, from his "Epistle to a Lady. On the Characters of Women," where he alludes to the creation of Eve: "Heav'n, when it strives to polish all it can / Its last best work, but forms a softer Man" (ll. 271–2).

Woman (see excerpt (**p. 22**) and *Rights of Woman*, chapter 5.4). This letter reveals the high esteem in which Wollstonecraft held Macaulay, compared to women who "only seek for flowers," i.e., to please and be pleased by men (see Wollstonecraft's comments on Anna Barbauld, chapter 4). Macaulay replied that she was pleased to learn that the *Rights of Men* (first published anonymously) "should have been written by a woman and thus to see my opinion of the powers and talents of the sex in your pen so early verified."[1]

Madam,

Now I venture to send you [*A Vindication of the Rights of Men*] with a name utterly unknown to you in the title page, it is necessary to apologize for thus intruding on you – but instead of an apology shall I tell you the truth? You are the only female writer who I coincide in opinion with respecting the rank our sex ought to endeavour to attain in the world. I respect Mrs Macaulay Graham because she contends for laurels whilst most of her sex only seek for flowers.

I am Madam,

Yours Respectfully

Mary Wollstonecraft

To Mary Hays (12 November 1792), on publishing

This frank letter to the feminist Hays, who would become Wollstonecraft's most devoted disciple (see Hays, **pp. 49–50**), reveals much about the difficult sexual dynamics of publishing at the turn of the nineteenth century. The tone echoes that in the *Rights of Woman*, and stands in interesting contrast to the letter to Godwin (**pp. 28–9**) in which Wollstonecraft defends herself against Godwin's similar charge that she had put too much of herself in her writings.

London Novr 12th [17]92

Dear Madam,—

I yesterday mentioned to Mr Johnson your request and he assented desiring that the title page might be sent to him—I, therefore, can say nothing more, for trifles of this kind I have always left to him to settle; and, you must be aware, Madam, that the *honour* of publishing, the phrase on which you have laid a stress, is the cant of both trade and sex; for if really equality should ever take place in society the man who is employed and gives a just equivalent for the money he receives will not behave with the obsequiousness of a servant.

I am now going to treat you with still greater frankness—I do not approve of

---

1   Macaulay to Wollstonecraft, 30 December 1790, quoted in Bridget Hill, "The Links Between Mary Wollstonecraft and Catharine Macaulay: new evidence," *Women's History Review* 4.2 (1995) 177–92, 178.

your preface[1]—and I will tell you why. If your work should deserve attention it is a blur on the very face of it.—Disadvantages of education &c ought, in my opinion, never to be pleaded (with the public) in excuse for defects of any importance, because if the writer has not sufficient strength of mind to overcome the common difficulties which lie in his way,[2] nature seems to command him, with a very audible voice, to leave the task of instructing others to those who can. This kind of vain humility has ever disgusted me—and I should say to an author, who humbly sued for forbearance, 'if you have not a tolerably good opinion of your own production, why intrude it on the public? we have plenty of bad books already, that have just gasped for breath and died.'

The last paragraph I particularly object to, it is so full of vanity. your male friends will still treat you like a woman—and many a man, for instance Dr Johnson, Lord Littelton, and even Dr Priestley, have insensibly been led to utter warm elogiums in private that they would be sorry openly to avow without some cooling explanatory ifs. An author, especially a woman, should be cautious lest she too hastily swallows the crude praises which partial friend and polite acquaintance bestow thoughtlessly when the supplicating eye looks for them. In short, it requires great resolution to try rather to be useful than to please. With this remark in your head I must beg you to pardon any freedom whilst you consider the purport of what I am going to add.—Rest, on yourself—if your essays have merit they will stand alone, if not the *shouldering up* of Dr this or that will not long keep them from falling to the ground. The vulgar have a pertinent proverb— 'Too many cooks spoil the broth', and let me remind you that when weakness claims indulgence it seems to justify the despotism of strength. Indeed the preface, and even your pamphlet, is too full of yourself.—Inquiries ought to be made before they are answered; and till a work strongly interests the public true modesty should keep the author in the back ground—for it is only about the character and life of a *good* author that anxiety is active—A blossom is but a blossom.

I am Madam

yours &c

MARY WOLLSTONECRAFT

To Gilbert Imlay (22 September 1794), on imagination

With her lover Imlay in London, Mary and her baby Fanny spent the winter of 1794 alone in Paris, where Wollstonecraft wrote her *Historical and Moral View of the ... French Revolution*. This letter contains an important statement on the value of imagination, as well as several digs at Imlay's commercialism (he was involved in importing goods, such as the alum and soap Wollstonecraft mentions); see Whale and Guest for discussions of imagination and commercialism, respectively **pp. 90–1 and 77–9**.

1 Mary Hays, *Preface to Letters and Essays, Moral and Miscellaneous* (1793).
2 Compare to Grant's response to Wollstonecraft (**pp. 48–9**).

[Paris] September 22 [1794]

I have just written two letters, that are going by other conveyances, and which I reckon on your receiving long before this. I therefore merely write, because I know I should be disappointed at seeing any one who had left you, if you did not send a letter, were it ever so short, to tell me why you did not write a longer—and you will want to be told, over and over again, that our little Hercules is quite recovered.

Besides looking at me, there are three other things, which delight her—to ride in a coach, to look at a scarlet waistcoat, and hear loud music—yesterday at the *fête*, she enjoyed the two latter; but, to honour J. J. Rousseau, I intend to give her a sash, the first she has ever had round her—and why not?—for I have always been half in love with him.[1]

Well, this you will say is trifling—shall I talk about alum or soap? There is nothing picturesque in your present pursuits; my imagination then rather chuses to ramble back to the barrier[2] with you, or to see you coming to meet me, and my basket of grapes.—With what pleasure do I recollect your looks and words, when I have been sitting on the window, regarding the waving corn!

Believe me, sage sir, you have not sufficient respect for the imagination—I could prove to you in a trice that it is the mother of sentiment, the great distinction of our nature, the only purifier of the passions—animals have a portion of reason, and equal, if not more exquisite, senses; but no trace of imagination, or her offspring taste, appears in any of their actions. The impulse of the senses, passions, if you will, and the conclusions of reason, draw men together; but the imagination is the true fire, stolen from heaven,[3] to animate this cold creature of clay, producing all those fine sympathies that lead to rapture, rendering men social by expanding their hearts, instead of leaving them leisure to calculate how many comforts society affords.

If you call these observations romantic, a phrase in this place which would be tantamount to nonsensical, I shall be apt to retort, that you are embruted by trade and the vulgar enjoyments of life—Bring me then back your barrier-face, or you shall have nothing to say to my barrier-girl; and I shall fly from you, to cherish the remembrances that will ever be dear to me; for I am yours truly

MARY

---

1   Wollstonecraft's mixed feelings for the French philosopher Rousseau are discussed in the headnote to the Contexts extract from his *Emile* (pp. 18–22), as well as in chapter 4 of *Rights of Woman*.
2   Wollstonecraft and Imlay used to meet at a toll gate, or barrier, in the Paris city wall.
3   This Romantic celebration of imagination alludes to the myth of Prometheus found in Hesiod's *Theogony* and Aeschylus' *Prometheus Bound*. *Prometheus* was a particular favorite of later writers like Percy Bysshe and Mary Shelley (Wollstonecraft's daughter and the author of *Frankenstein, or the Modern Prometheus*). Prometheus was a Titan who rebelled against Zeus by stealing fire and giving it to humans. He was punished by having his liver devoured daily while chained to a rock for 3,000 years; Zeus punished humanity by sending them Pandora, whose jar unleashed evils into the world (on Pandora, see p. 114).

To Gilbert Imlay (12 June 1795), on sex and sentiment

Written after her first suicide attempt and while she was en route to Scandinavia on secret business for her lover Imlay, this excerpt reveals Wollstonecraft's struggle to accept that Imlay's feelings for her are based on "appetite" (also known as "romantic wavering feelings" in *Rights of Woman*), i.e., ephemeral sexual desire unrefined by sentiment. Wollstonecraft's thoughts on imagination's role in transforming passion into love (here and in the previous letter), and on imagination as the route to spiritual and sexual rapture, anticipate the theories of imagination developed by William Wordsworth, Percy Bysshe Shelley, and Samuel Taylor Coleridge, the latter of whom was influenced by Wollstonecraft's most Romantic work, *Letters Written in Sweden* (1796).

[Hull] Friday, June 12 [1795]

I have just received yours dated the 9th, which I suppose was a mistake, for it could scarcely have loitered so long on the road. The general observations which apply to the state of your own mind, appear to me just, as far as they go; and I shall always consider it as one of the most serious misfortunes of my life, that I did not meet you, before satiety had rendered your senses so fastidious, as almost to close up every tender avenue of sentiment and affection that leads to your sympathetic heart. You have a heart, my friend, yet, hurried away by the impetuosity of inferior feelings, you have sought in vulgar excesses, for that gratification which only the heart can bestow.

The common run of men, I know, with strong health and gross appetites, must have variety to banish *ennui*,[1] because the imagination never lends its magic wand, to convert appetite into love, cemented by according reason—Ah! my friend, you know not the ineffable delight, the exquisite pleasure, which arises from a unison of affection and desire, when the whole soul and senses are abandoned to a lively imagination, that renders every emotion delicate and rapturous. Yes; these are emotions, over which satiety has no power, and the recollection of which, even disappointment cannot disenchant; but they do not exist without self-denial. These emotions, more or less strong, appear to me to be the distinctive characteristic of genius, the foundation of taste, and of that exquisite relish for the beauties of nature, of which the common herd of eaters and drinkers and *child-begeters*, certainly have no idea. You will smile at an observation that has just occurred to me:—I consider those minds as the most strong and original, whose imagination acts as the stimulus to their senses.

Well! you will ask, what is the result of all this reasoning? Why I cannot help thinking that it is possible for you, having great strength of mind, to return to nature, and regain a sanity of constitution, and purity of feeling—which would open your heart to me.—I would fain rest there!

Yet, convinced more than ever of the sincerity and tenderness of my attachment

---

1   Boredom, world-weariness.

to you, the involuntary hopes, which a determination to live has revived, are not sufficiently strong to dissipate the cloud, that despair has spread over futurity. I have looked at the sea, and at my child, hardly daring to own to myself the secret wish, that it might become our tomb; and that the heart, still so alive to anguish, might there be quieted by death. At this moment ten thousand complicated sentiments press for utterance, weigh on my heart, and obscure my sight.

Are we ever to meet again? and will you endeavour to render that meeting happier than the last? Will you endeavour to restrain your caprices, in order to give vigour to affection, and to give play to the checked sentiments that nature intended should expand your heart? I cannot indeed, without agony, think of your bosom's being continually contaminated; and bitter are the tears which exhaust my eyes, when I recollect why my child and I are forced to stray from the asylum, in which, after so many storms, I had hoped to rest, smiling at angry fate.—These are not common sorrows; nor can you perhaps conceive, how much active fortitude it requires to labour perpetually to blunt the shafts of disappointment.[. . .]

To William Godwin (4 September 1796), on her writing

This excerpt reveals the intellectual parity and honesty that characterized Wollstonecraft and Godwin's relationship; she defends her writing on the grounds of originality, resisting Godwin's rationalist criteria for good writing.

[London] Sunday Morning [4 September, 1796] Labouring all the morning, in vain, to overcome a depression of spirits, which some things you uttered yesterday, produced; I will try if I can shake it off by describing to you the nature of the feelings you excited.

I allude to what you remarked, relative to my manner of writing—that there was a radical defect in it—a worm in the bud—&c What is to be done, I must either disregard your opinion, think it unjust, or throw down my pen in despair; and that would be tantamount to resigning existence; for at fifteen I resolved never to marry for interested motives, or to endure a life of dependence. You know not how painfully my sensibility, call it false if you will, has been wounded by some of the steps I have been obliged to take for others. I have even now plans at heart, which depend on my exertions; and my entire confidence in Mr Imlay plunged me into some difficulties, since we parted, that I could scarcely away with.[1] I know that many of my cares have been the natural consequence of what, nine out of ten would termed folly—yet I cannot coincide in the opinion, without feeling a contempt for mankind. In short, I must reckon on doing some good, and getting the money I want, by my writings, or go to sleep for ever. I shall not be

---

1   Wollstonecraft had reluctantly accepted a bond from Imlay for Fanny, but he had not paid the interest as agreed, and had also sent her some of his bills.

content merely to keep body and soul together—By what I have already written Johnson, I am sure, has been a gainer. And, for I would wish you to see my heart and mind just as it appears to myself, without drawing any veil of affected humility over it, though this whole letter is a proof of painful diffidence, I am compelled to think that there is some thing in my writings more valuable, than in the productions of some people on whom you bestow warm elogiums—I mean more mind—denominate it as you will—more of the observations of my own senses, more of the combining of my own imagination—the effusions of my own feelings and passions than the cold workings of the brain on the materials procured by the senses and imagination of other writers—[. . .]

MARY

To Amelia Alderson (Opie) (11 April 1797), on marriage

After Wollstonecraft married Godwin in March 1797, many of their friends, including the writer Elizabeth Inchbald (1753–1821), shunned them because of the revelation that she seems not to have been married to Imlay. In the early 1790s, Amelia Alderson (Opie) was part of a radical Dissenting circle, and Godwin had proposed to her before his affair with Wollstonecraft; in 1805 she published a novel, Adeline Mowbray, based on Wollstonecraft's relationship with Godwin, in which the radical heroine, after rejecting marriage, repents and dies. Here Wollstonecraft justifies her decision to marry, despite her philosophical opposition to marriage.

[London] Tuesday Night [11 April 1797]

My dear Girl,

[. . .] I shall be sorry to resign the acquaintance of Mrs. and Mr. F. Twiss,[1] because I respect their characters, and feel grateful for their attention; but my conduct in life must be directed by my own judgment and moral principles: it is my wish that Mr. Godwin should visit and dine out as formerly, and I shall do the same; in short, I still mean to be independent, even to the cultivating sentiments and principles in my children's minds, (should I have more), which he disavows. The wound my unsuspecting heart formerly received is not healed. I found my evenings solitary; and I wished, while fulfilling the duty of a mother, to have some person with similar pursuits, bound to me by affection; and beside, I earnestly desired to resign a name which seemed to disgrace me.[2] Since I have been unfortunately the object of observation, I have had it in my power, more than once, to marry very advantageously; and of course, should have been courted by those, who at least cannot accuse me of acting an interested part, though I have

---

1 Francis Twiss and his wife Frances (Kemble) Twiss, sister of the actress Sarah Siddons, were some of Wollstonecraft's friends who shunned her.
2 Since registering as Imlay's wife in Paris to avoid imprisonment during the Revolution, Wollstonecraft had occasionally gone under the name of Mrs. Imlay, leading many to assume she was married.

not, by dazzling their eyes, rendered them blind to my faults. I am proud perhaps, conscious of my own purity and integrity; and many circumstances in my life have contributed to excite in my bosom an indignant contempt for the forms of a world I should have bade a long good night to, had I not been a mother. Condemned then to toil my hour out, I wish to live as rationally as I can; had fortune or splendor been my aim in life, they have been within my reach, would I have paid the price. Well, enough of the subject; I do not wish to resume it. Good night! God bless you.

MARY WOLLSTONECRAFT
femme Godwin.

2

Interpretations

2

Interpretations

Critical History

The immediate reception of *Rights of Woman* was largely positive, particularly when it was considered as a call for improving women's education. Periodicals like the *Analytical Review, Literary Magazine, New Annual Register*, and *Monthly Review* (excerpted below) reviewed it positively, and literary women like Anna Seward, Sarah Trimmer, and Mary Berry praised the book's emphasis on improving women's education.[1] A few responses, such as John Henry Colls's *Poetical Epistle Addressed to Miss Wollstonecraft* (*c.*1794), went even further, praising Wollstonecraft's elevation of female genius in terms which Elizabeth Barrett Browning would echo decades later:

> Thus WOLLSTONECRAFT, by fiery genius led,
> Entwines the laurel round the female's head;
> Contends with man for equal strength of mind,
> And claims the rights estrang'd from womankind;
> Dives to the depths of science and of art,
> And leaves to fools the conquest of the heart;
> Or mounts exulting through the fields of space,
> On faith's strong pinions, to the throne of grace.[2]

But once Godwin's *Memoirs* of Wollstonecraft appeared in 1798, revealing her suicide attempts and love affairs, conservatives successfully conflated her political and educational arguments with promiscuity and even atheism (via Godwin).

Critics like Richard Polwhele, Robert Bisset, and William Beloe established this longstanding reading of Wollstonecraft as fallen woman with which feminists have had to contend since Wollstonecraft's death (excerpted **pp. 44, 46, 53**). In

---

1   See R.M. Janes, "On the Reception of Mary Wollstonecraft's *A Vindication of the Rights of Woman*" (**p. 84**), and Nicola Trott, "Sexing the Critic: Mary Wollstonecraft at the Turn of the Century," *1798: The Year of the Lyrical Ballads*, ed. Richard Cronin (London: Macmillan, 1998) 32–67.
2   Colls, *A Poetical Epistle Addressed to Miss Wollstonecraft. Occasioned by Reading her Celebrated Essay on the Rights of Woman, and her Historical and Moral View of the French Revolution* (London: Vernor & Hood, *c.*1794) 19.

conservative hands, sexual propriety (or lack thereof) became the defining issue distinguishing dangerous feminists like Wollstonecraft from virtuous educational reformers like Hannah More, author of *Strictures on the Modern System of Female Education* (1799). Thus in his 1798 diatribe against feminists like Wollstonecraft (*The Unsex'd Females*, **pp. 44–6**), Richard Polwhele wrote that "Miss Hannah More may justly be esteemed, as a character, in all points, diametrically opposite to Miss Wollstonecraft." Yet in 1799 Mary Berry was still able to write that

> I have been able . . . to go entirely through Hannah More, and Mrs. Wollstonecraft immediately after her. It is amazing, but impossible, they should do otherwise than agree on all the great points of female education. H. More will, I dare say, be very angry when she hears this, though I would lay wager that she never read the book.[3]

More, an ardent propagandist against political reform, had indeed claimed not to have read the *Rights of Woman* because of its radical politics, but she herself would also face growing opposition to her educational and evangelical activities because of her gender.[4] Women's intensifying political activism, whether evangelical like More's or republican like Wollstonecraft's, came under increasing attack by the end of the eighteenth century, despite the efforts of conservatives like More and Polwhele to delineate an acceptable arena for women's public political influence.

The fusion of radical politics, feminism, and sexual transgression associated with Wollstonecraft's name after 1798 has remained central to the ongoing reception of *Rights of Woman*, from the conservative backlash at the turn of the nineteenth century and its oppositional More/Wollstonecraft model of femininity, to nineteenth-century suffragists who saw in Wollstonecraft's radical experiments a precedent for their own struggles.

The anarchist Emma Goldman was one such kindred spirit, who in 1911 voiced a competing, sympathetic reading of Wollstonecraft as a "Pioneer" of human progress, "a pathfinder" driven by "[i]ntense, yearning, burning faith" and "[i]n conflict with every institution" of her time. Like most feminist commentators since Wollstonecraft's death, Goldman saw her own contradictions and struggles amplified in Wollstonecraft's. Similarly, in her early years writing for the radical journal *The English Republic* (1854), Eliza Lynn Linton, who years later would become the antifeminist scourge of the independent "Girl of the Period," eulogized Wollstonecraft as "one of the priestesses of the future," and included a feminized engraving of Wollstonecraft in marked contrast to her Enlightenment

---

3   Mary Berry, as quoted in Harriet Guest, "The Dream of a Common Language: Hannah More and Mary Wollstonecraft," *Textual Practice* 9.2 (1995) 305; excerpted **pp. 77–9**.
4   Angela Keane, "The Anxiety of (Feminine) Influence: Hannah More and Counter-Revolution," in *Rebellious Hearts: British Women Writers and the French Revolution*, ed. Adriana Craciun and Kari Lokke (Albany: SUNY, 2001); Anne Mellor, *Mothers of the Nation: Women's Political Writing in England, 1780–1830* (Bloomington: Indiana University Press, 2000).

portrait of 1791 (Frontispiece). As the Victorian women's movement became more militant and divided on issues of natural sexual difference and rights, Wollstonecraft's contradictions and complexity allowed for commentators to see surprising affinities and objections in her work and, more commonly, in her life. The economist Harriet Martineau, for example, focused on Wollstonecraft's personal revelations and transgressions, sharply dismissing Wollstonecraft despite their shared commitment to increasing women's education and economic independence. In contrast, Wollstonecraft's emphasis on the cultural value of motherhood allowed women like the conservative novelist Margaret Oliphant to praise the *Rights of Woman* as "altogether free from revolutionary principles, either political or moral," and "full of the warmest religiousness."[5] Radical suffragist Millicent Garrett Fawcett saw Wollstonecraft as "remarkabl[y] . . . ahead of her time" because she "claims for women the right to share in the advantages of representation in Parliament, nearly seventy years before women's suffrage was heard of."[6] Yet she reassured readers that Wollstonecraft was "the essentially womanly woman," whose "chief claim to the regard of posterity" is that "she had a keen appreciation of the sanctity of women's domestic duties" (excerpted, **pp. 58–9**).

The list of nineteenth-century women who wrote on Wollstonecraft is instructive, and has not yet been fully accounted for in histories of the women's movement. John Stuart Mill's *The Subjection of Women* (1869) is typically named by Victorian feminists as the most influential text on the "Woman Question," but George Eliot, Margaret Fuller, Margaret Oliphant, and Virginia Woolf all wrote on Wollstonecraft's controversial role in the development of the women's movement in Britain.[7] Elizabeth Barrett Browning read her at an early age, and in her "Fragment of an 'Essay on Woman'" celebrated women's claim to genius in terms reminiscent of Wollstonecraft, and later to emerge in the best-known poem on women's genius, *Aurora Leigh* (see **p. 54**). Olive Schreiner, feminist author of *The Story of an African Farm* (1883), recommended Wollstonecraft to her readers as "one of ourselves," and wrote to sexologist Havelock Ellis that her forthcoming Wollstonecraft essay "is all poetry from the first to the last,"[8] inspired by the revolutionary example of her subject's life, not her writings. In the United States as well, Wollstonecraft was a shaping spirit in the early suffrage movement. Lucretia Mott, who had helped organize the 1848 Seneca Falls Convention with Elizabeth Cady Stanton, wrote in 1855 that "I have long wished and believed that the time would come, when Mary Wollstonecraft and Frances

---

5 Margaret Oliphant, *The Literary History of England*, 3 vols. (London: Macmillan, 1883) 2: 252.
6 Millicent Garrett Fawcett, "Introduction to the New Edition" of *A Vindication of the Rights of Woman* (New York: Scribner and Welford, 1890) 24.
7 George Eliot, "Margaret Fuller and Mary Wollstonecraft," *Leader* 6 (October 1855) 988–9; Margaret Fuller, *Woman in the Nineteenth Century* (1855; Norton, 1971); Oliphant, *The Literary History of England* (1882); Woolf is excerpted **pp. 60–1**).
8 Schreiner, quoted in Carolyn Burdett, "A Difficult Vindication: Olive Schreiner's Wollstonecraft Introduction" 178, 187, published with Schreiner's (hitherto unpublished) "Introduction to the Life of Mary Wollstonecraft and the Rights of Woman," *History Workshop Journal* 37 (1994) 177–93.

Wright, and Robert Owen, would have justice done them."[9] Mott and Susan B. Anthony hung a portrait of Wollstonecraft in the office of their paper *The Revolution*.

Wollstonecraft's influence on the suffrage movement and the women's movement in general remains understudied, in part because the irregular republication of her texts makes her reception difficult to trace. Nineteenth-century British editions of *Rights of Woman* appeared in 1841, 1844, 1891 (twice), 1892, and US editions in 1833, 1845, 1856, 1890, 1891.[10] The first full-scale biography was by Elizabeth Pennell (1885), who built on Charles Kegan Paul's sympathetic accounts earlier in 1876 and 1878, and saw Wollstonecraft as a precursor of Ibsen in her critique "of the falseness of the doll's house."[11] Before these late recuperations of Wollstonecraft as a serious enlightenment intellectual, writer, and feminist, nineteenth-century commentators struggled with the damaging legacy of her controversial life; in 1882 Oliphant wrote that earlier in the century Wollstonecraft had been "a name of horror, considered as that of a female atheist and libertine, an offence to God and man" (Oliphant 2:252).

As Victorian feminists shaped their feminisms around the ideologies of their day – idealized motherhood and womanhood – so twentieth-century feminisms have "accepted and been organized around the agendas which have dominated the societies or the circles from which feminists have come."[12] In the 1980s, feminist commentators on Wollstonecraft, such as Mary Poovey and Cora Kaplan, reveal the urgency with which sexual liberation and class politics were addressed at that critical stage of the women's moment. Thus Moira Gatens wrote in 1991 that "From our present perspective, the major problem with Wollstonecraft is that she does not go far enough."[13] As the "founding text of Anglo-American feminism," *Rights of Woman* was judged by Marxist feminists like Kaplan to be fatally flawed by its distinctly middle-class liberal limitations and priorities. French feminism, the other major strand of twentieth-century feminism, likewise could not embrace *Rights of Woman* because of the vehe-

9 Mott, as quoted in Virginia Sapiro, *A Vindication of Political Virtue* (Chicago: University of Chicago Press, 1992) 175. On Wollstonecraft and radical reception, see Barbara Taylor, *Eve and the New Jerusalem* (London: Virago 1983) and "An Impossible Heroine? Mary Wollstonecraft and female heroism," *Soundings* 3 (1996) 119–35. On Wollstonecraft's early American reception, see Marcelle Thiébaux, "Mary Wollstonecraft in Federalist America: 1791–1802," *The Evidence of the Imagination*, ed. Donald Reiman et al. (New York: New York University Press, 1978) 195–235.
10 John Windle, *Mary Wollstonecraft Godwin 1759–1797: A Bibliography*, 2nd edn, edited by Karma Pippin (New Castle: Oak Knoll, 2000); Janet Todd, *Mary Wollstonecraft: An Annotated Bibliography* (New York: Garland, 1976). In addition, a brief "Life of Wollstonecraft" and extract of the *Rights of Woman* appeared in the radical periodical *The National* (1839) 139–40, 144–5. More little-known accounts of Wollstonecraft in the radical press, like Eliza Linton's in *The English Republic* (excerpted pp. 55–6), probably exist, and require further investigation.
11 Elizabeth Pennell, "Prefatory Note" to *A Vindication of the Rights of Woman* (London: Walter Scott, 1891) xxiii; Pennell, *Mary Wollstonecraft* (London: Allen, 1885); Charles Kegan Paul, *William Godwin, His Friends and Contemporaries* (1876) and "Mary Wollstonecraft: A Vindication," *Fraser's Magazine* N.S. 17 (1878) 748–62. The latter three are excerpted in *Lives of the Great Romantics III*, ed. Jump.
12 Barbara Caine, *Victorian Feminists* (Oxford: Oxford University Press, 1993) 17.
13 Moira Gatens, *Feminism and Philosophy* (Cambridge: Polity, 1991) 24.

mence with which it attacks femininity, certain aspects of sensibility and sexuality, and because of its celebration of "masculinist" concepts of reason and language. As Pateman argues in "Wollstonecraft's Dilemma," (1989, **pp. 62–3**) Wollstonecraft represents the crossroads of this historical divergence in women's approaches to modern citizenship – based on their difference (from men) or their equality (to men). For this reason we could agree with Jerome McGann that "Wollstonecraft is a prophetic soul, and her contradictions are an index of her historical position and significance."[14] For Wollstonecraft to have reconciled these contradictions (difference vs. equality) would not only have been historically impossible, but the work of ideology (what Blake called alternately Cunning and Religion).[15]

In the 1990s feminist theory was increasingly informed by historicism, and Wollstonecraft's work proved fruitful in new ways, particularly in its discussions of commercialism, sensibility, slavery (literal and metaphorical), and the history of the body. Wollstonecraft's views of sexuality have been significantly reframed through these perspectives, as has the role of imagination in her politics and aesthetics. The familiar critical opposition between (masculine) reason and (feminine) imagination in *Rights of Woman*, and Wollstonecraft's supposed rejection of the latter, seems increasingly insufficient, particularly in consideration of women writers' significant roles in shaping the aesthetics of imagination in the Romantic period. "Reason and fancy," wrote Wollstonecraft in 1791, "are nearer akin than cold dulness is willing to allow," and "A writer of genius makes us feel; an inferior author reason."[16] In later works like the *Letters from Sweden*, her essay "On Poetry," and in the "Hints [Chiefly designed to have been incorporated in the Second Part of the Vindication of the Rights of Woman]" she elaborated her developing aesthetic and political theory of the imagination in which modern scholars are increasingly interested. This reading of Wollstonecraft as a Romantic writer was also available to her contemporaries; Anne Grant, who was clearly fascinated by Wollstonecraft and also disturbed by this fascination, described her in terms we would be wrong to associate solely with male Romantic writers: "There is a gloomy grandeur in her imagination, while she explores the regions of intellect without chart or compass, which gives one the idea of genius wandering through chaos" (**p. 49**).

The writers included in the twentieth-century responses eloquently illustrate these changing critical priorities and dialectical debates, reflecting feminism's ongoing transformations. Attesting to the interdisciplinary foundations of *Rights of Woman* (and indeed of women's studies itself), Wollstonecraft also increasingly appeals across modern disciplines: historians G.J. Barker-Benfield and Linda

---

14 McGann, *The Poetics of Sensibility: A Revolution in Literary Style* (Oxford: Clarendon, 1996) 107.
15 Blake, *Marriage of Heaven and Hell* (1790–3), plates 16–17, in *Romanticism: An Anthology*, 2nd edn, ed. Duncan Wu (Oxford: Blackwell, 2000) 90.
16 Review of William Gilpin's *Remarks on Forest Scenery* (1791) in *Works of Mary Wollstonecraft*, ed. Janet Todd and Marilyn Butler (London: Pickering, 1989) 7: 387); "Hints" no. 31 (**p. 164**).

Colley, political scientists Carole Pateman and Virginia Sapiro, and literary critics Claudia Johnson and Mary Poovey, as well as philosophers and anthropologists,[17] have all found Wollstonecraft to be a central figure in understanding the turn-of-the-century shift in gender roles.

---

17 These writers are excerpted below; see also Ruth Benedict, *An Anthropologist at Work*, ed. Margaret Mead (Boston: Houghton Mifflin, 1959) 491–519; Catriona Mackenzie, "Reason and Sensibility: The Ideal of Women's Self-Governance in the Writings of Mary Wollstonecraft," *Hypatia: A Journal of Feminist Philosophy* 8.4 (1993) 35–55.

Nineteenth-Century Responses

Romantic-Period Responses and Reviews

Review of *Rights of Woman* in *Monthly Review* n.s. 8 (1792) 198–209

This review of the *Rights of Woman* in the Whig *Monthly Review* is a good example of its favorable reception when judged on its own merits (and generally as a work on education), before the revelations of Wollstonecraft's private life in the 1798 *Memoirs* irreparably damaged her critical reputation (on other reviews see Janes 1978, **pp. 84–6**).

It will be easily perceived that the author is possessed of great energy of intellect, vigour of fancy, and command of language; and that the performance suggests many reflections, which well deserve the attention of the public, and which, pursued under the direction of good sense and sage experience, may greatly contribute to the improvement of the condition and character of the female world. We do not, however, so zealously adopt Miss W.'s plan for a REVOLUTION in female education and manners, as not to perceive that several of her opinions are fanciful, and some of her projects romantic. We do not see, that the condition or the character of women would be improved, by assuming an active part in civil government. It does not appear to us to be necessary, in order to enlighten the understandings of women, that we should prohibit the employment of their fingers in those useful and elegant labours of the needle, for which, from the days of Penelope,[1] they have obtained so much deserved applause. Certain associations, now too firmly established to be easily broken, forbid us to think that women are degraded by the trivial attention which the men are inclined to pay them; or that it would be any increase of the pleasures of society, if, "except where love animates

---

1 In Homer's *Odyssey*, Penelope is the chaste and faithful wife of Odysseus who, in his twenty-year absence, refused other suitors by saying she would marry again when she finished weaving her father-in-law's funeral robe. She never completed this, however, because by night she unraveled what she wove by day.

the behaviour, the distinction of sex were to be confounded." This distinction, we apprehend, will never be overlooked, till the time arrives, "when we shall neither marry nor be given in marriage, but be as the angels of God in heaven."[2] Notwithstanding all this, however, we entirely agree with the fair writer, that both the condition and the character of women are capable of great improvement; and that, by means of a more rational plan of female education, in which a judicious attention should be paid to the cultivation of their understanding and taste, as well as of their dispositions and manners, women might be rendered at once more agreeable, more respectable, and more happy in every station of life.

Thomas Taylor, *A Vindication of the Rights of Brutes* (London, 1792) iii–vii

Known as the "Platonist" because of his writings on neoplatonism, Taylor (1758–1835) was a friend of Wollstonecraft's in Walworth, south of London, in the late 1770s. Taylor parodied *Rights of Woman* and Thomas Paine's *Rights of Man* by taking their arguments to what he considered absurd extremes – rights for children and rights for animals – two "extremes" that emerged as significant social movements in the nineteenth century.

The particular design of the following sheets, is to evince by demonstrative arguments, the perfect equality of what is called the irrational species, to the human; but it has likewise a more general design; and this is no other, than to establish the equality of all things, as to their intrinsic dignity and worth. Indeed, after those wonderful productions of Mr. PAINE and Mrs. WOOLSTONCRAFT, such a theory as the present, seems to be necessary, in order to give perfection to our researches into the rights of things; and in such an age of discovery and independence as the present, the author flatters himself, that his theory will be warmly patronized by all the lovers of novelty, and friends of opposition, who are happily, at this period, so numerous both in France and England, and who are likely to receive an unbounded increase.

The author indeed, is well aware, that even in these luminous days, there are still many who will be so far from admitting the equality of brutes to men, that they will not even allow the equality of mankind to each other. Perhaps too, they will endeavour to support their opinion from the authority of Aristotle in his politics, where he endeavours to prove, that some men are naturally born slaves, and others free; and that the slavish part of mankind ought to be governed by the independent, in the same manner as the soul governs the body, that is, like a deposit or a tyrant. "For (says he) those who are born with strong bodily and weak mental powers, are born to Serve; and on the contrary, whenever the mind predominates over the body, it confers natural freedom on its possessor." But this

---

2   Matthew 22:30. Wollstonecraft used this phrase in the last sentence of her first novel, *Mary, a Fiction* (1788).

is a conclusion which will surely be ridiculed by every genuine modern, as it wholly proceeds on a Supposition, that mind and body are two distinct things, and that the former is more excellent than the latter; though almost every one is now convinced, that soul and body are only nominally distinguished from each other, and are essentially the same.[1]

Anna Laetitia Barbauld, "The Rights of Woman" (comp. c.1792, pub. 1825), *Oxford Book of Eighteenth Century Women's Poetry*, ed. Roger Lonsdale (Oxford: Oxford University Press, 1990) 305–6.

Barbauld (1743–1825) was part of a prominent Dissenting political circle that included Joseph Johnson (Wollstonecraft's publisher) and Joseph Priestley. Author of outspoken political works such as the anti-war *Eighteen Hundred and Eleven* (1812) and the antislavery *Epistle to William Wilberforce* (1790), Barbauld was most influential in children's books like *Hymns in Prose for Children* (1776–8). Though some of her poems were excerpted in Wollstonecraft's *Female Reader* (1789), they came under attack in *Rights of Woman*, notably Barbauld's poem "To a Lady, with some painted flowers" (**p. 131**). Barbauld replied to Wollstonecraft's critique with the following poem, published posthumously.

YES, injured Woman! rise, assert thy right!   1
Woman! too long degraded, scorned, oppressed;
O born to rule in partial Law's despite,
Resume thy native empire o'er the breast!

Go forth arrayed in panoply divine;   5
That angel pureness which admits no stain;
Go, bid proud Man his boasted rule resign,
And kiss the golden sceptre of thy reign.

Go, gird thyself with grace, collect thy store   9
Of bright artillery glancing from afar;
Soft melting tones thy thundering cannon's roar,
Blushes and fears thy magazine of war.

Thy rights are empire: urge no meaner claim,—   13
Felt, not defined, and if debated, lost;
Like sacred mysteries, which withheld from fame,
Shunning discussion, are revered the most.

---

1 Taylor's argument that "natural" differences exist between men, women, and children (as between body and soul), and implicitly between people of different races, attempts to justify the conclusion that social hierarchies are therefore natural. Abolitionists, feminists, and reformers typically insisted on spiritual equality for opposite reasons, either challenging the idea of essential physical difference, or seeing it as an unjust means of judging worth (i.e., might makes right).

Try all that wit and art suggest to bend   17
Of thy imperial foe the stubborn knee;
Make treacherous Man thy subject, not thy friend;
Thou mayst command, but never canst be free.

Awe the licentious, and restrain the rude;   21
Soften the sullen, clear the cloudy brow:
Be, more than princes' gifts, thy favours sued; —
She hazards all, who will the least allow.

But hope not, courted idol of mankind,   25
On this proud eminence secure to stay;
Subduing and subdued, thou soon shalt find
Thy coldness soften, and thy pride give way.

Then, then, abandon each ambitious thought,   29
Conquest or rule thy heart shall feebly move,
In Nature's school, by her soft maxims taught
That separate rights are lost in mutual love.

William Godwin, *Memoirs of the Author of A Vindication of the Rights of Woman* (London: Joseph Johnson, 1798) 108–14

After Wollstonecraft's death in 1797, her husband Godwin (1756–1836) published her *Posthumous Works* and his own *Memoirs* of her life. The *Memoirs* proved to be the most controversial assessment of her career, as its revelations about her passion for Henry Fuseli and especially Gilbert Imlay, and about her subsequent suicide attempts, gave conservatives the ammunition they needed to brand Wollstonecraft as not only politically subversive but morally corrupt as well (see Polwhele (**pp. 44–6**) and Bisset (**pp. 46–7**) in this section). In these *Memoirs* the bereaved Godwin constructed a vision of Wollstonecraft as romantic hero – "a female Werter" (see footnote 1 overleaf). Not merely the rational philosopher, already known to her audience through her published works, but the woman of sensibility, the devoted friend, and the adventurous radical emerge from Godwin's frank account. A second edition of the *Memoirs*, also in 1798, toned down some of the more sexually suggestive revelations, but the damage was done, and through its subsequent reception the *Memoirs* helped establish the two divergent nineteenth-century traditions of reading Wollstonecraft, as hero and as whore. This excerpt describes Wollstonecraft in 1793 Paris, when she and Imlay had begun living together.

Mary was now arrived at the situation, which, for two or three preceding years, her reason had pointed out to her as affording the most substantial prospect of happiness. She had been tossed and agitated by the waves of misfortune. Her childhood, as she often said, had known few of the endearments, which constitute the principal happiness of childhood. The temper of her father had early given to her mind a severe cast of thought, and substituted the inflexibility of resistance for the confidence of affection. The cheerfulness of her entrance upon womanhood, had been darkened, by an attendance upon the death-bed of her mother, and the still more afflicting calamity of her eldest sister. Her exertions to create a joint independence for her sisters and herself, had been attended, neither with the success, nor the pleasure, she had hoped from them. Her first youthful passion, her friendship for Fanny, had encountered many disappointments, and, in fine, a melancholy and premature catastrophe. Soon after these accumulated mortifications, she was engaged in a contest with a near relation, whom she regarded as unprincipled, respecting the wreck of her father's fortune. In this affair she suffered the double pain, which arises from moral indignation, and disappointed benevolence. Her exertions to assist almost every member of her family, were great and unremitted. Finally, when she indulged a romantic affection for Mr Fuseli, and fondly imagined that she should find in it the solace of her cares, she perceived too late, that, by continually impressing on her mind fruitless images of unreserved affection and domestic felicity, it only served to give new pungency to the sensibility that was destroying her.

Some persons may be inclined to observe, that the evils here enumerated, are not among the heaviest in the catalogue of human calamities. But evils take their rank more from the temper of the mind that suffers them, than from their abstract nature. Upon a man of a hard and insensible disposition, the shafts of misfortune often fall pointless and impotent. There are persons, by no means hard and insensible, who, from an elastic and sanguine turn of mind, are continually prompted to look on the fair side of things, and, having suffered one fall, immediately rise again, to pursue their course, with the same eagerness, the same hope, and the same gaiety, as before. On the other hand, we not unfrequently meet with persons, endowed with the most exquisite and delicious sensibility, whose minds seem almost of too fine a texture to encounter the vicissitudes of human affairs, to whom pleasure is transport, and disappointment is agony indescribable. This character is finely portrayed by the author of The Sorrows of Werter. Mary was in this respect a female Werter.[1]

She brought then, in the present instance, a wounded and sick heart, to take refuge in the bosom of a chosen friend. Let it not however be imagined, that she brought a heart, querulous, and ruined in its taste for pleasure. No; her whole character seemed to change with a change of fortune. Her sorrows, the depression of her spirits, were forgotten, and she assumed all the simplicity and the vivacity of a youthful mind. She was like a serpent upon a rock, that casts its slough, and appears again with the brilliancy, the sleekness, and the elastic activity of its happiest age.[2] She was playful, full of confidence, kindness and sympathy. Her eyes assumed new lustre, and her cheeks new colour and smoothness. Her voice became chearful; her temper overflowing with universal kindness; and that smile of bewitching tenderness from day to day illuminated her countenance, which all

---

1 Goethe's *Sorrows of Young Werther* (1774) was immensely popular, and featured a tragic love triangle in which the Romantic hero commits suicide. In 1795 Wollstonecraft would make two suicide attempts after discovering that Imlay had moved in with another woman.
2 The second edition omits this sentence.

who knew her will so well recollect, and which won, both heart and soul, the affection of almost every one that beheld it.

Mary now reposed herself upon a person, of whose honour and principles she had the most exalted idea. She nourished an individual affection, which she saw no necessity of subjecting to restraint; and a heart like hers was not formed to nourish affection by halves. Her conception of Mr Imlay's "tenderness and worth had twisted him closely round her heart;" and she "indulged the thought, that she had thrown out some tendrils, to cling to the elm by which she wished to be supported." This was "talking a new language to her;" but "conscious that she was not a parasite-plant," she was willing to encourage and foster the luxuriancies of affection.[3] Her confidence was entire; her love was unbounded. Now, for the first time in her life, she gave a loose to all the sensibilities of her nature.[4]

Richard Polwhele, *The Unsex'd Females* (London: Cadell & Davies, 1798) 14–20, 24–5

Polwhele's personal attack on Wollstonecraft and fellow feminists is well known, in part due to its near hysterical urgency and its thorough coverage of women writers at the close of the eighteenth century. Polwhele (1760–1838) was a conservative Anglican cleric like Beloe (**p. 53**); his *Unsex'd Females* helped establish the moralistic opposition between Hannah More and Wollstonecraft that recent criticism has challenged (see Guest 1995, **pp. 77–9**), as well as the passion versus reason dichotomy in Wollstonecraft (though Polwhele suggests, paradoxically, that she suffered from an excess of both). Polwhele's notes dwell on the personal details revealed in Godwin's *Memoirs*, and argue that "she died a death that strongly marked the distinction of the sexes, by pointing out the destiny of women, and the diseases to which they are liable" (*The Unsex'd Females*, p. 30). I have cut some of Polwhele's footnotes, modernized his punctuation, and noted line numbers for this excerpt.

See Wollstonecraft, whom no decorum checks,   1
Arise, the intrepid champion of her sex;
O'er humbled man assert the sovereign claim,
And slight the timid blush[1] of virgin fame.

---

3   "Her conception . . . affection": the second edition omits this description of Wollstonecraft's love for Imlay. Godwin quotes from Wollstonecraft's letters to Imlay, which he published in part in the *Posthumous Works*.

4   The second edition adds a justification here, including: "The mistake of Mary in this instance is easy of detection. She did not give full play to her judgement in this most important choice of life. She was too much under the influence of the melancholy and disappointment which had driven her from her native land; and, gratified with the first gleam of promised relief, she ventured not to examine with too curious a research into the soundness of her expectation."

---

1   [Polwhele's note.] That Miss Wollstonecraft was a sworn enemy to blushes, I need not remark. But many of my readers, perhaps, will be astonished to hear, that at several of our boarding-schools for young ladies, a blush incurs a penalty.

"Go, go (she cries) ye tribes of melting maids,   5
Go, screen your softness in sequester'd shades;
With plaintive whispers woo the unconscious grove,
And feebly perish, as depis'd ye love.
What tho' the fine Romances of Rousseau
Bid the flame flutter, and the bosom glow;   10
Tho' the rapt Bard, your empire fond to own,
Fall prostrate and adore your living throne,
The living throne his hands presum'd to rear,
Its seat a simper, and its base a tear;[2]
Soon shall the sex disdain the illusive sway,   15
And wield the sceptre in yon blaze of day;[3]
Ere long, each little artifice discard,
No more by weakness[4] winning fond regard;
Nor eyes, that sparkle from their blushes, roll,
Nor catch the languors of the sick'ning soul,   20
Nor the quick flutter, nor the coy reserve,
But nobly boast the firm gymnastic nerve;[5]
Nor more affect with Delicacy's fan
To hide the emotion from congenial man;
To the bold heights where glory beams, aspire,   25
Blend mental energy with Passion's fire,
Surpass their rivals in the powers of mind
And vindicate *the Rights of womankind*."
[. . .]
Alas! in every aspiration bold,
I saw the creature of a mortal mould: 30
Yes! not untrembling (tho' I half ador'd
A mind by Genius fraught, by Science stor'd)
I saw the Heroine mount the dazzling dome
Where Shakespeare's spirit kindled, to illume
His favourite FUSELI, and with magic might   35
To earthly sense unlock'd a world of light!
Full soon, amid the high pictorial blaze,
I saw a Sibyl-transport in her gaze:

---

2 [Polwhele's note.] According to Rousseau, the empire of women is the empire of softness – of
  address: their commands, are caresses; their menaces, are tears. [Ed.: See Rousseau's *Emile* in
  Contexts (**pp. 17–22**) and the poems by Barrett Browning (**pp. 54–5**) and Barbauld (**pp. 41–2**).]
3 [Polwhele's note.] Her visual nerve was purged with euphrasy: she could see the illumination fast
  approaching, unperceived as it was by common mortals.
4 [Polwhele's note.] "Like monarchs, we have been flattered into imbecillity, by those who wish to
  take advantage of our weakness;" says Mary Hays (Essays and Letters, p. 92). But, whether
  flattered or not, women were always weak: and female weakness hath accomplished, what the
  forced of arms could not affect . . .
5 [Polwhele's note.] Miss Wollstonecraft seriously laments the neglect of all muscular exercises, at
  our female Boarding-schools. [Ed.: this objection to Wollstonecraft's call for women to increase
  their physical strength was common among conservatives; see Craciun (**pp. 82–4**).]

To the great Artist, from his wondrous Art,
I saw transferr'd the whole enraptur'd Heart;   40
Till, mingling soul with soul, in airy trance,
Enlighten'd and inspir'd at every glance,[6]
And from the dross of appetite refin'd,
And, grasping at angelic food, all mind,
Down from the empyreal heights she sunk, betray'd   45
To poor Philosophy – a love-sick maid!

Robert Bisset, rev. of Godwin's *Memoirs of the Author of the Vindication of the Rights of Woman, Anti-Jacobin Review I* (1798) 94–108. Reprinted in *Lives of the Great Romantics III vol. 2: Wollstonecraft,* ed. Harriet Jump (London: Pickering & Chatto, 1999) 130–2

Bisset (1759–1805) was a frequent contributor to the arch-conservative *Anti-Jacobin Review*, and his writings include the *Life of Edmund Burke* (1798) and *A Defence of the Slave Trade* (1804). This influential review of Godwin's *Memoirs* of Wollstonecraft, like Polwhele's and the *British Critic*'s, established the dominant conservative tradition of reading Wollstonecraft's politics and writings as the effects of a transgressive sexual (im)morality.

Next succeeded her *Rights of Woman*, which the superficial fancied to be profound, and the profound knew to be superficial: it indeed had very little title to the character of ingenuity. Her doctrines are almost all obvious corollaries from the theorems of Paine. If we admit his principle, that all men have an equal right to be governors and statesmen, without any regard to their talents and virtues, there can be no reason for excluding women or even children. Such was the intellectual process by which Mary was led to her extravagant, absurd, and destructive theories. Mrs. W. having ardent sensibility, and a vigorous imagination, possessed no small excellence in description, but had neither materials nor habits of close reasoning and cautions investigation, and therefore ought to have avoided discussions in which these were necessary. [. . .]

The substance of Mrs. Wollstonecroft's moral sentiments and history was briefly this—the creature of impulse, some of her propensities were benevolent, and frequently operated to the good of those who were placed within the sphere of her actions. Not directed, however, by sound principles, she considered herself as exempted from those restraints on inclination, which are necessary to the welfare of society. Prompted by the feeling of the time, she even in her friendly acts proceeded much farther than virtue, guided by reason, would dictate. [. . .] Her constitution, as the philosopher, her husband, bears testimony, was very amorous. Her passions were farther inflamed "by the state of celibacy and

---

6   [Polwhele's note.] Philosophism has reduced the God of the Universe, to this pervading mind or spirit.

restraint in which she had hitherto lived, and to which the rules of polished society *condemn* an unmarried woman."[1] The amorous lady fell in love with a Mr. Fuseli, a married man, and continued long to have a violent affection for him: to what length it was indulged has not appeared.

Mary Robinson, *A Letter to the Women of England on the Injustice of Mental Subordination* (1799): *A Romantic Circles Hypertext Edition* (1998), eds. Adriana Craciun, Anne Close, Orianne Smith, Megan Musgrave www.rc.umd.edu/editions/robinson/cover.htm 1–2

A leading poet and popular novelist of the Romantic period, Robinson (1758–1800) also suffered from public scandal surrounding her extramarital relationships, most famously with the Prince of Wales. Robinson's *Letter to the Women of England on the Injustice of Mental Subordination* (1799) is a feisty feminist polemic that claims allegiance with Robinson's friend, the recently deceased Wollstonecraft, an unusual gesture of feminist solidarity after the publication of Godwin's controversial *Memoirs* in 1798.

Custom, from the earliest periods of antiquity, has endeavoured to place the female mind in the subordinate ranks of intellectual sociability. WOMAN has ever been considered as a lovely and fascinating part of the creation, but her claims to mental equality have not only been questioned, by envious and interested sceptics; but, by a barbarous policy in the other sex, considerably depressed, for want of liberal and classical cultivation. I will not expatiate largely on the doctrines of certain philosophical sensualists, who have aided in this destructive oppression, because an illustrious British female, (whose death has not been sufficiently lamented, but to whose genius posterity will render justice) has already written volumes in vindication of "The Rights of Woman."[1] But I shall endeavour to prove that, under the present state of mental subordination, universal knowledge is not only benumbed and blighted, but true happiness, originating in enlightened manners, retarded in its progress. Let WOMAN once assert her proper sphere, unshackled by prejudice, and unsophisticated by vanity; and pride, (the noblest species of pride,) will establish her claims to the participation of power, both mentally and corporeally.

---

1   William Godwin, *Memoirs of the Author of A Vindication of the Rights of Woman*, ed. Pamela Clemit and Gina Luria Walker (Peterborough: Broadview, 2001); Bisset's italics.

---

1   [Robinson's note.] The writer of this letter, though avowedly of the same school, disdains the drudgery of servile imitation. The same subject may be argued in a variety of ways; and though this letter may not display the philosophical reasoning with which "The Rights of Woman" abounded; it is not less suited to the purpose. For it requires a legion of Wollstonecrafts to undermine the poisons of prejudice and malevolence. [Ed.: the *Anti-Jacobin*'s review of Robinson's *Letter* concluded that: "It is *our* province, and our duty, to meet this legion; ('*for they are many!*') and, since '*no man can bind them, no, not with chains,*' to endeavour to '*cast them out!*' " (vol. 3 (1799) 146).]

Anne Grant, *Letters from the Mountains*, vol. 2 of 3, 2nd edn (London: Longman, Hurst, Rees & Orme, 1807) 268–70, 272–5. From letter 51, to Miss Oury

Anne Macvicar Grant (1755–1838) of Laggan, in the Scottish highlands, supported eight children through her prolific writings on Scottish subjects, most famously her *Letters from the Mountains* and her popular *Essay on the Superstitions of the Highlanders*. In 1814 she published a conservative reply to Anna Laetitia Barbauld's antinationalist poem, *Eighteen Hundred and Eleven*, titled *Eighteen Hundred and Thirteen*. (For Wollstonecraft's negative response to Barbauld's more traditional early poetry, see **p. 131**, and for Barbauld's poetic retort, **pp. 41–2**.) In her lengthy critique of the *Rights of Woman*, Grant reveals a fascination with Wollstonecraft's bold ideas, but finds the uncertainties of women's freedom frightening.

Glasgow, Jan. 2, 1794

[. . .] I have seen Mary Woolstonecroft's book, which is so run after here, that there is no keeping it long enough to read it leisurely, though one had leisure. [. . .] I consider this work as every way dangerous. First, because the author to considerable powers adds feeling, and I dare say a degree of rectitude of intention. She speaks from conviction on her own part, and has completely imposed on herself before she attempts to mislead you. Then because she speaks in such a strain of seeming piety, and quotes Scripture in a manner so applicable and emphatic that you are thrown off your guard, and surprised into partial acquiescence, before you observe that the deduction to be drawn from her position, is in direct contradiction, not only to Scripture, reason, the common sense and universal custom of the world, but even to parts of her own system, and many of her own assertions. [. . .] I think the great advantage that women, taken upon the whole, have over men, is, that they are more gentle, benevolent, and virtuous. Much of this only superiority they owe to living secure and protected in the shade. Let them loose, to go impudently through all the j[o]stling paths of politics and business, and they will encounter all the corruptions that men are subject to, without the same powers either of resistance or recovery; for, the delicacy of the female mind is like other fine things; in attempting to rub out a stain, you destroy the texture. I am sorry to tell you, *in a very low whisper*, that this intellectual equality that the Misses make such a rout about, has no real existence. [. . .] Where a woman has those superior powers of mind to which we give the name of genius, she will exert them under all disadvantages: Jean Jacques says truly, genius will educate itself, and, like flame, burst through all obstructions.[1] Certainly in the present state of society, when knowledge is so very attainable, a strong and vigorous intellect may soon find its level. Creating hot-beds for female genius, is merely another way of

---

1   As Wollstonecraft understood, Rousseau excluded women from this formulation of genius: "as regards works of genius, they are out of the reach of women" (*Emile* 386).

forcing exotic productions, which, after all, are mere luxuries, indifferent in their kind, and cost more time and expence than they are worth. As to superiority of mental powers, Mrs. W. is doubtless the empress of female philosophers; yet what has she done for philosophy, or for the sex, but closed a ditch, to open a gulf? There is a degree of boldness in her conceptions, and masculine energy in her style, that is very imposing. There is a gloomy grandeur in her imagination, while she explores the regions of intellect without chart or compass, which gives one the idea of genius wandering through chaos. [. . .] What, as I said before, has she done? shewed us all the miseries of our condition; robbed us of the only sure remedy for the evils of life, the sure hope of a blessed immortality; and left for our comfort the rudiments of crude, unfinished systems, that crumble to nothing whenever you begin to examine the materials of which they are constructed. [. . .] When the desired revolution is brought about, will not the most sanguine advocates of equality be satisfied, in the first national council, with having an equal number of each sex elected? Now I foresee that when this is done, (as girls, or very old women, will not be eligible for the duties of legislation, and mothers have certainly a greater stake in the commonwealth) a third of the female members will be lying-in, recovering, or nursing; for you can never admit the idea of a female philosopher giving her child to be nursed.

Mary Hays, "Memoirs of Mary Wollstonecraft" *The Annual Necrology for 1797–8* (London, 1800), reprinted in *Lives of the Great Romantics III vol. 2: Wollstonecraft*, ed. Harriet Jump (London: Pickering & Chatto, 1999) 177–8, 180–1, 183

After Godwin's *Memoirs* revealed the controversial details of Wollstonecraft's life, it was Hays (1760–1843) who became Wollstonecraft's most vocal disciple. In her autobiographical novel *The Memoirs of Emma Courtney* (1796), Hays had advocated that women's sexual passion was as important as their reason, a radical claim that led the author to be satirized like Wollstonecraft and Mary Robinson, and one which also epitomizes Hays's complex response to Wollstonecraft's faith in reason and ambivalence towards passion. Hays attended Wollstonecraft's deathbed, and afterwards published anonymously her own feminist polemic, the *Appeal to the Men of Great Britain in Behalf of Women* (1798), as well as several memoirs of Wollstonecraft. See also Wollstonecraft's letter to Hays (**pp. 24–5**).

The intrepid spirit, daring flights, lofty pretensions, and disdain of sanctioned opinions, which characterize the productions of the vindicator of the Rights of Woman, have combined to excite an extraordinary degree of attention; which some events, of a peculiar nature, in her personal history have had a tendency to increase. By the distinction which the reputation of superior talents confers, their possessors are exalted to a dangerous pre-eminence: attention is roused, curiosity excited, their claims are subjected to a scrutiny, in which all the nobler and all the baser passions become equally interested. [. . .] Persons of the finest and most exquisite genius have probably the greatest sensibility, consequently the strongest passions, by the fervor of which they are too often betrayed into error. Vigorous minds are with difficulty restrained within the trammels of authority; a spirit of enterprise; a passion for experiment, a liberal curiosity, urges them to quit beaten paths, to explore untried ways, to burst the fetters of prescription, and to acquire wisdom by an individual experience. [. . .]

Those whom a calmer temperament conduct in an even path, deviating neither to the right nor to the left, will find their reward in the safety of their course. But it is to speculative and enterprising spirits, whom stronger powers and more impetuous passions impel forward, regardless of established usages, that all great changes and improvements in society have owed their origin. If, intoxicated by contemplating the grand projects in their imagination, they deviate into extravagance, and lose sight of the nature of man, their theories remain to be corrected by experience, while, in the gratitude of posterity, the contemporary cry of interest will be absorbed and forgotten. [. . .]

The high masculine tone, sometimes degenerating into coarseness, that characterizes this performance [*A Vindication of the Rights of Woman*], is in a variety of parts softened and blended with a tenderness of sentiment, an exquisite delicacy of feeling, that touches the heart, and takes captive the imagination. [. . .]

In a case like this, a solitary individual affords no example; Mary Wollstonecraft's experiment was in a high degree perilous; it is improbable that another woman should exist, equal in fortitude and resource, similarly circumstanced: nor, for the credit of human nature, dare we believe, how profligate forever may be the state of society, that a conduct, originating in motives thus magnanimous, would in all instances have met with a similar reward. There are few rules so universal to admit of no exception. The mind of Mary Wollstonecraft was not formed on common principles.

William Blake, "Mary" (The Pickering Manuscript, 1801–5). *The Poetry and Prose of William Blake*, ed. David Erdman (Garden City: Doubleday Anchor, 1970) 478–9

The visionary poet and artist William Blake (1757–1827) was a member of Joseph Johnson's (and Wollstonecraft's) radical circle. Blake illustrated Wollstonecraft's *Original Stories from Real Life* (1788), published by Johnson, and this unpublished poem, "Mary," may be a reflection on his friend Wollstonecraft and her suffering in a sexually hypocritical and repressive society.

Sweet Mary the first time she ever was there   1
Came into the Ball room among the Fair
The young Men and Maidens around her throng
And these are the words upon every tongue

An Angel is here from the heavenly Climes   5
Or again does return the Golden times
Her eyes outshine every brilliant ray
She opens her lips tis the Month of May

Mary moves in soft beauty and conscious delight   9
To augment with sweet smiles all the joys of the Night
Nor once blushes to own to the rest of the Fair
That sweet Love and Beauty are worthy our care

In the Morning the Villagers rose with delight   13
And repeated with pleasure the joys of the night
And Mary arose among Friends to be free
But no Friend from henceforward thou Mary shalt see

Some said she was proud some calld her a whore   17
And some when she passed by shut to the door
A damp cold came oer her her blushes all fled
Her lillies and roses are blighted and shed

O why was I born with a different Face   20
Why was I not born like this Envious Race
Why did Heaven adorn me with bountiful hand
And then set me down in an envious Land

To be weak as a Lamb and smooth as a dove   25
And not to raise Envy is calld Christian Love
But if you raise Envy your Merits to blame
For planting such spite in the weak and the tame

I will humble my Beauty I will not dress fine   29
I will keep from the Ball and my Eyes shall not shine
And if any Girls Lover forsakes her for me
I'll refuse him my hand and from Envy be free

She went out in Morning attird plain and neat   33
Proud Marys gone Mad said the Child in the Street
She went out in Morning in plain neat attire
And came home in Evening bespatterd with mire

She trembled and wept sitting on the Bed side   37
She forgot it was Night and she trembled and cried
She forgot it was Night she forgot it was Morn
Her soft Memory imprinted with Faces of Scorn

With Faces of Scorn and with Eyes of disdain   41
Like foul Fiends inhabiting Marys mild Brain
She remembers no Face like the Human Divine
All Faces have Envy sweet Mary but thine

And thine is a Face of sweet Love in Despair   45
And thine is a Face of mild sorrow and care
And thine is a Face of wild terror and fear
That shall never be quiet till laid on its bier

Anonymous, *A Defence of the Character and Conduct of the Late Mary Wollstonecraft Godwin* (1803), reprinted in *Lives of the Great Romantics III vol. 2: Wollstonecraft*, ed. Harriet Jump (London: Pickering & Chatto, 1999) 221–3

While the author of this anonymous and rare defence of Wollstonecraft is not known, it may be Archibald Hamilton Rowan (1751–1834), an Irish radical whom Wollstonecraft knew in Paris (his account of Wollstonecraft was published in his *Autobiography* (Dublin, 1840)). The *Defence* celebrates Wollstonecraft's intolerance for injustice, and her courageous pursuit of a philosophical experiment, rare qualities to praise at a time when women's forbearance and resignation were increasingly called for by moralists.

The aspersors of Mary Wollstonecraft exult at her disappointment, regarding it as a demonstration of the fallacy of her system. That her system was imperfect, and by no means adapted, considering the present state of society and manners, for general application, has been already admitted; but that it is essentially erroneous, because it is incomplete, we must be permitted to doubt; till the objectors have produced at least one human system, that is complete in all its parts, and uniformly effective upon every application. Her's is certainly founded in Nature and Reason, and so far is consistent with Truth; it is therefore well adapted for the conscientious Moralist and Philosopher: but it is inapplicable to persons of gross appetites and vulgar apprehensions; that is, to the great mass of mankind. The failure of her experiment is no further attributable to herself, than in her mistaking a proper object of choice, and giving him credit for qualities and principles of heart, which lay only upon his tongue. For, with such feelings, sentiments, and views as appear to have actuated him, there is sufficient reason to suspect that he would have proved faithless, in *spite of legal obligations*; and in such case, she would have been for ever wedded to misery. In appealing to the laws of the country for redress (a measure which the loftiness of her spirit would never have permitted her to adopt,) she might very probably have failed of her object; and certainly would never have recovered her lost peace. You observe that I omit all supposition of her tamely enduring the indignity, as some women do from pliability or rather pusillanimity of disposition; pretending to be satisfied with a divided heart; because such a degradation of character was totally foreign to the whole tenor of her conduct, and to her declared hypothesis of equal rights.

William Beloe, "Chapter LII: Mary Wollstonecraft" *The Sexagenarian; or, the Recollections of a Literary Life*, 2 vols. (London: Rivington, 1818) 1: 348–9, 351–2

The conservative Anglican cleric Beloe (1756–1817) co-founded the *British Critic*; his sensationalized account of Wollstonecraft's affair with Imlay helps establish the misogynist tradition of reading her as a whore, and also explicitly links Wollstonecraft to Sappho, the woman of genius reduced to a fallen woman through her ungovernable passions. Mary Robinson's *Sappho and Phaon* (1796) had offered a very different vision of Sappho as a woman of superior passion and intellect, yet accounts of Sappho (and Wollstonecraft) like Beloe's persisted throughout the century.

Few individuals have combined qualities and talents so various, and so contradictory; very few females have experienced more or greater vicissitudes, and none ever employed their time and abilities on subjects so much at variance with the common feelings and opinions of mankind. [. . .]

At Paris our heroine fell in the way of a plain downright man of business from America, with no particular recommendation either of fortune, person, or talent; but strange to tell, she almost instantaneously conceived for him a passion yet more violent and uncontroulable than that which she had formerly experienced for Mr. [Imlay]. To him she sacrificed every thing, even her modesty; for though she without scruple lived with him as his wife, she refused to be married to him even according to the slight and unsatisfactory ceremonial then observed in France. Her reasons for this conduct were somewhat whimsical. She did not choose that he should be made liable to debts formerly incurred by her, and she also entertained the idea, that an avowed marriage with her, would expose him to certain family inconveniences and embarrassments.

But alas! for such hasty attachments! neither did our American return her passion with a suitable enthusiasm. [. . .] To be brief—he chose another companion, and recommended to her to do the same. This was rather too much to be endured. The lady did not indeed, in imitation of Sappho, precipitate herself from another Leucadian rock;[1] she chose a more vulgar mode of death; she put some lead into her pockets, and threw herself into the water. She did not, however, use lead enough, as there was still gas sufficient left in her head to counterpoise it. She was rescued from the watery bier, and lived again to experience the feverish varieties of the tender passion.

---

1   The Greek poet Sappho (*c*.600 BC) is generally regarded as the greatest lyric poet of antiquity, and was also known for the intensity of her passion for women. In his epistle "Sappho to Phaon," Ovid famously (and inaccurately) attributed her death to suicide by leaping from the cliffs of Leucas after her passion for Phaon was unrequited.

Victorian and Early Twentieth-Century Responses

Elizabeth Barrett Browning, "Fragment of an 'Essay on Woman'" (c.1821) (unpublished)

A highly regarded Victorian poet, Barrett Browning (1806–61) is best known for her "novel in verse," *Aurora Leigh* (1856), in which she explored the issues of women's intellectual, sexual, economic, and religious rights and duties in an epic poem about the poet Aurora Leigh and the "fallen woman" Marian Erle. Elizabeth and Robert Browning each wrote a poem about Wollstonecraft, their two responses illustrating the divergent traditions of reading her as either intellectual and political heroine, or victim of debilitating passions, respectively. Robert Browning's poem, "Mary Wollstonecraft and Fuseli," focused on Wollstonecraft's ill-fated love for the painter, revealed in John Knowles's *Life and Writings of Henry Fuseli* (1831). Elizabeth Barrett Browning, on the other hand, explored the central argument of the *Rights of Woman* regarding the destructive effects of women's lack of education and independence, asking the key question: "why must woman to be loved be weak?" Barrett Browning declared that "I read Mary Wollstonecraft when I was thirteen: no, twelve! ... and, through the whole course of my childhood, I had a steady indignation against Nature who made me a woman, & a determinate resolution to dress up in men's clothes as soon as ever I was free of the nursery, & go into the world 'to seek my fortune.'"[1]

Imperious Man! is this alone thy pride	1
T'Enslave the heart that lingers at thy side?	
Smother each flash of intellectual fire,	
And bid Ambition's noblest throb expire?	
Pinion the wing, that yearns for glory's light,	5
Then boast the strength of thy superior flight?	
Go! love the fabric of unmeaning clay,	
The flattered creature of an idle day!	
And as the trembling partner of thy lot	
Hangs on thy steps unheeded, or forgot,	10
Thy cradle rocks, and weeps upon thy grave,	
Tis thine to fetter, scorn, disdain, enslave!	
And while she smiles, submissive, on thy breast,	
Debase the faithful heart that loves thee best!	

---

1   Elizabeth Barrett Browning, letter to Mary Russell Mitford, 22 July [1842], *The Brownings' Correspondence*, vol. 6, ed. Philip Kelley and Ronald Hudson (Winfield, KS: Wedgestone Press, 1984) 42.

Teach her a lovely, abject thing, to be!   15
For such are *generous deeds*, and *worthy thee*!

Eternal Genius! thou mysterious tie,
That links the Mortal, and Divinity!
Say, hath thy sacred influence never stole
With radiance unobscured, on Woman's soul;   20
Till, waking into greatness, it hath caught
The glow of fancy, and the life of thought,
Breathing Conception, eloquence that fires,
And all that learning gives, & Heav'n inspires?
Is Woman doomed obscure, & lone, to sigh?   25
Comnena, Dacier, More, DeStael, reply![2]

Eliza Lynn Linton, "Mary Wollstonecraft" The English Republic 3 (1854) 418–24 (421, 424)

Linton (1822–1898) was a professional woman of letters who worked as a foreign correspondent, critic, and historical novelist, and married the republican publisher William Linton in 1858. The illustration that accompanied Linton's essay was based on John Opie's portrait, making Wollstonecraft look more traditionally feminine than Opie did, and was probably engraved by William Linton (see Frontispiece). Despite her praise for Wollstonecraft in this early essay in William's radical journal, Linton is best known for her vicious essays attacking feminists, whom she famously labeled "The Girl of the Period," particularly those who challenged what Linton considered to be women's "natural" duties and physical limitations. The violent contradictions of Linton's views on women (whose vanity and extravagance she mercilessly, one could say misogynistically, attacked) place her in an oddly parallel position to Wollstonecraft's regarding middle-class women's frivolity and idleness.

Out of the dead level of our modern fine-ladyism every now and then a woman rises like a goddess standing above the rest: a woman of fair proportions and unmutilated nature, a woman of strength, will, intellect, and courage, practically asserting by her own life the truth of her equality with man, and boldly claiming as her right also an equal share in the privileges hitherto reserved for himself alone. None stronger, more independent, or more noble, than Mary Wollstonecraft, one of the first, as she was one of the ablest, defenders of the Rights of Woman. [. . .]

---

2   Anna Comnena (1083–1148) was a Byzantine historian and physician; Anne Dacier (1654–1720) was a leading French classical translator; Hannah More (1745–1833) was Wollstonecraft's contemporary, an influential conservative moralist and educator; Madame de Staël (1766–1817) was the leading theorist and cultural critic of European Romanticism, and author of *Corinne* (1807).

She is one of our greatest women, because one of the first who stormed the citadel of selfishness and ignorance, because one of the bravest and one of the most complete. Hers was one of those great loving, generous souls that make no bargain between self and duty, that dare to follow out their own law and to walk by their own light, that refuse vicarious help and work out their salvation by their own strength, that appeal to God for judgement, not to man for approbation. She was one of the priestesses of the future; and men will yet gather constancy and truth from her example: so true it is that a good deed never dies out, but extends its influence as far as Humanity can reach. [. . .]

We have Mary Wollstonecrafts by the dozen among us in her abstract ability: how many in her moral courage? Yet we have the same fight to fight that she had, and the same things remain undone that she would fain have forwarded with a helping hand. Who will take this stigma of cowardice and the slave's degradation from the women of England? Who will show that we have minds as subtle and wills as strong as Mary Wollstonecraft of the past? Who will prove that if they will our women shall be free and noble, as Godwin's wife would have made them, as Godwin's wife did make herself? Whose voice will answer us from the distance, whose hand meet us in the darkness?

Harriet Martineau, *Harriet Martineau's Autobiography*, 3 vols. (London: Smith, Elder & Co., 1877), reprinted in *Lives of the Great Romantics III vol. 2: Wollstonecraft*, ed. Harriet Jump (London: Pickering & Chatto, 1999) 275–6

A prolific journalist and political economist, Martineau (1802–76) wrote widely on women's labor, public health, political economy, and history. Despite her advocacy for women's financial independence and education, Martineau saw Wollstonecraft as "a poor victim of passion" (p. 277) whose personal crises injured the cause of women's rights.

. . . I never could reconcile my mind to Mary Wollstonecraft's writings, or to whatever I heard of her. It seemed to me, from the earliest time when I could think on the subject of Woman's Rights and condition, that the first requisite to advancement is the self-reliance which results from self-discipline. Women who would improve the condition and chances of their sex must, I am certain, be not only affectionate and devoted, but rational and dispassionate, with the devotedness of benevolence, and not merely of personal love. But Mary Wollstonecraft was, with all her powers, a poor victim of passion, with no control over her own peace, and no calmness or content except when the needs of her individual nature were satisfied. I felt, forty years ago, in regard to her, just what I feel now in regard to some of the most conspicuous denouncers of the wrongs of women at this day;—that their advocacy of Woman's cause becomes mere detriment, precisely in proportion to their personal reasons for unhappiness, unless they have fortitude enough (which loud complainants usually have not) to get their own troubles under their feet, and leave them wholly out of the account in stating the state of their sex. Nobody can be further than I am from being satisfied with the condition of my own sex, under the law and custom of my own country; but I decline all fellowship and co-operation with women of genius or otherwise favourable position, who injure the cause by their personal tendencies. When I see an eloquent writer[1] insinuating to every body who comes across her that she is the victim of her husband's carelessness and cruelty, while he never spoke in his own defence: when I see her violating all good taste by her obtrusiveness in society, and oppressing every body about her by her epicurean selfishness every day, while raising in print an eloquent cry on behalf of the oppressed; I feel, to the bottom of my heart, that she is the worst enemy of the cause she professes to plead. The best friends of that cause are women who are morally as well as intellectually competent to the most serious business of life, and who must be clearly seen to speak from conviction of the truth, and not from personal unhappiness. The best friends of the cause are the happy wives and the busy, cheerful, satisfied single women, who have no injuries of their own to avenge, and no painful vacuity or mortification to relieve. The best advocates are yet to come,—in the persons of women who are obtaining access to real social business,—the female physicians and other professors in America, the women of business and the female artists of France; and the hospital administrators, the nurses, the educators and substantially successful authors of our own country.

Mathilde Blind, "Mary Wollstonecraft" *New Quarterly Magazine* 10 (July 1878) 390–412 (398–9, 412)

Blind (1841–96) was a feminist, poet, and sympathetic editor of Percy Shelley and Byron who grew up in a family of revolutionaries (her brother tried to assassinate Bismarck). Like many Victorian feminists, Blind tones down Wollstonecraft's radicalness, saying that her proposals "are neither startling nor subversive according to nineteenth-century ideas" because Wollstonecraft emphasizes the duties of women and the importance of domestic life.

Mary Wollstonecraft's 'Vindication of the Rights of Woman,' which has enjoyed the doubtful privilege of looming in the imagination of the reading world as a *terra incognita* of the most daring and subversive speculations concerning women, differs considerably from the works on the same subject published at the present day. Compared with the claims which have been advanced on behalf of the female sex by John Stuart Mill[1] and others, the rights vindicated by Mary

---

1 Caroline Norton (1808–77) was a successful poet whose husband charged her with committing adultery with the Prime Minister; her published revelations about her abusive husband were instrumental in bringing about the Married Women's Property and Divorce Act (1857).

1 Mill wrote *The Subjection of Women* (1869).

Wollstonecraft are, on the whole, of the most modest character, and but few of her demands, chiefly relating to the higher education of women, would be disputed by enlightened people of the present day: much of what she desired in that respect having, indeed, been put into practice – for example, in the classes opened for ladies at the London, Oxford, and Cambridge Universities and in the degrees now offered to them.[2]

Mary Wollstonecraft's treatise might perhaps with more justice be called the Duties instead of Rights of Woman. For its authoress is eloquent on the subject of the former; and it is in a great measure that they may properly fulfil their various duties as wives and mothers, sisters and daughters, that she claims for them certain rights, prominent amongst which she considers that of a thoroughly sound education. [. . .] Although her writings are at this day but little known and still less read, the spirit that animates them has, to a great extent, become part of the thought of our age, and at present many eminent men and women are putting into practice many of the theories she broached nearly a century ago.

Millicent Garrett Fawcett, "Introduction to the New Edition" of
A Vindication of the Rights of Woman (New York: Scribner & Welford, 1890) 1–30 (18–19, 20–1, 23, 24, 27–8)

Fawcett (1847–1929) was a writer and leader of the British suffrage movement, serving as head of the National Union of Women's Suffrage Societies from 1890 to 1919. In this introduction to a Victorian edition of *Rights of Woman* (1890), Fawcett praised Wollstonecraft's advocacy of women's economic and legal independence, and saw her as an important predecessor to Victorian suffragists: "The battle in which Mary Wollstonecraft took a leading part is still being waged." Yet Fawcett, like Blind (**pp. 57–8**) above, was keen to insist on Wollstonecraft's feminine propriety, describing her as "the essentially womanly woman," and in another essay, "The Emancipation of Women" (1891), compared her to the moralistic Harriet Martineau, who had attacked Wollstonecraft in her *Autobiography* (see **pp. 56–7**).[1]

Mary Wollstonecraft . . . does not claim for women intellectual or physical or moral equality with men. Her argument is that being weaker than men, physically and mentally, and not superior morally, the way in which women are brought up, and their subordination throughout life, first to their fathers, then to their husbands, prevents the due natural development of their physical, mental, and

---

2   Under the leadership of feminist and conservative Emily Davies, Girton College, Cambridge began admitting women in 1869.

---

1   Fawcett, "The Emancipation of Women" (*Fortnightly Review*, Nov. 1891) reprinted in *Criminals, Idiots, Women and Minors: Victorian Women's Writing on Women*, ed. Susan Hamilton (Peterborough: Broadview, 1995) 260.

moral capacities. How can the powers of the body be developed without physical exercise? [...] Mary Wollstonecraft pleaded that the lower degree of physical strength of women, and the strain upon that strength caused by maternity, ought to secure for them such conditions as regards exercise, clothing, and food as would make the most of that strength, and not reduce it to a vanishing point. [...]

Mary Wollstonecraft's great merit, however, lies in this, that with a detachment of mind from the prejudices and errors of her time, in regard to the position of women, that was quite extraordinary, she did not sanction any depreciation of the immense importance of the domestic duties of women. She constantly exalted what was truly feminine as the aim of woman's education and training; she recognized love and the attraction between the sexes as a cardinal fact in human nature, and "marriage as the foundation of almost every social virtue." Hence very largely from her initiative the women's rights movement in England has kept free from the excesses and follies that in some other countries have marred its course. Mary Wollstonecraft, in her writings as well as in her life, with its sorrows and errors, is the essentially womanly woman, with the motherly and wifely instincts strong within her, and caring for all she claims and pleads for on behalf of her sex, because she is convinced that a concession of a large measure of women's rights is essential to the highest possible conception and fulfilment of women's duties.

Emma Goldman, "Mary Wollstonecraft: Her Tragic Life and Her Passionate Struggle for Freedom" [1911] *Feminist Studies* 7.1 (1981) 114–21 (115–16, 121)

Goldman (1869–1940) was a leading anarchist feminist activist who published the anarchist journal *Mother Earth* and wrote widely, was imprisoned in the US in 1893, and deported to the USSR in 1919. Like most subsequent feminist commentators on Wollstonecraft, Goldman saw her own contradictions amplified in Wollstonecraft's. Goldman portrayed Wollstonecraft as a "Pioneer" and visionary who could see a promised land but never inhabit it, much like Goldman herself.[1]

Like the Falcon who soared through space in order to behold the Sun and then paid for it with his life, Mary drained the cup of tragedy, for such is the price of wisdom.

Much has been written and said about this wonderful champion of the eighteenth century, but the subject is too vast and still very far from being exhausted. The woman's movement of today and especially the suffrage movement will find in the life and struggle of Mary Wollstonecraft much that would show them the inadequacy of mere external gain as a means of freeing their sex. No doubt much

---

1   See Alice Wexler's Afterword to Goldman's essay in *Feminist Studies* 7.1 (1981) 122–33.

has been accomplished since Mary thundered against women's economic and political enslavement, but has that made her free? Has it added to the depth of her being? Has it brought joy and cheer in her life? Mary's own tragic life proves that economic and social rights for women alone are not enough to fill her life, nor yet enough to fill any deep life, man or woman. [. . .]

Mary Wollstonecraft, the intellectual genius, the daring fighter of the eighteenth, nineteenth, and twentieth Centuries, Mary Wollstonecraft, the woman and lover, was doomed to pain because of the very wealth of her being. With all her affairs she yet was pretty much alone, as every great soul must be alone—no doubt, that is the penalty for greatness.

Her indomitable courage in behalf of the disinherited of the earth has alienated her from her own time and created the discord in her being which alone accounts for her terrible tragedy with Imlay. Mary Wollstonecraft aimed for the highest summit of human possibilities. She was too wise and too worldly not to see the discrepancy between her world of ideals and her world of love that caused the break of the string of her delicate, complicated soul.

Virginia Woolf, "Mary Wollstonecraft" (1932), reprinted in *The Second Common Reader* (London: Hogarth Press, 1965) 156–63 (157–61)

Woolf is one of the best-known English novelists and essayists of the twentieth century, a member of the modernist Bloomsbury circle who was committed to expanding women's intellectual, political, and sexual rights. Woolf's famous essay follows in the nineteenth-century tradition of seeing Wollstonecraft's life as an experiment governed by a dialectic of theory and practice.

The Revolution thus was not merely an event that had happened outside her; it was an active agent in her own blood. She had been in revolt all her life—against tyranny, against law, against convention. The reformer's love of humanity, which has so much of hatred in it as well as love, fermented within her. The outbreak of revolution in France expressed some of her deepest theories and convictions, and she dashed off in the heat of that extraordinary moment those two eloquent and daring books—the *Reply to Burke* [*A Vindication of the Rights of Men*] and the *Vindication of the Rights of Woman*, which are so true that they seem now to contain nothing new in them—their originality has become our commonplace. [. . .]

The life of such a woman was bound to be tempestuous. Every day she made theories by which life should be lived; and every day she came smack against the rock of other people's prejudices. Every day too—for she was no pedant, no cold-blooded theorist—something was born in her that thrust aside her theories and forced her to model them afresh. She acted upon her theory that she had no legal claim upon Imlay; she refused to marry him; but when he left her alone week after week with the child she had borne him her agony was unendurable. [. . .] Tickling minnows he had hooked a dolphin, and the creature rushed him through the waters till he was dizzy and only wanted to escape. After all, though he had played at theory-making too, he was a business man, he depended upon soap and alum; "the secondary pleasures of life", he had to admit, "are very necessary to my comfort". [. . .]

Many millions have died and been forgotten in the hundred and thirty years that have passed since she was buried; and yet as we read her letters and listen to her arguments and consider her experiments, above all, that most fruitful experiment, her relation with Godwin, and realise the high-handed and hot-blooded manner in which she cut her way to the quick of life, one form of immortality is hers undoubtedly: she is alive and active, she argues and experiments, we hear her voice and trace her influence now among the living.

Twentieth-Century Responses

Wollstonecraft's Political and Social Arguments

Wollstonecraft's Dilemma: Equality vs. Difference, Carole Pateman

Carole Pateman, *The Disorder of Women: Democracy, Feminism and the Welfare State* (Cambridge: Polity, 1989) 196–7

Pateman is the author of *The Sexual Contract*, a landmark feminist critique of social contract theory. In this later essay, Pateman locates in Wollstonecraft's *Rights of Woman* the central dilemma faced by women in Western democracies, a choice between gaining access to rights through either "difference" from or "equality" with men. "Wollstonecraft's dilemma" between equality and difference, configured here as a question central to modern political theory, is likewise central to the development of twentieth-century feminist theory, often divided between French feminist theory (emphasizing women's difference through their distinctive experiences of sexuality, maternity, language) and Anglo-American feminist theory (emphasizing women's equality in terms of reason, rights, and public politics).

The extremely difficult problem faced by women in their attempt to win full citizenship I shall call 'Wollstonecraft's dilemma'. The dilemma is that the two routes toward citizenship that women have pursued are mutually incompatible within the confines of the patriarchal welfare state, and, within that context, they are impossible to achieve. For three centuries, since universal citizenship first appeared as a political ideal, women have continued to challenge their alleged natural subordination within private life. From at least the 1790s they have also struggled with the task of trying to become citizens within an ideal and practice that have gained universal meaning through their exclusion. Women's response has been complex. On the one hand, they have demanded that the ideal of citizenship be extended to them,[1] and the liberal-feminist agenda for a 'gender-neutral' social world is the logical conclusion of one form of this demand. On the other hand, women have also insisted, often simultaneously, as did Mary Wollstonecraft, that *as women* they have specific capacities, talents, needs and concerns, so that the expression of their citizenship will be differentiated from that of men. Their unpaid work providing welfare could be seen, as Wollstonecraft saw women's tasks as mothers, as women's work *as citizens*, just as their husbands' paid work is central to men's citizenship.[2]

The patriarchal understanding of citizenship means that the two demands are incompatible because it allows two alternatives only: either women become (like) men, and so full citizens; or they continue at women's work, which is of no value for citizenship. Moreover, within a patriarchal welfare state neither demand can be met. To demand that citizenship, as it now exists, should be fully extended to women accepts the patriarchal meaning of 'citizen', which is constructed from men's attributes, capacities and activities. Women cannot be full citizens in the present meaning of the term; at best, citizenship can be extended to women only as lesser men. At the same time, within the patriarchal welfare state, to demand proper social recognition and support for women's responsibilities is to condemn women to less than full citizenship and to continued incorporation into public life as 'women', that is, as members of another sphere who cannot, therefore, earn the respect of fellow (male) citizens.

Wollstonecraft and Liberal Individualism, Virginia Sapiro

Virginia Sapiro, *A Vindication of Political Virtue: The Political Theory of Mary Wollstonecraft* (Chicago: University of Chicago Press, 1992) 182–5, 167

Sapiro's analysis of Wollstonecraft's political theory argues against critics who see her as limited by bourgeois individualism and its narrow definitions of self and society (like Kaplan, **pp. 76–7**). As a political scientist Sapiro sees in Wollstonecraft's collective-minded critique an important response to Rousseau's ideal of the autonomous male citizen (see also Colley and Pateman **pp. 65–7 and 62–3**).

Mary Wollstonecraft incorporated individual autonomous human beings centrally into her political theory. [. . .] She seemed to place the full burden of sociopolitical

1   [Pateman's note.] I have discussed the earlier arguments in more detail in 'Women and Democratic Citizenship', The Jefferson Memorial Lectures, University of California, Berkeley, 1985, Lecture I.
2   [Pateman's note.] For example, Wollstonecraft writes, 'speaking of women at large, their first duty is to themselves as rational creatures, and the next, in point of importance, as citizens, is that, which includes so many, of a mother.' She hopes that a time will come when a 'man must necessarily fulfil the duties of a citizen, or be despised, and that while he was employed in any of the departments of civil life, his wife, also an active citizen, should be equally intent to manage her family, educate her children, and assist her neighbours.' *A Vindication of the Rights of Woman*, (Norton, New York, 1975), pp. 145, 146.

change on individuals and did not argue for any collective action on the part of the oppressed. It is little wonder that contemporary feminist theorists have generally accepted Zillah Eisenstein's view that Wollstonecraft's "liberal individualism overwhelms her insights into the reality of the sexual-class system."[1] Eisenstein probably summarizes the view of others in concluding, "Wollstonecraft tried to blend her feminism and her liberalism and what we see is an uneasy mix."[2]

In fact, it is not correct to treat Wollstonecraft's writing as a clear expression of stereotypical liberal individualism. Rather, it offers at least a medium through which we can see early skepticism about the adequacy of liberal individualism. Most important, it is a challenge securely grounded *within* that tradition. That skepticism is derived in large part from the centrality of women and women's day-to-day experiences in Wollstonecraft's understanding of the social world. [. . .]

Wollstonecraft lived at a time when the conceptual distinction between public and private was gaining force. [. . .] She saw "public" and "private" as integral parts of the same wholes, not just as different social spaces but, in some ways, as occupying the same space. [. . .]

Wollstonecraft's organic vision led her to a consistence in political critique that surpassed that of many other political theorists. She did not segment away a portion of life ("private life"), or the inhabitants of that portion (women), to lie beyond notions of justice. Although she expressed a sense of tension and fragility in balancing notions of the autonomous individual, the social individual, and the collective, she seemed to reach a kind of dynamic resolution that did not require posing the individual and the collective in constant opposition and competition. The integrated organic aspect of her view is especially remarkable because it did not lead her to conservatism, as such visions often have done for others. For Wollstonecraft, the interconnections made her try to throw light on intimate and family relations rather than allowing them to drag public life into the realm of untouchable mystery. Here we can conclude where we began, with Wollstonecraft's debate with Rousseau. She framed her debate with him by picking on passages containing at least a subterranean longing for a lost freedom and solitude of the original state. [. . .] In Rousseau's world men seem to hold a dream of the ideal and natural state of vigorous individualized autonomy. There, citizenship must be a problem because it is unnatural to men.[3] He certainly wrote that people are better off having chosen to give up natural in favor of moral and civic liberty, but the natural liberty of the original state nevertheless remains a romantic ideal in his writing. [. . .] But Wollstonecraft's perspective did not allow her

---

1   [Sapiro's note.] Eisenstein, *The Radical Future of Liberal Feminism* [Northeastern Illinois Press, 1981], p. 104.

2   [Sapiro's note.] Ibid., p. 105. This is a most unfortunate formulation of the problem. Wollstonecraft could not have "tried to blend her feminism and her liberalism" unless she understood these as particular and distinct categories of theory or ideology. In the historical context, it would have been remarkable had she done so.

3   [Sapiro's note.] Margaret Canovan, "Rousseau's Two Concepts of Citizenship," in *Women in Western Political Philosophy: Kant to Nietzsche*, ed. Ellen Kenney and Susan Mendus (St. Martin's Press, 1987), pp. 78–105.

Rousseau's regret for the lost original state. His natural man, this roving self-reliant but self-absorbed creature, is merely a brute until he can enter social relations, and will remain a brute as long as he exists only for his own pleasure. He may be cunning, but he cannot be wise. He will engage in some social relations and will reproduce himself, but only in a brutish fashion with less concern for his offspring than other species have and no possibility of friendship or love for his mate. His regret for the passing of this state is regret for lost, selfish hedonism.

Wollstonecraft seemed to understand that in this discussion *he* did not encompass *she*. Within this original state women, too, would have been brutes because they would also lack reason and virtue. But she seemed to be aware, as most male writers were not, that the facts of life mean that even if man could have a small regret for the passing of the original state woman could not. Rousseau's civilized world offered little solace for women either, because there women would be subjugated to men's pleasure by law and convention rather than by mere physical force. Women would be denied citizenship for the benefit of men's. For Rousseau and other male liberal theorists the subjugation of women by their private relations within civil society was a necessary or, at worst, trivial problem. For Wollstonecraft it was not.

For Wollstonecraft, becoming better human beings and becoming true citizens is much the same thing. Both require liberty. But, also, both humanity and citizenship must be common human projects; they require human sociability and cooperation. [. . .] For Wollstonecraft there was no such thing as submerging women in strictly private relationships and concerns for the benefit of the public good.

Wollstonecraft and Separate-Spheres Ideology, Linda Colley

Linda Colley, *Britons: Forging the Nation 1707–1837* (Yale University Press, 1992) 273–4, 280–1

The division between the "masculine" public sphere of politics and the "feminine" private sphere of domestic concerns is a central tenet of much modern political and literary history. Historian Linda Colley's landmark reassessment of this separate-spheres theory in *Britons* argues that in fact British women played a central role in public-sphere politics (such as abolition and the war effort against France), and that Wollstonecraft's critique is part of this increasing interchange between the public and private spheres (see also Pateman and Sapiro **pp. 62–3, 63–5**).

I have argued that the spread of separate-spheres ideology, which had been increasingly evident in prescriptive literature in Great Britain, as in so much of Europe and in North America from the 1770s onwards, could be drawn on in practice to defend the position of women. I have suggested, too, that the existence of prominent royal females who had to act out the roles of wife, daughter, sister or mother, helped other British women to assert the dignity and importance of these private relationships. But belief in a distinctive female sphere could also, paradoxically, legitimise women's intervention in affairs hitherto regarded as the preserve of men.

To understand why, we need to return to Rousseau. Subordinate and artificial though his ideal woman was, she was also indispensable to the well-being of the state through her private influence on her citizen husband and education of her children. Without the wholesome domesticity that she presided over, male citizenship would have no foundation, 'the legislative hallways would grow silent and empty, or become noisily corrupt'.[1] From these initial premises, two very different conclusions were drawn. As far as the Jacobins in France and the evangelical conservatives in Great Britain were concerned, since woman's place at home was so valuable, it was important that she stay there. But Rousseau's arguments could also be understood very differently, and this was why feminists like Georgiana, Duchess of Devonshire, and Mary Wollstonecraft found his writings so valuable. In previously prevailing political theory, citizenship had been linked with the possession of land and/or the ability to bear arms—in other words, as an inescapably masculine prerogative. By breaking away from this model and stressing instead the connexion between civic virtue and the family, Rousseau, whether he recognised it or not, supplied women with a rationale for intervening in political affairs. Confining women to the private sphere, he none the less helped to dissolve the distinction between it and the public. For if politics was indistinguishable from morality, as he always claimed, then surely women as guardians of morality must have some right of access to the political?

Wollstonecraft saw the potential in Rousseau's arguments very clearly and was careful to construct her claims for women's rights in the *Vindication* out of their contribution to the family. 'If children are to be educated to understand the principle of patriotism', she pointed out, then 'their mother must be a patriot' as well. Only if women were able to 'acquire a rational affection for their country', could they become truly useful in the home.[2] [. . .]

[B]eing thought of as moral exemplars is a lot better than being dismissed as merely inferior and irrelevant. There seems no doubt that, insofar as the position of women changed in Britain in the half-century after the American war, the effect was to increase—rather than diminish—their opportunities for participating in public life. The wars with revolutionary and Napoleonic France tempted much greater numbers of female Britons out of the home and into pro-war activism (and into pacifist agitation, too) than any previous conflict. A new idealisation of the female members of the Royal Family provided women from many different social backgrounds with their own distinctive brand of patriotism, as well as a way of celebrating by example their domestic roles as mothers, daughters, sisters and

---

1   [Colley's note.] Jean Bethke Elshtain, *Public Man, Private Woman* (1981), pp. 164–5; and see Joel Schwartz, *The Sexual Politics of Jean-Jacques Rousseau* (Chicago, 1984).
2   [Colley's note.] *Vindication*, p. 86.

wives. And, throughout this period, women were exposed as never before to the bustle and seductions of urban life, to newspapers, magazines, books and broadsheets, available in greater numbers and more cheaply than ever before, to new kinds of charitable, patriotic and political associations, and—of course—to new types of paid work. For many of them, as for many of their male contemporaries, the cumulative result of all these developments must have been wider access to people, information and ideas.

It is in this context that the renewed emphasis in a great deal of prescriptive literature on the importance of separate spheres must be understood. If British women were being urged to remain at home more stridently in this period than ever before, it was largely because so many of them were finding an increasing amount to do outside the home. The literature of separate spheres was more didactic than descriptive. Yet, as some women discovered, it could still serve a useful purpose. Proclaiming their reputed vulnerability and moral superiority—and men's duty to respect both—provided them with a means to legitimise their intervention in public affairs and a means, as well, of protecting themselves. Posing as the pure-minded Women of Britain was, in practice, a way of insisting on the right to public spirit.

Wollstonecraft and Sensibility, G.J. Barker-Benfield

G.J. Barker-Benfield, *The Culture of Sensibility: Sex and Society in Eighteenth-Century Britain* (Chicago: University of Chicago Press, 1992) 361–4

"Sensibility," writes Barker-Benfield in his authoritative study, "signified revolution, promised freedom, threatened subversion, and became convention. The word denoted the receptivity of the senses and referred to the psychoperceptual scheme, explained and systematized by Newton and Locke" (*Culture of Sensibility*, p. 1). Despite its materialist basis, "proponents of the cultivation of sensibility came to invest it with spiritual and moral values" (ibid, p. 1), specifically, middle-class values. By Wollstonecraft's era, sensibility was hotly debated: conservatives like Hannah More linked it with the French Revolution and radicals like Wollstonecraft associated it with the claustrophobic sensuality of middle-class women's sheltered lives. Sensibility remains one of the most productive fields of inquiry in eighteenth-century studies, and it is central to the ongoing debate over Wollstonecraft's perspective on women's sexuality and corporeality.

Women's publication of so many works personifying sense and sensibility in characters who struggled for readers' minds suggests the widespread existence of conflict within women, parallel to the attacks made on them by men, between a sensibility governed by reason and a sensibility dangerously given over to fantasy and the pursuit of pleasure. This had been a dynamic that characterized the culture of sensibility all along, two parts of wished-for selves, capitalizing on literacy and consumerism to make sense of women's new social circumstances and their attempts to improve them.

As we have seen, Wollstonecraft was capable of distinguishing very clearly between these two versions of sensibility. Her adherence to sensibility's value and her insistent aspiration to modify sensibility with reason was, in many respects, a more passionate and developed version of a well-known view among her contemporaries, one to which both sentimental and antisentimental writers subscribed.[1] Wollstonecraft's distinction was to take "Sense" further in her defense of woman's mind, and to be still more damning in her analysis of the damage an exaggerated "Sensibility" could do to women. Moreover, in addition to her advocacy of the softening influence of mothers in improved domestic surroundings, Wollstonecraft insisted that women toughen themselves by fully entering the world and subjecting themselves individually to all of the experiences possible to men. Basing her call for women's rights on the "Commonwealthman" ideal of a *populo armato*, Wollstonecraft invoked a picture of women warriors, capable of burnishing their arms as well as their reason. To become "real" heroines of "public virtue" (in contrast to fiction's segregated fantasies), women should actually take "the field" to "march and counter-march like soldiers, or wrangle in the senate to keep their faculties from rusting." Women were capable of this range of roles, from sentimental yet tough-minded wife and mother to Commonwealth patriot and warrior.[2]

Despite the clarity with which Wollstonecraft distinguished between the good and bad versions of sensibility, she was also torn between them. Her demand that women subject sensibility to reason expressed her deepest personal struggle, evident throughout her published works and her letters.[3] The conflict can be discerned even in the *Rights of Woman*, where on occasion she used the same sentimental clichés that elsewhere are her target as "sentimental rant," and "turgid bombast"—the "sentimental jargon" induced in women by their reading sentimental novels. This had always been a major target in her reviews of novels.[4] [. . .]

Wollstonecraft's private letters show her awareness of this deep conflict. She had not mastered the presentation of herself as a woman of sensibility as one of a repertoire of roles, comparable, say, to the ability she saw in Imlay to present a "commercial face," an ability she condemned in accordance with sensibility's values. She wrote him privately what she demonstrated publicly in *Letters from Sweden*, that "those affections and feelings" which "seem to have been given to vivify my heart" were in fact "the source of so much misery." "That being," said Wollstonecraft, "who moulded my heart thus, knows that I am unable to tear up by the roots the propensity to affection which has been the torment of my

---

1 [Barker-Benfield's note.] For the relationship between Austen's ideas and those of Wollstonecraft see Roberts, *Jane Austen*, 156–7.
2 [Barker-Benfield's note.] Wollstonecraft, *Rights of Woman*, 258.
3 [Barker-Benfield's note.] Barker-Benfield, "Mary Wollstonecraft's Depression and Diagnosis: The Relation between Sensibility and Women's Susceptibility to Nervous Disorders," *Psychohistory Review* 13, no. 4 (Spring 1985): 15–31 [. . .].
4 [Barker-Benfield's note.] Wollstonecraft, *Rights of Woman*, 192, 82, 309.

life."[5] She knew that "an accumulation of disappointments and misfortunes seem to suit the habit of my mind." She connected her adult misery to her own father's treatment of her as a child, but she also explained it as the result of the conventional rearing and education of middle-class females, their sensibilities developed at the expense of reason, their ambitions confined to love and marriage. She said that educated, middle-class women in general were subjected to the same "continual conflicts" between sensibility and reason. Precisely because Wollstonecraft showed herself able to make the most radical analysis of the dangers the culture of sensibility posed to women, her difficulty in disentangling herself from them dramatized the power of its hold.[6]

Wollstonecraft and Slavery, Moira Ferguson

Moira Ferguson, "Mary Wollstonecraft and the Problematic of Slavery" in *Colonialism and Gender Relations from Mary Wollstonecraft to Jamaica Kincaid* (New York: Columbia University Press, 1993) 8–9, 28–9, 33

Ferguson argues that Wollstonecraft's extensive use of the discourse of slavery and subjugation throughout *Rights of Woman* must be understood in the larger cultural debate on colonial slavery and abolition. Britain's participation in the slave trade (which did not end until 1807) and its extensive profits from colonial slavery came under increasing attack from politicians, reformers, and writers (many of them women) at the end of the eighteenth century. Wollstonecraft had spoken out firmly against slavery in her *Vindication of the Rights of Men* (1790), but in *Rights of Woman* she goes even further and draws "connections between colonial slavery and sexual abuse" (Ferguson, p. 14), at one point hinting at the dangerous potential for female revolution when she compares female resistance against patriarchal oppression to a slave revolt (see **p. 140**).

In contrast to A *Vindication of the Rights of Men* in 1790, which drew primarily on the language of natural rights for its argument, A *Vindication of the Rights of Woman* (1792) favored a discourse on slavery that foregrounded female subjugation. Whereas *The Rights of Men* refers to slavery in a variety of contexts only four or five times, *The Rights of Woman* contains more than eighty references; the constituency Wollstonecraft champions—white, middle-class women—is constantly characterized as slaves. By utilizing an antislavery discourse to talk about white women's rights, Wollstonecraft underscores epistemological differences,

---

5   [Barker-Benfield's note.] Wollstonecraft to Gilbert Imlay, 17 June 1795 and 4 October 1795, *The Collected Letters of Mary Wollstonecraft*, ed. Ralph M. Wardle (Ithaca: Cornell University Press, 1979), 296, 316.

6   [Barker-Benfield's note.] Wollstonecraft, *Rights of Woman*, 179; it could be argued that Wollstonecraft came to terms with her lifelong conflict in her late thirties. The best evidence for this is a letter Wollstonecraft wrote to Godwin, 4 September 1796.... [Ed.: this letter is included in Contexts (**pp. 28–9**).]

how white women and slaves discern their situations differently and how she connects them. For her major polemic Mary Wollstonecraft decided to adopt and adapt the terms of contemporary political debate. Over a two-year period that debate had gradually reformulated its terms as the French Revolution in 1789, which highlighted aristocratic hegemony and bourgeois rights, was followed by the San Domingo Revolution, which focused primarily on colonial relations.[1]

Wollstonecraft's evolving commentaries on the status of European women in relation to slavery were made in response to four interlocking activities and events: first, intense agitation over the question of slavery in England, which included the case of the slave James Somerset in 1772 and Phillis Wheatley's visit in 1773; second, the French Revolution in 1789; third, Catharine Macaulay's *Letters on Education* (1790), which argued forthrightly against sexual difference; and fourth, the successful revolution by slaves in the French colony of San Domingo in 1791. [. . .]

Specifically Wollstonecraft talks about resistance only by talking about slaves. The successful revolution by slaves in San Domingo taught the British public that slaves and freed blacks could collectively overthrow systematic tyranny. By equating slaves with laboring-class "mobs" and using highly inflated diction for rebels, Wollstonecraft censures slaves' reaction. "For the same reason," states Wollstonecraft, quoting from Jean-Jacques Rousseau, "women have, or ought to have, but little liberty; they are apt to indulge themselves excessively in what is allowed them. Addicted in every thing to extremes, they are even more transported at their diversions than boys." She continues this response to Rousseau: "The answer to this is very simple. Slaves and mobs have always indulged themselves in the same excesses, when once they broke loose from authority.—The bent bow recoils with violence, when the hand is suddenly relaxed that forcibly held it."[2]

Yet, since Wollstonecraft disdains passivity and servitude, she may be embedding an unconscious desire about female resistance that corresponds to her own. She could be hinting that women should emulate the San Domingo insurgents and fight back. That nuance is stressed pictorially by the sexual overtones of female compliance in "bent bow." Just as important, the image resonates with the previous textual image of women from earliest times with necks bent under a yoke.

Put succinctly, what slaves can do, white women can do; as she asserts in *The Rights of Woman*, authority and the reaction to it push the "crowd of subalterns forward."[3] Sooner or later tyranny incites retaliation. San Domingo instructs women in the importance of connecting physical and moral agency. Struggle creates a potential bridge from ignorance to consciousness and self-determination. In the most hard-hitting sense, the San Domingo revolutionaries loudly voice by their bold example—to anyone ready to listen—that challenge to oppression is not an option but a responsibility. [. . .]

---

1   [Ferguson's note.] C.L.R. James, *The Black Jacobins*, p. ix.
2   [Ferguson's note.] Wollstonecraft, *The Rights of Woman*, p. 144.
3   [Ferguson's note.] Ibid., p. 17.

By theorizing about women's rights using old attributions of harem-based slavery in conjunction with denotations of colonial slavery, Wollstonecraft was a political pioneer, fundamentally altering the definition of rights and paving the way for a much wider cultural dialogue.

Wollstonecraft and Religion, Daniel Robinson

Daniel Robinson, "Theodicy versus Feminist Strategy in Mary Wollstonecraft's Fiction" Eighteenth-Century Fiction 9.2 (1997) 183–202 (183, 187, 190, 197–9)

Modern scholars typically underemphasize the degree to which Wollstone-craft's political and feminist polemic was inspired by spirituality. Godwin's atheism is often attributed to Wollstonecraft yet, as Robinson shows, her thinking remained informed by a sense of religious faith, something she shared with earlier feminists like the politically conservative Mary Astell (author of A Serious Proposal to the Ladies, 1697) and radical contemporaries like Catharine Macaulay (see **pp. 22–3**). While at times her idea of a deity seems to mean reason, her religious thought is also connected to her likewise underestimated interest in the sensual world and in imagination (see Whale, **pp. 90–1**).

Biographies of the last twenty years or so have tended to downplay Wollstone-craft's religious thought because it is difficult to trace. Most biographies can pinpoint her religion as conventionally Church of England until 1787 when, as Godwin reports in his *Memoir*, she stopped attending church services regularly. The details of Wollstonecraft's faith are sketchy after this date, though her writing evinces proof that she maintained a general spiritual faith in providence over doctrine as Godwin grudgingly writes, "Her religion was in reality little allied to any system of forms; and, as she has often told me, was founded rather in taste, than in the niceties of polemical discussion."[1] Modern biographers do little to correct the misconception, initiated by Godwin, that Wollstonecraft was a god-less woman after 1787 (or 1792), though at least one is overtly defensive about it.[2] This was also the year when, at Newington Green, Wollstonecraft met Richard Price, the dissenting preacher, mathematician, and political thinker, who, it seems, had some influence on Wollstonecraft's lapsing involvement in her church; she would go occasionally to hear him preach to the local Presbyterian congregation.[3] Price stood for a moral religion that included among duties to God duties to society, a conscientious benevolence required in order to be truly

---

1 [Robinson's note.] William Godwin, *Memoirs of the Author of A Vindication of the Rights of Woman* (1798; reprinted New York: Garland, 1974) pp. 35, 33.
2 [Robinson's note.] C. Kegan Paul opens his "prefatory memoir," *Mary Wollstonecraft* (New York; Haskell House 1971), with a vague defence of Wollstonecraft's faith. [. . .]
3 [Robinson's note.] Godwin, *Memoirs*, pp. 32–35; Emily Sunstein, *A Different Face: The Life of Mary Wollstonecraft* (New York: Harper, 1975), pp. 96–97.

virtuous; Wollstonecraft responded to his liberal platform and his emphasis on "God-given reason." [. . .]

Though she is not a consistent rationalist, Wollstonecraft, during her most polemical phase, followed the lead of Enlightenment thinkers in seeking a rational explanation for her faith in the face of evil; as she explained in *A Vindication of the Rights of Men* (1790), [. . .] her God is equivalent to reason: "it is not to an arbitrary will, but to unerring reason I submit." Evil for Wollstonecraft, like most Enlightenment theodicists, is part of the grand design: "That both physical and moral evil were not only foreseen, but entered into the scheme of providence, when this world was contemplated in the divine mind, who can doubt, without robbing Omnipotence of a most exalted attribute?"[4] To question the divine justice of God in permitting evil is impertinence. [. . .]

Claire Tomalin writes of Wollstonecraft's faith in providence that "had such Christian resignation prevailed with her there would have been no *Vindication*."[5] [. . .] It is important to remember, however, that the *Vindication* is in many ways an ostensibly religious work.[6] She bases her argument upon her own rational Christianity that asserts "God is Justice itself"; thus "women were destined by providence to acquire human virtues" and thus to receive education on equal terms with all humans (pp. 100, 20). Wollstonecraft maintains her faith in providence throughout but limits the work's explicit language of theodicy only to its opening chapters. She attacks Rousseau's illogical thinking on the basis of its inconsistency with rational theodicy; Rousseau's assertion in *Émile* that humankind introduced evil and defiled God's immaculate creation is a prime target for Wollstonecraft's justification of the divine will of God. Mounting her attack on Rousseau's illogic, she asserts that, when God created humanity:

> he could see that present evil would produce future good. Could the helpless creature whom he called from nothing break loose from his providence, and boldly learn to know good by practising evil, without his permission? No. – How could that energetic advocate for immortality argue so inconsistently?

She distinctly establishes her faith in God's omnipotence, benevolence, and justice at the outset of her *Vindication*: "Firmly persuaded that no evil exists in the world that God did not design to take place," she proudly exclaims, "I build my belief on the perfection of God" (pp. 14–15). And she elsewhere points out that morality chiefly is derived from "the character of the supreme Being" and that God "must be just, because he is wise, he must be good, because he is omnipotent" (p. 46). Thus, Wollstonecraft reasons her faith. [. . .]

---

4   [Robinson's note.] "A Vindication of the Rights of Men," *A Wollstonecraft Anthology*, ed. Janet Todd (Bloomington: Indiana University Press, 1977), pp. 75, 79.
5   [Robinson's note.] Tomalin, p. 59.
6   [Robinson's note.] Wollstonecraft invokes religion for her attack on the Bible and on Rousseau, Milton, Pope, and others. She mounts her attack on Rousseau on the grounds that, when he misunderstands woman, he misunderstands the nature of God and humanity as well. [. . .]

By the time she wrote the *Vindication*, . . . her individual concern about faith becomes a question of injustice, and resignation is not a defence in the face of such a formidable foe. It is clearly a message she did not wish to send. Rather, Wollstonecraft looked towards a future state on earth, refusing to accept that all is for the best in the best of all possible worlds: "Rousseau exerts himself to prove that all *was* right originally: a crowd of authors that all *is* now right: and I, that all will *be* right" (p. 15).

Wollstonecraft and Nationalism, Jan Wellington

Jan Wellington, "Blurring the Borders of Nation and Gender: Mary Wollstonecraft's Character (R)evolution" in *Rebellious Hearts: British Women Writers and the French Revolution*, eds. Adriana Craciun and Kari Lokke (Albany, NY: State University of New York Press, 2001) 34–5, 50–1

Wollstonecraft's dedication of *Rights of Woman* to the French politician Talleyrand quickly launched into a critique of the French national character as precisely the effeminate, dissipated, and superficial character that Wollstonecraft wanted to reform in British men and women. Such anti-French rhetoric was common in 1790s British politics (radical and conservative) yet, as Wellington shows, it is a mistake to read Wollstonecraft as a straightforward nationalist. Just as Wollstonecraft challenged her age's prevailing notions about sexual character, she also challenged the idea of "national character," finding much to value in French (and by extension in "feminine") culture.

Like her fellow English, Wollstonecraft often characterized the French, both implicitly and explicitly, as effeminate. I intend to show that, while the English, prior to and during the Revolution, often deployed gendered characterizations of the French in order to differentiate and disempower the national 'other,' Wollstonecraft, who seemed at times to engage in the same project, had something different in mind. Although she shared with her more nationalistic contemporaries a measure of the distaste they felt for a nation whose habits and manners were in many ways alien, her writing during the revolutionary years reveals an important difference. Swimming against the tide of nationalist propaganda, Wollstonecraft deployed unflattering characterizations as part of her attempt to recuperate character on multiple levels, in the process dismantling the barriers of nation and gender so many of her contemporaries labored to erect. Her arguments concerning nationality and gender feed and reinforce each other: France's struggle to throw off its effeminate character inspired her to urge women to do the same; her critique of sexual character shaped her opinions of the French, which her border-crossing experiences in Scandinavia forced her to revise. In each case her arguments hinge on a vision of character as a sociohistorical construct open to change. [. . .]

Significantly, it was in France that Wollstonecraft found satisfaction of her own sensations: her seduction (by an American) and the resultant burgeoning of her sexuality were surely assisted by the freer moral atmosphere there. In a sense, she was seduced by France: empowered by its moral liberty to plunge into a relationship in which physical passion, elevated above mere appetite by imagination, and sanctioned by reason, contributed to the synthesis of sentiment and principle she considered humanity's noblest expression. And though her sensations blinded her to the unworthiness of her partner, this passion-driven experience set the stage for a revaluation of the national character she had earlier disparaged.[1]

In the clarifying light of her own sexual experience (including the birth and nurturing of her daughter) and her observations in Sweden, Norway, and Denmark, Wollstonecraft is ready to rethink her alignment of the French character with all that is characterless in women. The hints at revaluation sprinkled throughout *Letters Written in Sweden* culminate, by her journey's end, in the admission that "I believe I should have been less severe in the remarks I have made on the vanity and depravity of the French, had I travelled towards the north before I visited France" (*LWS*, 326). The context of this passage is significant. Earlier in the same letter, Wollstonecraft described the freedom and intimacy allowed young Danish couples during the period of their engagement, which she refers to as "a kind of interregnum" between parental and spousal tyranny and "the only period of freedom and pleasure that the women enjoy" (326). Not only does she approve of the sexual intimacy these couples engage in, she sees it as conducive to character. Unlike the dull, mindless peccadilloes of their philandering elders, the innocent sensuality of the affianced, she suggests, is prompted by "an exuberance of life, which often fructifies the whole character when the vivacity of youthful spirits begins to subside into strength of mind" (326). Wollstonecraft makes a revealing mental transition when she moves from the virtuous sexual liberty of the Danish youth to the exuberance of the revolutionary French. She writes, "[w]e talk of the depravity of the French ... yet where has more virtuous enthusiasm been displayed than during the last two years, by the common people of France, and in their armies? I am obliged sometimes to recollect the numberless instances which I have either witnessed, or heard well authenticated, to balance the account of horrours, alas! but too true" (326). What Wollstonecraft seems to have concluded since her 1793 "Letter Introductory" is that the voluptuousness she earlier portrayed as stifling the moral emotions is not necessarily one of the "gross vices" (*LWS*, 326) that contributed to the Revolution's horrors. Further, she has been forced to concede that the "simplicity of manners" she so values (and failed to find among the generality of French) is all too often allied with gross vice and ignorance (326). This recognition prompts her, in turn, to be more forgiving of effeminate French vanity and artifice.

---

1   Wellington's note omitted.

Wollstonecraft on the Body and Sexuality

Wollstonecraft and Self-Control, Mary Poovey

Mary Poovey, *The Proper Lady and the Woman Writer: Ideology as Style in the Works of Mary Wollstonecraft, Mary Shelley, and Jane Austen* (Chicago: University of Chicago Press, 1984) 79

Mary Poovey's influential account of the Romantic period's best-known women writers of prose joins Marxist and feminist critiques to examine how these women "became professional writers despite the strictures of propriety" that ostensibly made genius incompatible with women (p. x). Poovey, like Kaplan (pp. 76–7), sees Wollstonecraft's focus on self-control (i.e., the control of female sexuality and emotion) and reason as the source of "her inability to acknowledge or fully assimilate the profoundly unreasonable longings of her own emotional or physical being," consequently weakening her argument and preventing her from seeking a collective solution that would resist the narrow claims of bourgeois individualism (p. 77).

An even more severe consequence of Wollstonecraft's refusal to acknowledge female sexuality is her reluctance to consider women as a group capable of achieving solidarity or taking the initiative for social reform. Because she considers the root of a culture's values to be *men's* sexual desire, she continues to portray social reform strictly in terms of individual men's acts of self-denial and self-control.

Certainly her understanding of the determinate relationship between the individual and institutional or historical forces is more sophisticated in *The Rights of Woman* than in *The Rights of Men*. In it she explicitly acknowledges, for example, the limited efficacy of individual effort (especially in education; see pp. 21, 157) and the necessity for society-wide changes in legal, political, and employment policies (see pp. 145, 147, 148). But when she calls for change, her summons always encourages an alteration in *individual*, particularly *male*, attitudes. "Let men become more chaste and modest" (p. 11), let the nobility "prefer" the practice of reason (p. 22), let "mankind become more reasonable" (p. 56); only then can social change begin. The terms used may pass as generic nouns and pronouns, but they most frequently designate males. Wollstonecraft is generally *not* challenging women to *act*. When she calls for a "revolution in female manners" (p. 45), for example, she is not advocating a feminist uprising to overthrow manners but rather a general acquiescence in the gradual turning that the word "revolution" was commonly taken to mean in the eighteenth century. Women are simply to wait for this revolution to *be* effected, for their dignity to *be* restored, for their reformation to *be* made necessary. The task is primarily men's, and it involves not confrontation but self-control. Wollstonecraft defers her discussion of legal inequality to the promised second volume (which she never wrote) because, in her scheme, social legislation is less effective than individual self-control. And in *The Rights of Woman*, Wollstonecraft emphasizes independence rather than equality both because she conceives of society as a collection of individual attitudes rather than legal contracts and because she imagines relationships to be fundamentally antagonistic rather than cooperative. The major antagonism, however, is not against an external force but against one's own self—against fear and, especially, against desire.

Wollstonecraft and Sexuality, Cora Kaplan

Cora Kaplan, "Wild Nights: Pleasure/Sexuality/Feminism" in *Sea Changes: Essays in Culture and Feminism* (London: Verso, 1986) 38–9, 45–6

> Kaplan's immensely influential political critique locates in *Rights of Woman*, "the founding text of Anglo-American feminism" (p. 34), a central dilemma faced by modern middle-class feminism. "Where both right and left sexual ideologies converge," writes Kaplan, "associating women's desire with weakness, unreason and materialism, it has been noticeably hard to insist on positive social and political meanings for female sexuality" (p. 33). Wollstonecraft fails to incorporate female sexuality and pleasure in her political vision, argues Kaplan, revealing the class-bound limitations of liberal humanism. Wollstonecraft ultimately remains trapped in Rousseau's misogynist construct of female sexuality as dangerous, according to Kaplan (see Poovey (**pp. 75–6**) for a similar reading and Sapiro (**pp. 63–5**) for a contrasting one).

Even in its own day *A Vindication* must have been a short, sharp shock for women readers. Men might be able to mobilize reason and passion, in them equitably combined, to change the world immediately; women, crippled and stunted by an education for dependence, must liberate themselves from a slavish addiction to the sensual before their 'understandings' could liberate anyone else. At later moments of political crisis feminists could, and would, portray women as vanguard figures, subordinated members of the propertied class who understood more about oppression, as a result, than their bourgeois male comrades. Not here. Read intertextually, heard against the polyphonic lyricism of Paine, Godwin and the dozens of ephemeral pamphleteers who were celebrating the fact and prospect of the revolution, *A Vindication* was a sobering read. Wollstonecraft sets out on an heroic mission to rescue women from a fate worse than death, which was, as she saw it, the malicious and simultaneous inscription of their sexuality and inferiority as innate, natural difference. This was how her political mentor and gender adversary Rousseau had placed them, too weak by nature to reach or be reached by sweet reason. Rousseau's influence was great, not least on Wollstonecraft herself. She accepts Rousseau's ascription of female inferiority and locates it even more firmly than he does in an excess of sensibility. Since lust and narcissism were evil they must belong to social relations rather than human nature; this was Rousseau's own position in relation to men. Accordingly, female sexuality insofar as it is vicious is inscribed in *A Vindication* as the effect of culture on an essentially ungendered nature. By tampering with the site of degrading sexuality without challenging the moralising description of sexuality itself, Wollstonecraft sets up heartbreaking conditions for women's liberation—a little death, the death of desire, the death of female pleasure. [. . .]

It is unfortunate that Wollstonecraft chose to fight Rousseau in his own terms, accepting his paradigm of a debased, eroticized femininity as fact rather than ideological fiction. Woman's reason may be the psychic heroine of *A Vindication*, but its gothic villain, a polymorphous perverse sexuality, creeping out of every paragraph and worming its way into every warm corner of the text, seems in the end to win out. It is again too easy to forget that this suffusing desire is a permanent male conspiracy to keep women panting and dependent as well as housebound and pregnant. What the argument moves towards, but never quite arrives at, is the conclusion that it is male desire that must be controlled and contained if women are to be free and rational. This conclusion cannot be reached because an idealized bourgeois male is the standard towards which women are groping, as well as the reason they are on their knees. Male desire may be destructive to women, but it remains a part of positive male identity. A wider education and eros-blunting forays into the public world of work and politics keeps the rational in control of the sensual in men, and is the recommended remedy for women too. Wollstonecraft thought gender difference socially constructed but she found practically nothing to like in socially constructed femininity. With masculinity it was quite different—'masculine' women are fine as long as they don't hunt and kill. Yet there could be nothing good about feminized men, since the definitions of the feminine available in *A Vindication* are shot through with dehumanizing and immoral sensuality. It's not surprising that women together—girls in boarding schools and women in the home—can only get up to unsavory personal familiarities, 'nasty, or immodest habits.' This description backs up an argument, possibly forceful in its own time, for mixed education and a freer association of adult men and women; it rounds off the denigration of women's world in *A Vindication*.

Wollstonecraft and (Anti)Commercialism, Harriet Guest

Harriet Guest, "The Dream of a Common Language: Hannah More and Mary Wollstonecraft," *Textual Practice* 9 (2) (1995) 303–23 (309–10, 320)

Wollstonecraft and the conservative polemicist Hannah More have been seen as polar opposites in terms of their politics, beginning with the reactionary Richard Polwhele and William Beloe, who both used this moralistic contrast at the turn of the nineteenth century (see **pp. 44–6** and **53**). Increasingly, modern scholars (such as Mitzi Myers in a landmark 1988 essay)[1] have seen many productive connections between these two formidable public figures and their similar calls for increasing female education, ethical responsibility, and

---

1 Mitzi Myers, "Reform or Ruin: 'A Revolution in Female Manners'," noted in Further Reading.

rationality. Guest's essay focuses on the central thread of anticommercialism running through both More's and Wollstonecraft's works, a critique of effeminizing luxury that for Guest links conservative and radical alike. What many critics have seen as Wollstonecraft's anti-sexuality or anti-femininity stance emerges in this historically grounded essay as a distinctly 1790s anticommercialism (see also Wollstonecraft's letter to Imlay, **pp. 25–6**).

What Wollstonecraft's comments here serve to confirm is that by the 1790s economic considerations have taken priority in the characterization of corrupted femininity. The problem is not that absorption in self-adornment may encourage an insatiable sexual rapacity disturbing to the social confidence placed in the system of propertied inheritance, though that remains an important ingredient of the discursive construction at issue. In these years, when fortunes may be more likely to be acquired through commercial speculation than as a result of inherited landed estates, the dangers of social disruption that cluster and find focus in the familiar figure of feminine excess, at least in the context of the polemical genre of vindications, appeals and strictures, result from the vices of consumerism, rather than the more colourful sins of bad sexuality. The figure of corrupted femininity, I suggest, needs to be understood primarily as a set of gendered characteristics appropriated to the requirements of the discourse of commerce and its feared inverse, the anti-commercial horrors of profiteering, greed and consumerism run riot. In the late eighteenth century, the discourse of commerce projects out of itself the image of its own amoralism, producing the figure of insatiable feminine desire that shadows the morality of middle-class men and women, and that, in its confirmed and acknowledged immorality, works to consolidate the shaky moral values of commerce itself. The vices of commerce are embodied in the figure of immorally desirous femininity, which serves, as it were, to draw that poison off from the system of commerce itself. [. . .]

The apparently misogynistic discourse that is common to both Wollstonecraft and More, and to a less marked extent to Hays, in their polemical texts if not in their writing in other genres, needs to be understood, I think, as peculiar to the late century. As I have mentioned, the general terms in which it characterizes corrupt femininity are common to writing about women throughout the eighteenth century. Mary Astell, for example, has some very similar things to say about fashionable women at the beginning of the century. But in Mary Astell's writing the image is not misogynistic, it is not a representation of all femininity. It is a set of terms appropriated, broadly speaking, to those women who are seen to be surplus to the marriage market, marriageable women who may be made redundant by the newly emerging relationship between the city and the landed gentry. By the late century, however, the requirements of anti-commercial discourse appropriate the image of corrupt femininity, and extend it into the nightmare of a language that represents all women, and all forms of feminine desire. It is important, I think, to recognize the specific uses to which the notion of feminine corruption is put, in the course of the eighteenth century. For if we accept its terms as common to all forms of femininity, then, in a sense, we accept their status as somehow essential to gender difference. We then tend to privilege from among the cluster of characteristics that make up the image those which we most nearly accept as essential to femininity ourselves – such as sexuality – and overlook the extent to which feminisms of the past have changed their nature to suit the specific historical circumstances in which they operate. We overlook the flexible self-image which is surely necessary to feminist polemical texts.

Wollstonecraft and Sexual Distinction, Claudia Johnson

Claudia Johnson, *Equivocal Beings: Politics, Gender and Sentimentality in the 1790s* (Chicago: University of Chicago Press, 1995) 23–4, 29–30

A central tenet of most of Wollstonecraft scholarship (and of her contemporaries' objections) is that she argued against distinctions based on sex, instead insisting that women have access to larger "human" virtues and rights. Johnson argues instead that the main thrust of Wollstonecraft's argument is to reinforce distinctions based on sex, particularly in men, whom she saw as dangerously feminized by sentimentality. To the extent that Johnson emphasizes Wollstonecraft's desire that women have access to "masculine" reason, strength, and self-control, however, she is part of an important tradition that reads Wollstonecraft as an antisentimental republican advocate of masculine Enlightenment values.

Although Wollstonecraft ridicules the "distinction of sexes" (VRW 24) as presently understood, she is far from arguing that no distinction exists. A militantly antisentimental work, the *Rights of Woman* denounces the collapse of proper sexual distinction as the leading feature of her age, and as the grievous consequence of sentimentality itself. The problem undermining society in her view is feminized men, and they are not to be corrected by easy seducements, but by bracing, even humiliating, exhortations to manlier duties and sterner pleasures. [. . .]

But even though the work's status as an educational tract determines its major targets (authorities on female education such as Rousseau, Fordyce, and Gregory) and its emphasis on domestic concerns (Wollstonecraft promised to write about the legal status of women in a sequel), *Rights of Woman* is also a republican manifesto, addressed principally to men. The few early reviewers who recognized this aim damned the book as insurrectionary.[1] Wollstonecraft's primary concern throughout, in other words, is not to discuss women's condition per se, much less female sexuality. Rather, it is to consider the future, indeed the very possibility of, liberal democracy, in her view the only political arrangement which enables men and women to fulfill their God-given purpose as "human creatures" placed "on

1   Johnson cites Janes, "On the Reception of Mary Wollstonecraft's *A Vindication of the Rights of Woman*," included here (**pp. 84–6**), and Mitzi Myers, "Reform or Ruin," noted in Further Reading.

this earth to unfold their faculties" (VRW 8) and to "acquire the dignity of conscious virtue" (VRW 26).

Thus, although *Rights of Woman* frequently insists that women must be granted educational, legal, and political rights because it is unfair and inconsistent to deny them, Wollstonecraft's principal argument is that the establishment of a democratic republic depends on the extirpation of hereditary, patriarchal structures, which have systematically vitiated men's character and deformed women's along with it. [. . .] *Rights of Woman* is preoccupied with championing a kind of masculinity into which women can be invited rather than with enlarging or inventing a positive discourse of femininity. Wollstonecraft posits rationality, independence, and productive bodily vigor as man's "true" nature, which culture has perverted into trifling sentimentality, dependence, and weakness. Accordingly she heaps abuse upon "unsexed" males, men who have been rendered effeminate by their excessive and voluptuous attentions to women, or men who "attend the levees of equivocal beings, to sigh for more than female languor" (VRW 138). [. . .]

To emancipate men and women alike, then, she must replace the "unmanly servility" (VRM 50) of courtly males "emasculated by hereditary effeminacy" (VRM 97) with republican manhood, for the same sentimental categories used by men to circumscribe women are also used by monarchs in turn to feminize men and consolidate their power. This is Wollstonecraft's agenda in *Rights of Woman*. [. . .]

Wollstonecraft is infinitely more disturbed by the permeability of the lines of sexual differentiation from the male side than outraged by insurmountable division between men and women: "From every quarter have I heard exclamations against masculine women," she observes, "but where are they to be found?" (VRW 8). Wollstonecraft finds none. But what really worries her is that under the sentimental dispensation she cannot find masculine men either. It is bad enough that women, she reiterates, have been brought up to be weak, idle, spoiled, dependent, and self-indulgent. But when *men* typify women's worst faults, we cannot wonder to find mankind enthralled by tyrants: "Educated in slavish dependence, and enervated by luxury and sloth," she writes, teasing the unwary into assuming that she is talking about women, "where shall we find men who will stand forth to assert the rights of man; – or claim the privilege of moral beings?" (VRW 45). If Wollstonecraft could find them, she wouldn't have to vindicate either the rights of women or the rights of men.

Wollstonecraft and Physical Abuse, Carol Poston

Carol Poston, "Mary Wollstonecraft and 'The Body Politic'" in *Feminist Interpretations of Mary Wollstonecraft*, ed. Maria Falco (Penn State University Press, 1996) 85–104 (89–90, 93–6)

Poston's important editions of *Rights of Woman* (Norton, 1975 and 1988) helped mobilize interest in Wollstonecraft, and this recent essay places Wollstonecraft in a distinctly modern context, that of women's writings on physical abuse. Poston reads *Rights of Woman* as inspired by Wollstonecraft's experience as a physically, emotionally, and possibly sexually abused woman. Wollstonecraft's difficulty in conceiving of her revolutionary female subject as an embodied and sexual subject, Poston suggests, grows out of her childhood experience of physical abuse and powerlessness.

A lack of power and control in Wollstonecraft's early life give birth, I believe, to her later conception of tyranny where she "reframes resistance" as an adult (Gilligan, Rogers, and Tolman, 1991). Is there a politically less powerful place than the body of a female child? That voice of the adult woman who has not forgotten domestic tyranny pervades the *Vindication*: Examples are frequent that link childhood abuse and adult political tyranny: "In this style, argue tyrants of every denomination, from the weak king to the weak father of a family" (*VROW* 5). Tyranny, or the blind phallic usurpation of power, poisons every relationship, political and personal: "All power inebriates weak man; and its abuse proves that the more equality there is established among men, the more virtue and happiness will reign in society" (*VROW* 16). It is telling here that Wollstonecraft uses the word "inebriates." We know from Godwin's *Memoirs* that Edward John Wollstonecraft was an alcoholic, a wife-batterer and a domestic tyrant, so the association of inebriation with power has a double edge.

But we also see here the domestic power struggle that informs her politics. In later life she revealed what we now understand to be a typical triad of domestic abuse: abusing father, passive mother, and a child who becomes a "little mother" in a role reversal that causes the child to lose her childhood. The young Wollstonecraft, Godwin related, often slept in front of her mother's bedroom door to protect her from the drunken assaults of the father. But Wollstonecraft also wrote to her friend Jane Arden in 1779 about "his ungovernable temper." In this letter she silences herself even as she tries to reveal her torment by beginning the sentence, "I will not say much of his ungovernable temper," then adding, "tho' that has been the source of much uneasiness misery to me;—his passions were seldom directed at me, yet I suffered more than any of them" (*Letters* 66).[1] "Passions" in this context means overt physical violence, while "I suffered more than any" suggests an unspeakable injury not of an overt nature, possibly the secret of sexual abuse. [. . .]

The personality effect of such betrayal and entrapment in childhood occurs around the issue of trust: in adulthood, the formerly deprived and abused child will distrust men, if they have been the abusers, but that failure to trust is augmented significantly if the child perceives that the mother has failed to protect the child from the abuser. The passivity of the mother usually results in a lack of trust, of both women and men, on the part of the adult daughter. The distrust of women

---

1   Poston's note omitted.

comes not from violence but from fear of abandonment, of being left to the mercy of the abuser.

However we may sympathize with a woman who had little choice but to live with a drunken tyrant in the eighteenth century, we must also acknowledge that Mary Wollstonecraft's mother fits into the abuse triad. Practiced readers of Wollstonecraft could surely point out a host of phrases and words that recur from work to work, but the prize must surely go to the phrase Wollstonecraft said that her mother uttered on her deathbed: "Yet a little while and all will be over." It is the phrase of a long-suffering victim. Wollstonecraft seems mesmerized by it; she repeats it several times in her published work and, quite tellingly, in a letter to Imlay when she says "Have but a little patience, and I will remove myself where it will not be necessary for you to talk – of course, not to think of me" (*Letters* 319). [. . .]

For Wollstonecraft, as for many survivors of abuse, the adult consequence of tyranny yoked with docility is not only a frightening lack in trust of men or women, but also a distrust of the self. Adults abused in childhood need love and attention, but they also fear getting it: the so-called go-away-closer phenomenon, where victims seek attention and love, yet cannot accept intimacy when offered for fear of being hurt again. We see this same kind of yearning uncertainty often in Wollstonecraft, who asserts her independence even as she is asking for shelter and love. That need for love and constancy is not limited to her frenzied pursuit of Gilbert Imlay. Understanding her as a woman whose body was taken from her as a child helps us understand, for example, her proposal to live in the Fuseli household having only a platonic relationship with Henry Fuseli. Nearly all her biographers find the proposal disingenuous, even laughable, but the offer makes perfect sense for a woman denying her sexuality while at the same time seeking out protection and love. She preferred to present herself as the intellectual she was, and not at all as a sexual being.

Wollstonecraft and Physical Strength, Adriana Craciun

Adriana Craciun, "Violence Against Difference: Mary Wollstonecraft and Mary Robinson" in *Making History: Textuality and the Forms of Eighteenth Century Culture*, ed. Greg Clingham (*Bucknell Review* 42.1) (1997) 111–41 (122, 125, 126–7, 128)

Arguing against the current of Wollstonecraft criticism of the 1980s that emphasized Wollstonecraft's distrust, if not disgust, of physicality and sexuality, Craciun examines the significance of physical strength in *Rights of Woman*. According to Craciun, Wollstonecraft saw women's physical strength and exercise as a crucial part of her program for political reform. Women's education and deprivation cultivated not only weak minds but also weak bodies; thus, increasing strength was one potential means of further diminishing the limitations of sexual difference and of empowering women.

Mary Wollstonecraft's "deep ambivalence about sexuality"[1] in *Vindication of the Rights of Woman* has become an accepted and much lamented fact, argued for most eloquently by Cora Kaplan and Mary Poovey. Such a reading of Wollstonecraft's strategic repression of women's passions, however, threatens to conflate sexuality with corporeality. This reduction of the corporeal to its sexual dimensions makes possible the exaggerated further assertion that Wollstonecraft offered women a disembodied subjectivity, and that on the female body she offered only warnings against the passions, setting up nineteenth-century feminism's "heartbreaking conditions for women's liberation—a little death, the death of desire, the death of female pleasure" ("WN," 39) [. . .] Wollstonecraft, like Mary Robinson, offered women much more on the subject of the body than warnings about the need to suppress it in order for women to gain access to equal political rights as rational citizens. [. . .]

Central to Wollstonecraft's *Rights of Woman* is a debate on the nature of strength and weakness: "I wish to persuade women to endeavour to acquire strength, both of mind and body, and to convince them that the soft phrases, susceptibility of heart, delicacy of sentiment, and refinement of taste, are almost synonymous with epithets of weakness" (*VRW*, 9). Wollstonecraft repudiates traditional *ancien régime* femininity as an unnatural effect of women's oppression; weakness of body and mind has been constructed and should be reconstructed, she argues throughout. We are accustomed to focusing on her "strength" as mental or moral—yet what does she mean by physical strength? The strength to regulate the passions? The strength to endure injury and abuse? The strength to remain impregnable under attack? The strength to labor in any profession? The strength to retaliate, attack or kill? The strength to grow larger? [. . .] Throughout Wollstonecraft's *Rights of Woman*, "strength" and "weakness" oscillate between these long-standing masculine and feminine connotations so that a curious subtext of women's possible physical reformation emerges. Because strength refers simultaneously to masculine force and feminine forbearance, the term endows strong women with an ambiguity extending to their biology.

"In the government of the physical world," writes Wollstonecraft in her introduction, "it is observable that the female in point of strength is, in general, inferior to the male. This is the law of nature; and it does not appear to be suspended or abrogated in favour of woman. A degree of physical superiority cannot, therefore, be denied" (*VRW*, 8). She thus first establishes strength as a physical and masculine quality, governed by immutable laws in favor of men. [. . .] Following her concession in the introduction to the *Rights of Woman* that a "law of nature" renders women inferior to men in physical strength, she continues to make this concession, yet, curiously, in conditional terms. But it is not clear why such conditionals should be necessary if a natural law were in operation—"acknowledging the inferiority of woman, according to

---

1   Cora Kaplan, "Wild Nights: Pleasure/Sexuality/Feminism," in *Sea Changes: Essays on Culture and Feminism* (London: Verso, 1986), 41; hereafter "WN," cited in the text. [Ed.: Kaplan's essay is excerpted, **pp. 76–7**.]

the present *appearance* of things" (*VRW* 35), "their *apparent* inferiority with respect to bodily strength" (*VRW* 11), "bodily strength *seems* to give man a natural superiority over woman" (*VRW* 39; my emphases). Wollstonecraft places the natural law of male superior strength in conditional terms precisely because she knows it is not natural. Like so many of the other rhetorical concessions in the *Rights of Woman*, physical incommensurability is an assurance to her readers that her argument for women's advancement has limits. [. . .]

Wollstonecraft's assurance of "naturally" superior male strength is not only placed in conditional terms, but as her critics realized, leaves open the disturbing possibility that women may continue to push the limits of corporeal distinctions to such a degree that the sexual order itself would be threatened on its supposedly most incontestable ground, that of natural corporeal difference. For when she assures her audience that "men have superior strength of body" she immediately proposes: "Let us then, by being allowed to take the same exercise as boys, not only during infancy, but youth, arrive at perfection of body, that we may know how far the natural superiority of man extends" (*VRW*, 85). For all her assurances to the contrary, then, Wollstonecraft does leave open the possibility of an ever receding limit to women's corporeal strength, and thus an eventual end to men's "natural superiority."

Wollstonecraft and Literary Traditions

Wollstonecraft's Early Reception, Regina Janes

Regina Janes, "On the Reception of Mary Wollstonecraft's *A Vindication of the Rights of Woman*" *Journal of the History of Ideas* 39 (1978) 293–302 (293–4, 297–9)

Janes's important essay corrected modern assumptions that the *Rights of Woman* was widely and immediately denounced. Looking carefully at contemporary reviews, Janes argues that it was actually Godwin's (retrospectively unwise) publication of her *Memoirs*, with their details of sex and suicide, that actually damaged her subsequent critical reputation.

With one important exception, every notice the *Rights of Woman* received when it first appeared was favorable. The reviews were split along party lines. Periodicals of radical inclination, sharing Wollstonecraft's philosophical assumptions, sympathetic towards the rights of man and events in France, distressed by Edmund Burke's lack of consistency, approved the work. Enthusiasts of the rights of man, they did not greet the rights of woman with horror. Wollstonecraft had written for the *Analytical Review* since 1788. Joseph Johnson who had published both the *Analytical* and the book, reviewed it positively, of course, as did the *Literary Magazine*, the *General Magazine*, the *New York Magazine*, the *Monthly*

Review, and the *New Annual Register*. These periodicals had also favorably noticed her *Vindication of the Rights of Men*, one of the first answers to Burke's *Reflections on the Revolution in France*. The single journal that had favorably reviewed her *Rights of Men* and ignored the *Rights of Woman* was the *English Review*.[1] Although periodicals less politically or more conservatively committed did not in the main choose to review the work, the *Critical* Review attacked it in two passionate installments. [. . .]

As should now be commonly known, Wollstonecraft's reputation collapsed as a consequence of two separate events: the course of the revolution in France and consequent repudiation of the vocabulary of revolution in England; and Godwin's publication of her posthumous works, including *Maria Or The Wrongs of Woman* and his *Memoirs of the Author of a Vindication of the Rights of Woman*. When she died in 1797, generous obituaries appeared in the *Gentleman's Magazine*, the *Monthly Magazine*, the *European Magazine*, and *New York Magazine*.[2] When Godwin's *Memoirs* appeared the following year, they were picked up for review by far more periodicals than had taken up the *Rights of Woman* itself.

The *Memoirs* revealed that Wollstonecraft had borne a child out of wedlock and then been deserted by her lover (Gilbert Imlay), that she had pursued him and had attempted suicide on two occasions, that she had found consolation with Godwin and had engaged in sexual relations with him before marriage. This series of actions found no approval at the time from any political persuasion. The periodicals that had been favorably disposed towards the *Rights of Woman* united in wishing the *Memoirs* unwritten, unpublished, and unread. If the *Memoirs* were "a singular tribute of respect to the memory of a well beloved wife,"[3] the vindication of adultery in *Maria* was scarcely more palatable. The most sympathetic readings of the *Memoirs* attempted to palliate her acts by attributing them to virtuous though mistaken motives. Having shared Wollstonecraft's political principles, this set of reviewers did not insist upon a necessary connection between her politics and her sexual divagations. [. . .]

To a considerable extent, it was the *Memoirs* rather than the *Rights of Woman* that shaped and colored Wollstonecraft's subsequent reputation. At the extremes

---

1   [Janes's note.] The *English Review* clarified its position in supporting Mirabeau's *Treatise of Public Education*, which restated Talleyrand's view that women should be confined to a domestic education "in opposition to some modern philosophers, or rather what the Italians call *filosolas iri*, who would wish to put into soft female hands the rod of government, and the sword of justice," XIX (1792), 56. The *Gentleman's Magazine* had a good laugh over the *Rights of Men*: "We should be sorry to raise a horse-laugh against a fair lady; but we were always taught to suppose that the *rights of woman* were the proper theme of the female sex; and that, while the Romans governed the world, the women governed the Romans." When the fair lady descended to her proper subject, the reviewer was not there to meet her. Both Wollstonecraft and the *Analytical* had anticipated the jocularity of the wits. *Gentleman's Magazine*, 61, pt. 1 (1791), 151; *Analytical Review*, 12 (1792), 241–49, 13 (1792), 481–89; *Literary Magazine*, 1 (1792), 133–39; *General Magazine*, 6 (1792), 187–91; *New York Magazine*, 4 (1793), 77–81; *Monthly Review*, 8 (1792), 198–209; *New Annual Register* (1792), p. [298]; *Critical Review*, N.S. 4 (1792), 389–98, N.S. 5 (1792), 132–41.

2   [Janes's note.] *Gentleman's Magazine*, 68, pt. 2 (1797), 894; *Monthly Magazine*, 4 (1797), 232–33; *European Magazine*, 32 (1797), 215; *New York Magazine*, N.S. 2 (1797).

3   [Janes's note.] *New Annual Register* (1798), p. [271]. The *Monthly Review* wisely considered the opinions on marriage and religion to be those of Godwin, not of his wife, 27 (1798), 321–24.

of approval and disapproval were those like Godwin and the *Anti-Jacobin* who considered her acts an illustration of Jacobin morality in action. Between the ideologues were those like Matilda Betham who represented Wollstonecraft as an amiable eccentric who had refused to marry Imlay as a matter of principle, those who approved her principles and were embarrassed by her actions, and those who found both her life and principles reprehensible.[4] The range of attitudes has remained much the same from the beginning of the nineteenth century to the last quarter of the twentieth.

Wollstonecraft as Literary Critic, Mitzi Myers

Mitzi Myers, **"Sensibility and the 'Walk of Reason': Mary Wollstonecraft's Literary Reviews as Cultural Critique"** in *Sensibility in Transformation*, ed. Syndy Conger (London: Associated University Presses, 1990) 120–44 (130, 131, 132–3)

> Myers, like John Whale **(pp. 90–1)**, represents an important shift in revisionary interpretations of Wollstonecraft's aesthetics. As a reviewer for Joseph Johnson's progressive *Analytical Review*, Wollstonecraft wrote hundreds of pieces on a wide variety of subjects, including literature, politics, religion, and education. Myers argues that contrary to the prevailing modern tendency to read her as a staunch opponent of women's novels in particular (Chapter 13.2), Wollstonecraft in fact objected to the affected and imitative qualities of mass-marketed sentimental fiction, not to its imaginative qualities.

Wollstonecraft offers her female audience a resistant model of reading that counters their cultural predisposition toward submersion in the events of the text. She asks them to close the gap between their lives and their fantasies, to critique rather than internalize the shopworn images of women in literature, and her strictures on submissive female reading postures slide easily into a broader cultural analysis of female submission. [. . .]

Wollstonecraft's reviews, then, imply not just alternative models of reading

---

4   [Janes's note.] Mary Matilda Betham, *Dictionary of Celebrated Women* (London, 1804), 374–77. Betham's principal source was the *Analytical Review* which, with the *Monthly Mirror*, had waxed rhapsodic about the letters to Imlay and had acclaimed their author another Werther. *Analytical Review*, 27 (1798), 235–45; *Monthly Mirror*, 5 (1798), 153–57. The *Monthly Mirror* is most familiar from its attempt to do a "cover story" on Wollstonecraft in its second issue for which a portrait was engraved, 1 (1796), 131–33, but it was also conducted by Thomas Bellamy, hosier turned bookseller, who had conducted the *General Magazine*, one of the periodicals to review the *Rights of Woman* favorably on its first appearance. The *Critical Review* and *Gentleman's Magazine* disapproved of what they read, but were surprisingly restrained in their animadversions. The *Critical* even praised her genius and "undaunted and masculine spirit." *Critical*, N. S. 22 (1798), 414–19; *Gentleman's Magazine* 68, pt. 1 (1798), 186–87. More injurious was Alexander Chalmers, *General Biographical Dictionary*, rev. and enl. XVI (London, 1814), 54–55. That article followed the language of the *British Critic* in finding Wollstonecraft "a voluptuary and sensualist without refinement." [. . .]

and female selfhood, but also an alternative aesthetics. Most significantly, her favorite critical counters range themselves firmly against the ways of knowing and valuing she attributes to popular literature. The derivative, prescriptive, imitative, and affected—false because copied rather than freshly seen: these are her foils for originality, individuality, independence, spontaneity; for the natural, innovative, imaginative, and real, true feeling—good because uniquely felt at firsthand. These are the characteristics of "genius"—always a standard of value for Wollstonecraft and the heart of the revisionist aesthetics she refines throughout her literary progression: direct observation, independent thought, the primacy of the individual imagination as the source of aesthetic truth. To think and to feel for oneself: such phrases inform her reviews and her whole career, from the preface to her first novel, a neat little piece of expressivist aesthetics which unmistakably enrolls Wollstonecraft among the first English Romantics, to her "Hints" for the *Rights of Woman*, part two, probably written during her reviewing years and packed with maxims about originality, spontaneity, creativity, and imagination; from her personal letters to her final aesthetic manifesto, "On Poetry," initially and more appropriately entitled "On Artificial Taste." Like many of her reviews, the *Hints* connect strong passions and strong minds, "enthusiastic flights of fancy" and individuality: "a writer of genius makes us feel—an inferior author reason"; the "flights of the imagination" grant access to truths beyond the "laboured deductions of reason," necessary though these are.[1]

And much as her reviews critique hackneyed sentimental fiction as a symptom of cultural malaise, of that overrefined "state of civic society ... in which sentiment takes place of passion, and taste polishes away the native energy of character," "On Poetry" contrasts two styles of feeling and stages of society, the natural and the artificial, into a definitive exposition of Wollstonecraft's aesthetic values. (It is justly described by one biographer as a virtual call for a romantic revival in poetry.) Here she talks again about the natural as the "transcript of immediate sensations, in all their native wildness and simplicity," about "real perceptions" versus bookish declamation, revealing once more how much she values strong feelings, exquisite sensibility, and original genius. The last two are equivalent, she suggests, but she also insists that the "effusions of a vigorous mind" reveal an "understanding ... enlarged by thought" as well as "finely fashioned nerves" that "vibrate acutely with rapture." Indeed, the understanding, she argues, "must bring back the feelings to nature."[2] [...]

Her habitual contrasts of "warmth of imagination" and "truth of passion" with "romantic rants of false refinement" or "cold romantic flights" and "false enervating refinement" must be read as the thoughtful cultural critique that they are, as legitimate concern over the impact (especially on women and the

---

1   Myers cites MW's "Hints" (see p. 161).
2   [Myers' note.] Review of *Amusement: A Poetical Essay*, by Henry James Pye, *Analytical Review* 6 (March 1790): 326–27 (M is next signature); Wardle, *Mary Wollstonecraft*, p. 285; "On Poetry, and Our Relish for the Beauties of Nature," *Memoirs and Posthumous Works*, 2: 255, 254, 260, 256, 264. [...]

young) of sensibility as literary and behavioral cliché. Like Jane Austen, Maria Edgeworth, and other female contemporaries who expose the literary dependence of feminine feelings, Wollstonecraft deplores a congealing of literary language into jargon, a hardening of the emotional arteries so that women feel and act by rote, casting themselves as derivative sentimental heroines and losing touch with cultural realities and their own thoughts and feelings. Wollstonecraft's real quarrel with women writers centers around affectation, falsity and imitation; it is never with sensibility, passion, imagination, or fiction per se and certainly not with narrative that feelingly renders female experience. That was the aspiration in *Maria*: "it is the delineation of finer sensations which, in my opinion, constitutes the merit of our best novels. This is what I have in view" she states in the preface, and the novel values (perhaps even overvalues) the heroine's "true sensibility, the sensibility which is the auxiliary of virtue, and the soul of genius."

Wollstonecraft's Discourse, Gary Kelly

Gary Kelly, *Revolutionary Feminism: The Mind and Career of Mary Wollstonecraft* (London: Macmillan, 1992) 108, 109–10, 112

> Kelly's close examination of Wollstonecraft's use of language and genres remains one of the best, and his account of her "double voiced discourse," using both masculine and feminine genres, is a useful guide to appreciating the wide variety of intellectual traditions on which Wollstonecraft drew to create her interdisciplinary polemic.

[. . .] *A Vindication* had to be an experiment in feminist writing for its time—a revolution in discourse to support and to exemplify 'a revolution in female manners'. [. . .] In order to do this she not only attacks oppression directly but also exemplifies in the way she makes her attack how women may convert the conditions of their inferiority and subordination into means for emancipation. For there was no neutral, ungendered discourse, style or genre available to her. All forms of writing were already strongly associated with either 'masculine' or 'feminine' culture, or would become primarily gendered discourse as soon as she applied them to a topic such as 'the rights of woman'. Thus she avoids an objective, detached, learned, syllogistic or sarcastic and sharply polemical style that could be considered as that which a man would use. That could 'unsex' her, undermining her rhetorical authority. But she also avoids what would be considered as a woman's belletristic, domestic, personal style and relative lack of formal argument. That could undermine her claim that women given the same education, culture and rights as men would be able to take an equal if different role in culture and society with men. [. . .]

[. . .] Wollstonecraft determined to compose a quasi-treatise, a discourse that would be seen to have attributes of both 'men's' and 'women's' writing—not an 'androgynous' form but one that converts the conventional limitations of women's education, 'mind' and writing into techniques for advancing and exemplifying women's claim to minds and careers equal to if different from those of men.[1] In order to carry out this rhetorical task Wollstonecraft feminizes 'philosophy', polemics and the politics of a particular moment in the evolution of the French Revolutionary state and the British cultural revolution's debate on the French Revolution. She incorporates the themes of earlier conduct books and educational writing but resituates them in the context of the Revolutionary decade and a feminism for such a decade. By means of a relentless sociological analysis she relates this feminism to the major themes of contemporary social and cultural criticism and to the major political issues of the day.

The text has several traits of a 'philosophical' work. Wollstonecraft calls it 'a treatise', describes the 'three parts' she plans to write, divides it into chapters in an orderly sequence, refers to her 'arguments' and 'principles', and uses terms found in philosophical argument, such as 'hence', 'inference' and 'therefore'. There are even footnotes. On the other hand, the title suggests a combative, 'engaged' and perhaps personal work. The chapters vary greatly in breadth, particularity and length, and often have polemical titles. The footnotes are not so much citations of sources and evidence as asides and exclamations. For example one note, to a quotation from Rousseau, reads simply, 'What nonsense!'[2] These traits suggest something other than a treatise—some discursive 'other' exemplifying the book's argument that domestic woman is the 'other' to patriarchy in law, society, culture and writing. The text moves from chapter to chapter in an orderly and progressive way, though the order is not rigid and the progression is not emphasized. The argument proceeds by incremental repetition, recurring to certain topics, themes and images, restating them in a different form and in relation to different topics. [. . .]

This use of language parallels Wollstonecraft's use of 'women's' genres, including the conduct book, the 'rhapsody', the anecdote (personal, confessional and domestic), the familiar letter, the maxim, devotional prose, the familiar essay and prose fiction. She had already assembled such genres into a curriculum of self-formation for women in the *Female Reader*, and *A Vindication* could be seen as another 'Female Reader', but using a bricolage of sub-literary 'women's' writing to emancipate its readers from the intellectual and cultural subordination usually associated with and reproduced by such writing. For example, *A Vindication* incorporates elements of the conduct book but is itself a meta-conduct book—a commentary and critique on conduct books as instruments in the construction of woman for oppression.

1   Kelly cites Poovey's *The Proper Lady and the Woman Writer*, excerpted **pp. 75–6**.
2   [Kelly's note.] Mary Wollstonecraft, *A Vindication of the Rights of Woman*, ed. Carol Poston, 2nd edn. (New York: WW Norton, 1988) p. 78 note 3. [. . .]

Wollstonecraft and Imagination, John Whale

John Whale, "Preparations for Happiness: Mary Wollstonecraft and Imagination," Reviewing Romanticism, eds. Philip Martin and Robin Jarvis (New York: St Martin's Press, 1992) 170–89 (172–3, 180–1)

Until recently Wollstonecraft has been consistently portrayed as an Enlightenment rationalist with only negative things to say about quintessentially Romantic preoccupations such as imagination, passion, sensibility and genius. Yet, as Whale demonstrates, Rights of Woman (particularly the appended Hints for a projected second volume) and later texts such as the Letters from Sweden place great value on imagination and genius. While Wollstonecraft was wary of what she termed "romantic wavering feelings" and the ideological illusions of romance, she saw imagination as the Promethean "true fire, stolen from heaven" that rendered "men social by expanding their hearts" (see her letter to Imlay, **pp. 25–6**). Whale makes an important case for reading Wollstonecraft more subtly, as an important theorist of Romantic aesthetics (see also Mitzi Myers's essay (**pp. 86–8**) for a similar revisionary reading of Wollstonecraft's literary criticism).

Across the range of her writings Wollstonecraft sees imagination not only as a passive faculty operated on for good or ill by outside forces—so that a false refinement of taste can make it libidinous or a healthy respect for religion can exalt it above an appetite of the sense. She can also refer to it as a dynamic force in its own right, a faculty which has its own transforming power. Close to offering her own version of genius here she makes imagination approximate to some of its more famous Romantic definitions. In a letter to Imlay she upbraids him for not paying it enough respect.

> I could prove to you in a trice that it is the mother of sentiment, the great distinction of our nature, the only purifier of the passions ... the imagination is the true fire, stolen from heaven, to animate this cold creature of clay, producing all those fine sympathies that lead to rapture, rendering men social by expanding their hearts, instead of leaving them leisure to calculate how many comforts society affords.
>
> If you call these observations romantic I shall be apt to retort, that you are embruted by trade and the vulgar enjoyments of life. (*Letters* 263) [letter included **pp. 25–6**]

Clearly, imagination in its positive manifestation is closely associated with her idea of improvement, her idealism; and in its negative manifestation it is awkwardly situated in relation to her commitment to the politics of the present. As far as it can be associated with creative genius it gives some evidence of the strength of her idealism, the rapture of happiness; but in this association it begins to unsettle any idea of egalitarian ideals of improvement. [. . .]

In her penchant for the Romantic artist it seems Wollstonecraft loses track of her moral thesis. Her descriptions of creative genius seem to contradict her careful elaboration of the relative value of emotions which we have already witnessed. Where is her insistence on the stabilising influence of reason and its allies on the side of virtue—principle, conscience, and duty? Her enthusiasm for the truth of powerful feeling certainly appears to contradict her celebration of divinely sanctioned rationality. But if one concentrates instead on the distinction made between material and visionary in such statements, there is less of a conflict. Liberation from the 'material shackles' need not look like a vague escapism. As I have suggested already, Wollstonecraft's writing frequently contains something more than a static categorising; there is also a temporal scheme, a latent narrative built into her language of morality.

The titular heroine of *Mary* claims (in what the narrator self-consciously calls a 'rhapsody') that sensibility provides ineffable moments of spiritual expansion tinged with exquisite sadness.

> Sensibility is the most exquisite feeling of which the human soul is susceptible: when it pervades us we feel happy; and could it last unmixed, we might form some conjecture of the bliss of those paradisiacal days when the obedient passions were under the domain of reason. . . . It is this quickness, this delicacy of feeling, which enables us to relish the sublime touches of the poet, and the painter; it is this, which expands the soul. . . . (1, 59)

Such moments support a belief in the hereafter; they provide intimations of immortality. As is often the case with these moments their ineffable quality—'it is only to be felt; it escapes discussion' (1, 60)—is not solely a result of the primacy given to feeling: language is considered to be inadequate for other reasons as well. So, too, their sadness, and indeed their transitoriness, provide an awareness of the limitations of mortality, a resigned acceptance of material shackles; resignation because the melancholy of such moments is assuaged by their promise—'Sensibility is indeed the foundation of all our happiness', (1, 59) Mary says, leaving unspoken the fact that happiness is elsewhere and hereafter. Sensibility's delicious melancholy is triggered by the difference between temporal and eternal.

Although such statements in Wollstonecraft's work often take the form of affective outbursts or lyrical intrusions, it would be wrong to see a total disconnection between her rationalistic moral theses and these 'lapses'. Much of Wollstonecraft's puritanical suppression of pleasure and her correctives of contemporary libertinism are underscored by the logic to be found in such intimations. Though her polemics are addressed to the malpractices of the present—to conduct, manners, taste, as well as revolution—they are far from pragmatic and materialist in basis. In the case of *A Vindication* this is difficult to see if one assumes that Wollstonecraft is engaged in an act of ventriloquism; that she is adopting the macho language of the Enlightenment rationalist and suppressing her feelings. But the assumption that reason is completely antithetical to emotion is too stark to do justice to the particular historical moment and the configuration of discourses in which Wollstonecraft's texts are situated.

3

Key Passages

Introduction

Rights of Woman is an interdisciplinary polemic that addresses a political crisis – the revolutionary demands for rights of man put into practice in France and increasingly called for by British reformers. Wollstonecraft's previous work, the *Vindication of the Rights of Men* (1790), had defended republican liberty, equality, and manliness. *Rights of Woman* extends this republican argument of the rights of man to women, with revolutionary implications not just for gender relations but for social and class relations in general. Wollstonecraft's polemic engages with a complex set of debates, traditions, and genres, leading Gary Kelly to describe it as a "revolutionary discursive project" that crosses boundaries of gender and genre: it is both polemic and letter, philosophical and educational treatise, conduct book and feminist essay (see Kelly in Interpretations, **pp. 88–9**).

Many of Wollstonecraft's early reviewers and commentators read the *Rights of Woman* predominantly as an educational treatise, and in the eighteenth century educational theory was central to larger political and philosophical debates. The *Rights of Woman* is dedicated to the French statesman Bishop Talleyrand (1754–1838), who had recently published his recommendation for state-supported education in France, *Rapport sur l'instruction publique* (1791). Talleyrand argued for universal public education until age eight, when girls "should confine themselves in the paternal home" because "The paternal home is better for the education of women; they have less need to deal with the interests of others, than to accustom themselves to a calm and secluded life. Destined to domestic cares, it is in the bosom of their family that they should receive their first lessons and their first examples."[1] This Rousseauesque ideology of the separate spheres, and of women remaining within the idealized domestic sphere, was the single most important object of Wollstonecraft's critique of Rousseau (and Talleyrand).

Wollstonecraft drew on the liberatory potential of seventeenth-century philosopher John Locke's theory of the *tabula rasa*, in which physical sensation and experience, not innate ideas, shape moral character. Throughout her writings, Wollstonecraft emphasized the importance of experience (not the absence of

---

1 Talleyrand, *Rapport sur l'instruction publique*, in Appendix B.1 in Wollstonecraft, *The Vindications*, eds. D.L. Macdonald and Kathleen Scherf (Peterborough: Broadview, 1997) 399, 398.

experience, i.e., innocence, in the "paternal home") as the source of virtue for both women and men. In opposition to the arguments of Rousseau, Fordyce, and Gregory that natural sexual difference (physical, intellectual, and moral) rendered women subordinate to men, feminists like Wollstonecraft and Macaulay argued that education and environment, not nature, were responsible for women's intellectual and physical "inferiority."

Reason is central to Wollstonecraft's argument, for this most important of all attributes, she argued, is not a "sexual" one, i.e., a sex-based one, but a human one. Wollstonecraft's faith in the "perfectibility of human reason" grounded simultaneously her political and religious beliefs: "the nature of reason must be the same in all, if it be an emanation of divinity, the tie that connects the creature with the Creator" (**p. 130**). God she defined alternatively as reason and justice, and central to the "ineffable delight" of passion.[2] Like Macaulay and Mary Astell[3] before her, Wollstonecraft's feminism grew from a conviction of women's spiritual equality with men. Wollstonecraft and Macaulay joined this longstanding tradition of women's spiritual equality to the burgeoning theories of human rights developed in the revolutionary 1790s. The French Revolution of 1789 and the San Domingo revolution of 1791, in which slaves rose up and demanded their liberty, were the immediate catalysts for the intensifying interest in the rights of woman.

Indeed, the *Rights of Woman* was as dangerous as Thomas Paine's *Rights of Man*, warned conservatives like Robert Bisset and Thomas Taylor. In France, this connection between the rights of women and of men had already been made even more radically by Condorcet and Olympe de Gouges, the latter of whom published in 1791 a militant *Rights of Woman*, which it seems Wollstonecraft did not know, declaring that

> The Law should be the expression of the general will; all the Female and Male Citizens should concur personally, or by their representatives, in its formation; it should be the same for all: all the female and all the male citizens, being equal in its eyes, should be equally admissible to all honours, positions and public employments, according to their capacities.[4]

---

2   "[I]t is not to an arbitrary will, but to unerring *reason* I submit" (*Rights of Men*, in *The Vindications* 66); "They, therefore, who complain of the delusions of passion, do not recollect that they are exclaiming against a strong proof of the immortality of the soul" (chapter 4); "God is justice itself" (chapter 5.4); on imagination and divinity, see also her letters to Imlay (**pp. 25–6**) and Godwin (**pp. 28–9**), and for her religious views see Robinson (**pp. 71–3**).

3   Astell, the author of *A Serious Proposal to the Ladies* (1697), was an early feminist educationalist and political conservative; see John McCrystal, "Revolting Women: The Use of Revolutionary Discourse in Mary Astell and Mary Wollstonecraft Compared," *History of Political Thought* 14.2 (1993) 189–203. On definitions of "woman" and feminism from the seventeenth to the twentieth century, see Denise Riley, *Am I That Name?: Feminism and the Category of 'Women' in History* (Minneapolis: Minnesota University Press, 1988).

4   Olympe de Gouges, *The Rights of Woman*, article 6, reprinted in Wollstonecraft, *The Vindications*, ed. Macdonald and Scherf, 382. The Marquis de Condorcet wrote in favor of universal suffrage and education in *Lettres d'un bourgeois de Newhaven* (1787) and *Sur l'admission des femmes au droit de Cité* (1790).

The revolutionary climate in France was to turn sharply against women's interests by 1793, when the Jacobins executed notable publicly active women like de Gouges, Madame Roland, Charlotte Corday, and banned women's political clubs, thus ruthlessly enforcing the divisive doctrine of the separate spheres that Rousseau had inspired.[5] Yet *A Vindication of the Rights of Woman* emerged in this brief window of revolutionary opportunity and, in chapter 9, Wollstonecraft suggests that women are entitled to political representatives, an early and rare British call for representation that would not get taken up seriously until the mid-nineteenth century. Anne Grant, Benjamin Silliman, and the *Anti-Jacobin* objected to this radical aspect of Wollstonecraft's argument, while *Town and Country*'s positive review admitted that this section of the text "arrested our attention very forcibly."[6] While Mary Robinson hinted towards women's representation in her *Letter to the Women of England* (1799),[7] for the most part this aspect of Wollstonecraft's argument was ignored by nineteenth-century activists on women's issues, many of whom saw Wollstonecraft as concerned largely with moderate educational rights and duties (see Fawcett and Blind in Interpretations, **pp. 58–9** and 57–8), or were themselves concerned with issues other than suffrage.[8]

More substantial, and closer to the mainstream of the nineteenth-century women's movements, is Wollstonecraft's argument for women's economic independence through increased professional opportunities, beyond that of milliner, mantua maker, governess, and of course the oldest professions, "common and legal prostitution," i.e., marriage (**p. 150**).[9] The full horror of women's descent into poverty, sexual vulnerability, and abuse due to their lack of economic opportunities was a theme taken up by women writers throughout this period, from Mary Robinson in *The Natural Daughter* (1799) to Fanny Burney in *The Wanderer* (1814), and indeed Wollstonecraft's most powerful exploration of this

---

5   Madelyn Gutwirth, *The Twilight of the Goddesses: Women and Representation in the French Revolutionary Era* (New Brunswick: Rutgers University Press, 1992); Adriana Craciun and Kari Lokke, eds., *Rebellious Hearts: British Women Writers and the French Revolution* (Albany: SUNY, 2001).

6   See Grant (**pp. 48–9**); Benjamin Silliman, *Letters of Shahcoolen* (Boston: Russell & Cutler, 1802), facsimile ed. by Ben Harris McClary (Gainseville: Scholars' Facsimiles and Reprints, 1962) 24; rev. of *Posthumous Works*, *Anti-Jacobin Review* 1 (1798) 94–108; *Town and Country* (Dec. 1793) 556–9.

7   Robinson asked, "How comes it, that in this age of reason we do not see statesmen and orators selecting women of superior mental acquirements as their associates?"; she also asked, "Why are women excluded from the auditory part of the British senate?" and noted that "Many of the American tribes admit women into their public councils, and allow them the privileges of giving their opinions, first, on every subject of deliberation" (*A Letter to the Women of England on the Injustice of Mental Subordination: A Romantic Circles Edition*, ed. Adriana Craciun, Anne Close, Megan Musgrave and Orianne Smith (Romantic Circles, 1997) www.rc.umd.edu/editions/robinson/cover.htm 14, 89; excerpt in Interpretations.)

8   For precedents to Wollstonecraft's call for representatives, see Elaine Chalus, "Women, Electoral Privilege and Practice in the Eighteenth Century" in *Women in British Politics 1760–1860*, ed. Kathryn Gleadle and Sarah Richardson (London: Macmillan, 2000) 19–38; Claire Tomalin, Appendix I in *The Life and Death of Mary Wollstonecraft*, rev. edn (1974; Harmondsworth: Penguin, 1992) 341–3.

9   Wollstonecraft also refers to marriage as "legal prostitution" in *Rights of Men* (*The Vindications*, 53) and in chapter 4 of *Rights of Woman* speaks of women "whose persons often [are] legally prostituted" in marriage.

deplorable situation appears in her own unfinished novel, *The Wrongs of Woman, or Maria*. But the outline of her desired "REVOLUTION in female manners" emerges in the later chapters of the *Rights of Woman*, where she explores educational and economic reforms with some specificity.

⌐   In her assertion that women should have equal right to education, intellectual development, physical exercise, legal and moral responsibility, political representation, and economic opportunities, Wollstonecraft radically challenged deeply held beliefs that such rights and duties should differ according to sex and class. Conservative attacks and subsequent feminist praise, especially in the late twentieth century, have typically focused on these radical aspects of the *Rights of Woman.*/Wollstonecraft's argument on motherhood and femininity, on the other hand, has opened divisions within what might (erroneously) seem to be politically homogeneous groups, revealing how gender and class interests can often be at odds. Wollstonecraft's painfully honest critique of women of leisure has long been likened to that of misogynist satirists. Her complex view of motherhood remains even more controversial. Discussing the social benefits of universal education, Wollstonecraft argued that women's inadequate educations made them bad mothers, for "whatever tends to incapacitate the maternal character, takes woman out of her sphere" (**p. 155**). Yet she repeatedly insisted that a wife is "also an active citizen" and that "if you take away natural rights, . . . duties become null" (**p. 149**). The Victorian feminist Mathilde Blind complained that *Rights of Woman* "might perhaps with more justice be called the Duties instead of Rights of Woman," (**p. 58**) yet Wollstonecraft makes it quite clear what relation rights and duties bear to one another: "The being who discharges the duties of its station is independent; and, speaking of women at large, their first duty is to themselves as rational creatures, and the next, in point of importance, as citizens, is that, which includes so many, of a mother" (**p. 149**). Maternal duties are therefore one part of many "*human* duties" of an active female citizen, and they are inseparable from the rights of citizens as conceived by radical male republicans at the time (chapter 3). The most revolutionary claim is that female citizens' first duty "is to themselves as rational creatures;" this refusal to celebrate the self-sacrificing ideals of domestic motherhood, to center women's lives around the nurturing of children and men, places Wollstonecraft far in advance of a culture that demanded and enforced women's idealized subjugation to maternal duties and domesticity.

This fundamental question, of motherhood's relationship to citizenship, is central to Wollstonecraft's revision of republican theories (such as Rousseau's and Talleyrand's) of the gendered separate spheres. This question also explains the vehemence of early nineteenth-century attacks on Wollstonecraft as a dangerous example of a woman who abandoned the traditional roles of mother and wife for that of philosopher and citizen, as well as Victorian responses that sometimes patronizingly acknowledged her "essentially womanly" support of women's traditional duties as mothers and wives. In the Interpretations section, Carole Pateman, Virginia Sapiro, and Linda Colley, among others, discuss the ongoing debates over this tension regarding separate-spheres ideology (sometimes called "republican motherhood") in Wollstonecraft's work.

The thirteen chapters of the *Rights of Woman* are each represented here with extracts highlighting key aspects in Wollstonecraft's discursive and at times diffuse argument. She planned to write a second volume focusing on women's lack of legal rights, but this was never completed and instead emerged in the argument of her most radical work, the novel *The Wrongs of Woman, or Maria*, which Godwin published after her death. She did, however, leave behind notes for the second volume, which Godwin also published as "Hints [Chiefly designed to have been incorporated in the Second Part of the Vindication of the Rights of Woman.]" (**pp. 161–4**). These "Hints" reveal the new directions Wollstonecraft's work was taking (for example, towards an increasing appreciation of the Romantic imagination and aesthetics) and *Rights of Woman* should be read with this ongoing intellectual exploration in mind.

A

VINDICATION

OF THE

RIGHTS OF WOMAN:

WITH

STRICTURES

ON

POLITICAL AND MORAL SUBJECTS.

By MARY WOLLSTONECRAFT.

VOL. I.

THE SECOND EDITION.

LONDON:

PRINTED FOR J. JOHNSON, Nº. 72, ST. PAUL'S CHURCH YARD.

1792.

TO

M. TALLEYRAND-PÉRIGORD,[1]

LATE BISHOP OF AUTUN.

SIR,

HAVING read with great pleasure a pamphlet which you have lately published, I dedicate this volume to you; to induce you to reconsider the subject, and maturely[2] weigh what I have advanced respecting the rights of woman and national education: and I call with the firm tone of humanity; for my arguments, Sir, are dictated by a disinterested spirit—I plead for my sex—not for myself. Independence I have long considered as the grand blessing of life, the basis of every virtue—and independence I will ever secure by contracting my wants, though I were to live on a barren heath.

It is then an affection for the whole human race that makes my pen dart rapidly along to support what I believe to be the cause of virtue: and the same motive leads me earnestly to wish to see woman placed in a station in which she would advance, instead of retarding, the progress of those glorious principles that give a substance to morality. My opinion, indeed, respecting the rights and duties of woman, seems to flow so naturally from these simple principles, that I think it scarcely possible, but that some of the enlarged minds who formed your admirable constitution, will coincide with me.

In France there is undoubtedly a more general diffusion of knowledge than in any part of the European world, and I attribute it, in a great measure, to the social intercourse which has long subsisted between the sexes. It is true, I utter my sentiments with freedom, that in France the very essence of sensuality has been extracted to regale the voluptuary, and a kind of sentimental lust has prevailed, which, together with the system of duplicity that the whole tenour of their political and civil government taught, have given a sinister sort of sagacity to the French character,[3] properly termed finesse; from which naturally flow a polish of

---

1 Charles Maurice de Talleyrand-Périgord (1754–1838), Bishop of Autun from 1788 to 1791, published his *Rapport sur l'instruction publique* in 1791, arguing for universal education until age eight, when women would return to the paternal home and remain there. Condorcet had argued for equal education and for women's political representation (as had the feminist Olympe de Gouges), but Talleyrand remained faithful to the educational philosophy of Rousseau. See chapter 12 for Wollstonecraft's more detailed discussion of Talleyrand's plans, and chapters 2 and 5 on Rousseau.

2 "I dedicate . . . maturely": This is the longest emendation made, presumably by Wollstonecraft, to the second edition. The first edition read:

> on National Education, I dedicate this volume to you – the first dedication that I have ever written, to induce you to read it with attention; and, because I think that you will understand me, which I do not suppose many pert witlings will, who may ridicule the arguments they are unable to answer. But, Sir, I carry my respect for your understanding still farther; so far, that I am confident you will not throw my work aside, and hastily conclude that I am in the wrong, because you did not view the subject in the same light yourself.—And, pardon my frankness, but I must observe, that you treated it in too cursory a manner, contended to consider it as it had been considered formerly, when the rights of man, not to advert to woman, were trampled on as chimerical—I call upon you, therefore, now to

3 This characterization of the French as artificial and effeminate is common in British writing of the time. After writing the *Rights of Woman*, Wollstonecraft moved to France, where her views began to change; see Wellington (pp. 73–4).

manners that injures the substance, by hunting sincerity out of society.—And, modesty, the fairest garb of virtue! has been more grossly insulted in France than even in England, till their women have treated as *prudish* that attention to decency, which brutes instinctively observe.

Manners and morals are so nearly allied that they have often been confounded; but, though the former should only be the natural reflection of the latter, yet, when various causes have produced factitious and corrupt manners, which are very early caught, morality becomes an empty name. The personal reserve, and sacred respect for cleanliness and delicacy in domestic life, which French women almost despise, are the graceful pillars of modesty; but, far from despising them, if the pure flame of patriotism have reached their bosoms, they should labour to improve the morals of their fellow-citizens, by teaching men, not only to respect modesty in women, but to acquire it themselves, as the only way to merit their esteem.

Contending for the rights of woman, my main argument is built on this simple principle, that if she be not prepared by education to become the companion of man, she will stop the progress of knowledge and virtue; for truth must be common to all, or it will be inefficacious with respect to its influence on general practice. And how can woman be expected to co-operate unless she know why she ought to be virtuous? unless freedom strengthen her reason till she comprehend her duty, and see in what manner it is connected with her real good? If children are to be educated to understand the true principle of patriotism, their mother must be a patriot;[4] and the love of mankind, from which an orderly train of virtues spring, can only be produced by considering the moral and civil interest of mankind; but the education and situation of woman, at present, shuts her out from such investigations.

In this work I have produced many arguments, which to me were conclusive, to prove that the prevailing notion respecting a sexual[5] character was subversive of morality, and I have contended, that to render the human body and mind more perfect, chastity must more universally prevail, and that chastity will never be respected in the male world till the person of a woman is not, as it were, idolized, when little virtue or sense embellish it with the grand traces of mental beauty, or the interesting simplicity of affection.

Consider, Sir, dispassionately, these observations—for a glimpse of this truth seemed to open before you when you observed, "that to see one half of the human race excluded by the other from all participation of government, was a political phaenomenon that, according to abstract principles, it was impossible to explain."[6] If so, on what does your constitution[7] rest? If the abstract rights of man

---

4 On this view of motherhood as an agent of civic education, known as "republican motherhood" in France and the US, see Pateman (**pp. 62–3**), Sapiro (**pp. 63–5**), and Colley (**pp. 65–7**).

5 i.e., sex-based or sex-specific.

6 Talleyrand, *Rapport sur l'instruction publique*, in Appendix B.1 in Wollstonecraft's The *Vindications*, ed. D.L. Macdonald and Kathleen Scherf (Peterborough: Broadview, 1997) 396. Talleyrand goes on to claim that "it seems incontestible to us that the common happiness, especially that of women, requires that they do not aspire to the exercise of political rights and duties" (397).

7 The French Constitution of 1791 granted citizenship only to men over twenty-five, thus disenfranchising all women until 1944 when women won the vote.

will bear discussion and explanation, those of woman, by a parity of reasoning, will not shrink from the same test: though a different opinion prevails in this country, built on the very arguments which you use to justify the oppression of woman—prescription.

Consider, I address you as a legislator, whether, when men contend for their freedom, and to be allowed to judge for themselves respecting their own happiness, it be not inconsistent and unjust to subjugate women, even though you firmly believe that you are acting in the manner best calculated to promote their happiness? Who made man the exclusive judge, if woman partake with him the gift of reason?

In this style, argue tyrants of every denomination, from the weak king to the weak father of a family; they are all eager to crush reason; yet always assert that they usurp its throne only to be useful. Do you not act a similar part, when you *force* all women, by denying them civil and political rights, to remain immured in their families groping in the dark? for surely, Sir, you will not assert, that a duty can be binding which is not founded on reason? If indeed this be their destination, arguments may be drawn from reason: and thus augustly supported, the more understanding women acquire, the more they will be attached to their duty—comprehending it—for unless they comprehend it, unless their morals be fixed on the same immutable principle as those of man, no authority can make them discharge it in a virtuous manner. They may be convenient slaves, but slavery will have its constant effect, degrading the master and the abject dependent.

But, if women are to be excluded, without having a voice, from a participation of the natural rights of mankind, prove first, to ward off the charge of injustice and inconsistency, that they want reason—else this flaw in your NEW CONSTITUTION will ever shew that man must, in some shape, act like a tyrant, and tyranny, in whatever part of society it rears its brazen front, will ever undermine morality.

I have repeatedly asserted, and produced what appeared to me irrefragable arguments drawn from matters of fact, to prove my assertion, that women cannot, by force, be confined to domestic concerns; for they will, however ignorant, intermeddle with more weighty affairs, neglecting private duties only to disturb, by cunning tricks, the orderly plans of reason which rise above their comprehension.

Besides, whilst they are only made to acquire personal accomplishments, men will seek for pleasure in variety, and faithless husbands will make faithless wives; such ignorant beings, indeed, will be very excusable when, not taught to respect public good, nor allowed any civil rights, they attempt to do themselves justice by retaliation.

The box of mischief thus opened in society, what is to preserve private virtue, the only security of public freedom and universal happiness?

Let there be then no coercion *established* in society, and the common law of gravity prevailing, the sexes will fall into their proper places. And, now that more equitable laws are forming your citizens, marriage may become more sacred: your young men may choose wives from motives of affection, and your maidens allow love to root out vanity.

The father of a family will not then weaken his constitution and debase his sentiments, by visiting the harlot, nor forget, in obeying the call of appetite, the purpose for which it was implanted. And, the mother will not neglect her children to practise the arts of coquetry, when sense and modesty secure her the friendship of her husband.

But, till men become attentive to the duty of a father, it is vain to expect women to spend that time in their nursery which they, "wise in their generation,"[8] choose to spend at their glass; for this exertion of cunning is only an instinct of nature to enable them to obtain indirectly a little of that power of which they are unjustly denied a share: for, if women are not permitted to enjoy legitimate rights, they will render both men and themselves vicious, to obtain illicit privileges.

I wish, Sir, to set some investigations of this kind afloat in France; and should they lead to a confirmation of my principles, when your constitution is revised the Rights of Woman may be respected, if it be fully proved that reason calls for this respect, and loudly demands JUSTICE for one half of the human race.

I am, SIR,

Your's respectfully,

M.W.

8   Luke 16:8.

ADVERTISEMENT.

WHEN I began to write this work, I divided it into three parts, supposing that one volume would contain a full discussion of the arguments which seemed to me to rise naturally from a few simple principles; but fresh illustrations occurring as I advanced, I now present only the first part to the public.

Many subjects, however, which I have cursorily alluded to, call for particular investigation, especially the laws relative to women, and the consideration of their peculiar duties. These will furnish ample matter for a second volume, which in due time will be published, to elucidate some of the sentiments, and complete many of the sketches begun in the first.[9]

CONTENTS.

CHAP. I.
The rights and involved duties of mankind considered

CHAP. II.
The prevailing opinion of a sexual character discussed

CHAP. III.
The same subject continued

CHAP. IV.
Observations on the state of degradation to which woman is reduced by various causes

CHAP. V.
Animadversions on some of the writers who have rendered women objects of pity, bordering on contempt

CHAP. VI.
The effect which an early association of ideas has upon the character

CHAP. VII.
Modesty. Comprehensively considered, and not as a sexual virtue

CHAP. VIII.
Morality undermined by sexual notions of the importance of a good reputation

CHAP. IX.
Of the pernicious effects which arise from the unnatural distinctions established in society

---

9   Part 2 of the *Rights of Woman* was never written, but Wollstonecraft did focus on legal injustices in her unfinished novel, *The Wrongs of Woman, or Maria* (published posthumously by Godwin in 1798); see also Wollstonecraft's "Hints. [Chiefly designed to have been incorporated in the Second Part of the Vindication of the Rights of Woman.]" (pp. 161–4).

CHAP. X.
Parental affection

CHAP. XI.
Duty to parents

CHAP. XII.
On national education

CHAP. XIII.
Some instances of the folly which the ignorance of women generates; with concluding reflections on the moral improvement that a revolution in female manners might naturally be expected to produce

INTRODUCTION.

AFTER considering the historic page, and viewing the living world with anxious solicitude, the most melancholy emotions of sorrowful indignation have depressed my spirits, and I have sighed when obliged to confess, that either nature has made a great difference between man and man, or that the civilization which has hitherto taken place in the world has been very partial. I have turned over various books written on the subject of education, and patiently observed the conduct of parents and the management of schools; but what has been the result?—a profound conviction that the neglected education of my fellow-creatures is the grand source of the misery I deplore; and that women, in particular, are rendered weak and wretched by a variety of concurring causes, originating from one hasty conclusion. The conduct and manners of women, in fact, evidently prove that their minds are not in a healthy state; for, like the flowers which are planted in too rich a soil, strength and usefulness are sacrificed to beauty; and the flaunting leaves, after having pleased a fastidious eye, fade, disregarded on the stalk, long before the season when they ought to have arrived at maturity.—One cause of this barren blooming I attribute to a false system of education, gathered from the books written on this subject by men who, considering females rather as women than human creatures, have been more anxious to make them alluring mistresses than affectionate wives and rational mothers; and the understanding of the sex has been so bubbled by this specious homage, that the civilized women of the present century, with a few exceptions, are only anxious to inspire love, when they ought to cherish a nobler ambition, and by their abilities and virtues exact respect.

In a treatise, therefore, on female rights and manners, the works which have been particularly written for their improvement must not be overlooked; especially when it is asserted, in direct terms, that the minds of women are enfeebled by false refinement; that the books of instruction, written by men of genius, have had the same tendency as more frivolous productions; and that, in the true style of Mahometanism, they are treated as a kind of subordinate beings, and not as a part of the human species, when improveable reason is allowed to be the dignified distinction which raises men above the brute creation, and puts a natural sceptre in a feeble hand.[1]

Yet, because I am a woman, I would not lead my readers to suppose that I mean violently to agitate the contested question respecting the equality or inferiority of the sex; but as the subject lies in my way, and I cannot pass it over without subjecting the main tendency of my reasoning to misconstruction, I shall stop a moment to deliver, in a few words, my opinion.—In the government of the physical world it is observable that the female in point of strength is, in general, inferior to the male.[2] This is the law of nature; and it does not appear to be

---

1   A common belief at the time that in Islam women did not have souls; feminists in particular used women's imagined position in Islam (particularly in the harem) to indicate the worst degree of women's sexual subjugation.
2   "that the female . . . the male": in the first edition, this phrase was followed by "The male pursues, the female yields."

suspended or abrogated in favour of woman. A degree of physical superiority cannot, therefore, be denied—and it is a noble prerogative! But not content with this natural pre-eminence, men endeavour to sink us still lower, merely to render us alluring objects for a moment; and women, intoxicated by the adoration which men, under the influence of their senses, pay them, do not seek to obtain a durable interest in their hearts, or to become the friends of the fellow creatures who find amusement in their society.

I am aware of an obvious inference:—from every quarter have I heard exclamations against masculine women; but where are they to be found? If by this appellation men mean to inveigh against their ardour in hunting, shooting, and gaming, I shall most cordially join in the cry; but if it be against the imitation of manly virtues, or, more properly speaking, the attainment of those talents and virtues, the exercise of which ennobles the human character, and which raise females in the scale of animal being, when they are comprehensively termed mankind;—all those who view them with a philosophic eye must, I should think, wish with me, that they may every day grow more and more masculine.

This discussion naturally divides the subject. I shall first consider women in the grand light of human creatures, who, in common with men, are placed on this earth to unfold their faculties; and afterwards I shall more particularly point out their peculiar designation.

I wish also to steer clear of an error which many respectable writers have fallen into; for the instruction which has hitherto been addressed to women, has rather been applicable to *ladies*, if the little indirect advice, that is scattered through Sandford and Merton, be excepted; but, addressing my sex in a firmer tone, I pay particular attention to those in the middle class, because they appear to be in the most natural state. Perhaps the seeds of false-refinement, immorality, and vanity, have ever been shed by the great. Weak, artificial beings, raised above the common wants and affections of their race, in a premature unnatural manner, undermine the very foundation of virtue, and spread corruption through the whole mass of society! As a class of mankind they have the strongest claim to pity; the education of the rich tends to render them vain and helpless, and the unfolding mind is not strengthened by the practice of those duties which dignify the human character.—They only live to amuse themselves, and by the same law which in nature invariably produces certain effects, they soon only afford barren amusement.

But as I purpose taking a separate view of the different ranks of society, and of the moral character of women, in each, this hint is, for the present, sufficient; and I have only alluded to the subject, because it appears to me to be the very essence of an introduction to give a cursory account of the contents of the work it introduces.

My own sex, I hope, will excuse me, if I treat them like rational creatures, instead of flattering their *fascinating* graces, and viewing them as if they were in a state of perpetual childhood, unable to stand alone. I earnestly wish to point out in what true dignity and human happiness consists—I wish to persuade women to endeavour to acquire strength, both of mind and body, and to convince them that the soft phrases, susceptibility of heart, delicacy of sentiment, and refinement of taste, are almost synonymous with epithets of weakness, and that those beings who are only the objects of pity and that kind of love, which has been termed its sister, will soon become objects of contempt.

Dismissing then those pretty feminine phrases, which the men condescendingly use to soften our slavish dependence, and despising that weak elegancy of mind, exquisite sensibility, and sweet docility of manners, supposed to be the sexual characteristics of the weaker vessel, I wish to shew that elegance is inferior to virtue, that the first object of laudable ambition is to obtain a character as a human being, regardless of the distinction of sex; and that secondary views should be brought to this simple touchstone.

This is a rough sketch of my plan; and should I express my conviction with the energetic emotions that I feel whenever I think of the subject, the dictates of experience and reflection will be felt by some of my readers. Animated by this important object, I shall disdain to cull my phrases or polish my style;—I aim at being useful, and sincerity will render me unaffected; for, wishing rather to per-suade by the force of my arguments, than dazzle by the elegance of my language, I shall not waste my time in rounding periods, or in fabricating the turgid bombast of artificial feelings, which, coming from the head, never reach the heart.—I shall be employed about things, not words!—and, anxious to render my sex more respectable members of society, I shall try to avoid that flowery diction which has slided from essays into novels, and from novels into familiar letters and conversation.[3]

These pretty superlatives, dropping glibly from the tongue, vitiate the taste, and create a kind of sickly delicacy that turns away from simple unadorned truth; and a deluge of false sentiments and overstretched feelings, stifling the natural emotions of the heart, render the domestic pleasures insipid, that ought to sweeten the exercise of those severe duties, which educate a rational and immortal being for a nobler field of action.

The education of women has, of late, been more attended to than formerly; yet they are still reckoned a frivolous sex, and ridiculed or pitied by the writers who endeavour by satire or instruction to improve them. It is acknowledged that they spend many of the first years of their lives in acquiring a smattering of accomplishments; meanwhile strength of body and mind are sacrificed to libertine notions of beauty, to the desire of establishing themselves,—the only way women can rise in the world,—by marriage. And this desire making mere animals of them, when they marry they act as such children may be expected to act:—they dress; they paint, and nickname God's creatures.—Surely these weak beings are only fit for a seraglio!—Can they be expected to govern a family with judgment, or take care of the poor babes whom they bring into the world?

If then it can be fairly deduced from the present conduct of the sex, from the

---

3 Style was an intensely political issue at this time; Wollstonecraft distinguishes her radical writing (here and in the *Vindication of the Rights of Men*) from the effeminate and elaborate diction of conservative writers like Edmund Burke. Reviewers and nineteenth-century critics often noted her forthright style as inappropriate or at the very least unusual for a woman; see Kelly (**pp. 88–9**) and Wollstonecraft's letters to Hays and Godwin (**pp. 24–5, 28–9**).

prevalent fondness for pleasure which takes place of ambition and those nobler passions that open and enlarge the soul; that the instruction which women have hitherto received has only tended, with the constitution of civil society, to render them insignificant objects of desire—mere propagators of fools!—if it can be proved that in aiming to accomplish them, without cultivating their understandings, they are taken out of their sphere of duties, and made ridiculous and useless when the short-lived bloom of beauty is over,[4] I presume that *rational* men will excuse me for endeavouring to persuade them to become more masculine and respectable.

Indeed the word masculine is only a bugbear: there is little reason to fear that women will acquire too much courage or fortitude; for their apparent inferiority with respect to bodily strength, must render them, in some degree, dependent on men in the various relations of life; but why should it be increased by prejudices that give a sex to virtue, and confound simple truths with sensual reveries?

Women are, in fact, so much degraded by mistaken notions of female excellence, that I do not mean to add a paradox when I assert, that this artificial weakness produces a propensity to tyrannize, and gives birth to cunning, the natural opponent of strength,[5] which leads them to play off those contemptible infantine airs that undermine esteem even whilst they excite desire. Let men become more chaste and modest, and if women do not grow wiser in the same ratio, it will be clear that they have weaker understandings.[6] It seems scarcely necessary to say, that I now speak of the sex in general. Many individuals have more sense than their male relatives; and, as nothing preponderates where there is a constant struggle for an equilibrium, without it has naturally more gravity, some women govern their husbands without degrading themselves, because intellect will always govern.

VINDICATION OF THE RIGHTS OF WOMAN.
PART I.

CHAP. I.
THE RIGHTS AND INVOLVED DUTIES OF MANKIND CONSIDERED.
IN the present state of society it appears necessary to go back to first principles in search of the most simple truths, and to dispute with some prevailing prejudice every inch of ground. To clear my way, I must be allowed to ask some plain questions, and the answers will probably appear as unequivocal as the axioms on which reasoning is built; though, when entangled with various motives of action, they are formally contradicted, either by the words or conduct of men.

---

4   [MW's note.] A lively writer, I cannot recollect his name, asks what business women turned of forty have to do in the world? [untraced]
5   This (gendered) opposition between cunning and strength is central to Wollstonecraft's argument, and similar to William Blake's in *The Marriage of Heaven and Hell* (1790–3): "The weak in courage is strong in cunning" (in *Romanticism: An Anthology*, 2nd edn, ed. Duncan Wu (Oxford: Blackwell, 2000) 88, 90). On strength, see Craciun (**pp. 82–4**).
6   "Let men . . . understandings": Instead of this sentence, the first edition read: "Do not foster these prejudices, and they will naturally fall into their subordinate, yet respectable station, in life."

In what does man's pre-eminence over the brute creation consist? The answer is as clear as that a half is less than the whole; in Reason.[1]

What acquirement exalts one being above another? Virtue; we spontaneously reply.

For what purpose were the passions implanted? That man by struggling with them might attain a degree of knowledge denied to the brutes; whispers Experience.

Consequently the perfection of our nature and capability of happiness, must be estimated by the degree of reason, virtue, and knowledge, that distinguish the individual, and direct the laws which bind society: and that from the exercise of reason, knowledge and virtue naturally flow, is equally undeniable, if mankind be viewed collectively.

The rights and duties of man thus simplified, it seems almost impertinent to attempt to illustrate truths that appear so incontrovertible; yet such deeply rooted prejudices have clouded reason, and such spurious qualities have assumed the name of virtues, that it is necessary to pursue the course of reason as it has been perplexed and involved in error, by various adventitious circumstances, comparing the simple axiom with casual deviations.

Men, in general, seem to employ their reason to justify prejudices, which they have imbibed, they can scarcely trace how, rather than to root them out. The mind must be strong that resolutely forms its own principles; for a kind of intellectual cowardice prevails which makes many men shrink from the task, or only do it by halves. Yet the imperfect conclusions thus drawn, are frequently very plausible, because they are built on partial experience, on just, though narrow, views.

Going back to first principles, vice skulks, with all its native deformity, from close investigation; but a set of shallow reasoners are always exclaiming that these arguments prove too much, and that a measure rotten at the core may be expedient. Thus expediency is continually contrasted with simple principles, till truth is lost in a mist of words, virtue, in forms, and knowledge rendered a sounding nothing, by the specious prejudices that assume its name.

That the society is formed in the wisest manner, whose constitution is founded on the nature of man, strikes, in the abstract, every thinking being so forcibly, that it looks like presumption to endeavour to bring forward proofs; though proof must be brought, or the strong hold of prescription will never be forced by reason; yet to urge prescription as an argument to justify the depriving men (or women) of

---

1 Wollstonecraft's point that men and women have equal capacity for reason is accompanied by a simultaneous denial that nonhuman animals possess reason or "mind." She argues at length against such claims for reason extending across species barriers in her review of Smellie's *The Philosophy of Natural History* (1790), which argued that "among mankind . . . the scale of intellect is very extensive" and that a "great chain of being" connects human and nonhuman animals (William Smellie, *Philosophy of Natural History*, 522; Wollstonecraft, *Works* 7: 293–300). This chain of being hypothesis had conservative uses at the time (seeing social inequality and slavery as results of natural inequality) but Wollstonecraft's concern is that such a chain robs humanity of its distinctive immortality: "in his ardour to prove that animals have minds similar to the human intellect," Smellie is in danger of "depriv[ing] us of souls" (*Works* 7: 296). See Sapiro (pp. 63–5), Pateman (pp. 62–3) and Colley (pp. 65–7) on Wollstonecraft's relationship to Enlightenment values and Londa Schiebinger on the great chain of being (*Nature's Body: Gender in the Making of Modern Science* (Boston: Beacon, 1993) 145–60).

their natural rights, is one of the absurd sophisms which daily insult common sense.

The civilization of the bulk of the people of Europe is very partial; nay, it may be made a question, whether they have acquired any virtues in exchange for innocence, equivalent to the misery produced by the vices that have been plastered over unsightly ignorance, and the freedom which has been bartered for splendid slavery. The desire of dazzling by riches, the most certain pre-eminence that man can obtain, the pleasure of commanding flattering sycophants, and many other complicated low calculations of doting self-love, have all contributed to overwhelm the mass of mankind, and make liberty a convenient handle for mock patriotism. For whilst rank and titles are held of the utmost importance, before which Genius "must hide its diminished head," it is, with a few exceptions, very unfortunate for a nation when a man of abilities, without rank or property, pushes himself forward to notice.—Alas! what unheard of misery have thousands suffered to purchase a cardinal's hat for an intriguing obscure adventurer, who longed to be ranked with princes, or lord it over them by seizing the triple crown!

Such, indeed, has been the wretchedness that has flowed from hereditary honours, riches, and monarchy, that men of lively sensibility have almost uttered blasphemy in order to justify the dispensations of providence. Man has been held out as independent of his power who made him, or as a lawless planet darting from its orbit to steal the celestial fire of reason; and the vengeance of heaven, lurking in the subtile flame, like Pandora's pent up mischiefs, sufficiently punished his temerity, by introducing evil into the world.[2]

Impressed by this view of the misery and disorder which pervaded society, and fatigued with jostling against artificial fools, Rousseau[3] became enamoured of solitude, and, being at the same time an optimist, he labours with uncommon eloquence to prove that man was naturally a solitary animal. Misled by his respect for the goodness of God, who certainly—for what man of sense and feeling can doubt it!—gave life only to communicate happiness, he considers evil as positive, and the work of man; not aware that he was exalting one attribute at the expence of another, equally necessary to divine perfection.

Reared on a false hypothesis his arguments in favour of a state of nature are plausible, but unsound. I say unsound; for to assert that a state of nature is preferable to civilization, in all its possible perfection, is, in other words, to arraign supreme wisdom; and the paradoxical exclamation, that God has made all things right, and that error has been introduced by the creature, whom he formed, knowing what he formed, is as unphilosophical as impious.

---

2   The Titan Prometheus, who stole the "celestial fire" from the gods, was a favorite of later Romantics like Percy Bysshe Shelley and Mary Shelley (Wollstonecraft's daughter and the author of *Frankenstein, or The Modern Prometheus*). After Prometheus stole the celestial fire to give to humans, Zeus punished humanity by sending Pandora. Pandora had a jar she was forbidden to open; unable to restrain her curiosity she opened the jar, releasing all the evils into the world. The best-known versions of the Prometheus and Pandora myths are found in Hesiod's *Theogony* and in Aeschylus' *Prometheus Bound*.

3   On Jean-Jacques Rousseau (1712–78) and solitude, see *Discourse on the Origin and Foundations of Inequality Among Men* (1755), *Reveries of the Solitary Walker* (1776–8), and *Confessions* (1781–8); on Rousseau's influence on Wollstonecraft, see headnote to *Emile* (p. 17).

When that wise Being who created us and placed us here, saw the fair idea, he willed, by allowing it to be so, that the passions should unfold our reason, because he could see that present evil would produce future good. Could the helpless creature whom he called from nothing break loose from his providence, and boldly learn to know good by practising evil, without his permission? No.—How could that energetic advocate for immortality argue so inconsistently? Had mankind remained for ever in the brutal state of nature, which even his magic pen cannot paint as a state in which a single virtue took root, it would have been clear, though not to the sensitive unreflecting wanderer, that man was born to run the circle of life and death, and adorn God's garden for some purpose which could not easily be reconciled with his attributes.

But if, to crown the whole, there were to be rational creatures produced, allowed to rise in excellence by the exercise of powers implanted for that purpose; if benignity itself thought fit to call into existence a creature above the brutes,[4] who could think and improve himself, why should that inestimable gift, for a gift it was, if man was so created as to have a capacity to rise above the state in which sensation produced brutal ease, be called, in direct terms, a curse? A curse it might be reckoned, if the whole of our existence were bounded by our continuance in this world; for why should the gracious fountain of life give us passions, and the power of reflecting, only to imbitter our days and inspire us with mistaken notions of dignity? Why should he lead us from love of ourselves to the sublime emotions which the discovery of his wisdom and goodness excites, if these feelings were not set in motion to improve our nature, of which they make a part,[5] and render us capable of enjoying a more godlike portion of happiness? Firmly persuaded that no evil exists in the world that God did not design to take place, I build my belief on the perfection of God.

Rousseau[6] exerts himself to prove that all *was* right originally: a crowd of authors that all *is* now right: and I, that all will *be* right. [. . .]

---

4   [MW's note.] Contrary to the opinion of anatomists, who argue by analogy from the formation of the teeth, stomach, and intestines, Rousseau will not allow a man to be a carnivorous animal. And, carried away from nature by a love of system, he disputes whether man be a gregarious animal, though the long and helpless state of infancy seems to point him out as particularly impelled to pair, the first step towards herding. [Ed.: See *Emile*, 57–8, 153–5. Throughout *Rights of Woman*, Wollstonecraft quotes from Rousseau's *Emilius and Sophia; or, A New System of Education*, trans. William Kenrick (London, 1763). My page references are to Allan Bloom's translation, *Emile, or On Education* (New York: Basic Books, 1979). Catharine Macaulay wrote that "I can from my own experience affirm with Rousseau, that the taste of flesh is not natural to the human palate," being "a diet only fit for savages; and must naturally tend to weaken our sympathies" (*Letters on Education* (New York: Garland, 1974) 38–9); on sensibility and animal cruelty, see Barker-Benfield, *The Culture of Sensibility* (Chicago: University of Chicago Press, 1992) 231–6.]

5   [MW's note.] What would you say to a mechanic whom you had desired to make a watch to point out the hour of the day, if, to shew his ingenuity, he added wheels to make it a repeater, &c. that perplexed the simple mechanism; should he urge, to excuse himself—had you not touched a certain spring, you would have known nothing of the matter, and that he should have amused himself by making *an experiment* without doing you any harm: would you not retort fairly upon him, by insisting that if he had not added those needless wheels and springs, the accident could not have happened?

6   Here and in the previous few paragraphs, Wollstonecraft is disputing Rousseau's influential theory of the state of nature, as expressed in the first sentence of *Emile*: "Everything is good as it leaves the hands of the Author of things; everything degenerates in the hands of man" (37).

After attacking the sacred majesty of Kings, I shall scarcely excite surprise by adding my firm persuasion that every profession, in which great subordination of rank constitutes its power, is highly injurious to morality.

A standing army, for instance, is incompatible with freedom; because subordination and rigour are the very sinews of military discipline; and despotism is necessary to give vigour to enterprizes that one will directs. A spirit inspired by romantic notions of honour, a kind of morality founded on the fashion of the age, can only be felt by a few officers, whilst the main body must be moved by command, like the waves of the sea; for the strong wind of authority pushes the crowd of subalterns forward, they scarcely know or care why, with headlong fury.

Besides, nothing can be so prejudicial to the morals of the inhabitants of country towns as the occasional residence of a set of idle superficial young men, whose only occupation is gallantry, and whose polished manners render vice more dangerous, by concealing its deformity under gay ornamental drapery. An air of fashion, which is but a badge of slavery, and proves that the soul has not a strong individual character, awes simple country people into an imitation of the vices, when they cannot catch the slippery graces, of politeness. Every corps is a chain of despots, who, submitting and tyrannizing without exercising their reason, become dead weights of vice and folly on the community. A man of rank or fortune, sure of rising by interest, has nothing to do but to pursue some extravagant freak; whilst the needy *gentleman*, who is to rise, as the phrase turns, by his merit, becomes a servile parasite or vile pander. [. . .]

May I be allowed to extend the comparison to a profession where more mind is certainly to be found; for the clergy have superior opportunities of improvement, though subordination almost equally cramps their faculties? The blind submission imposed at college to forms of belief serves as a novitiate to the curate, who must obsequiously respect the opinion of his rector or patron, if he mean to rise in his profession. Perhaps there cannot be a more forcible contrast than between the servile dependent gait of a poor curate and the courtly mien of a bishop. And the respect and contempt they inspire render the discharge of their separate functions equally useless.

It is of great importance to observe that the character of every man is, in some degree, formed by his profession. A man of sense may only have a cast of countenance that wears off as you trace his individuality, whilst the weak, common man has scarcely ever any character, but what belongs to the body; at least, all his opinions have been so steeped in the vat consecrated by authority, that the faint spirit which the grape of his own vine yields cannot be distinguished.

Society, therefore, as it becomes more enlightened, should be very careful not to establish bodies of men who must necessarily be made foolish or vicious by the very constitution of their profession.

In the infancy of society, when men were just emerging out of barbarism, chiefs and priests, touching the most powerful springs of savage conduct, hope and fear, must have had unbounded sway. An aristocracy, of course, is naturally the first form of government. But, clashing interests soon losing their equipoise, a monarchy and hierarchy break out of the confusion of ambitious struggles, and the foundation of both is secured by feudal tenures. This appears to be the origin of monarchical and priestly power, and the dawn of civilization. But such combustible materials cannot long be pent up; and, getting vent in foreign wars and intestine insurrections, the people acquire some power in the tumult, which obliges their rulers to gloss over their oppression with a shew of right. Thus, as wars, agriculture, commerce, and literature, expand the mind, despots are compelled, to make covert corruption hold fast the power which was formerly snatched by open force.[7] And this baneful lurking gangrene is most quickly spread by luxury and superstition, the sure dregs of ambition. The indolent puppet of a court first becomes a luxurious monster, or fastidious sensualist, and then makes the contagion which his unnatural state spread, the instrument of tyranny.

It is the pestiferous purple which renders the progress of civilization a curse, and warps the understanding, till men of sensibility doubt whether the expansion of intellect produces a greater portion of happiness or misery. But the nature of the poison points out the antidote; and had Rousseau mounted one step higher in his investigation, or could his eye have pierced through the foggy atmosphere, which he almost disdained to breathe, his active mind would have darted forward to contemplate the perfection of man in the establishment of true civilization, instead of taking his ferocious flight back to the night of sensual ignorance.

CHAP. II.

THE PREVAILING OPINION OF A SEXUAL CHARACTER DISCUSSED.

TO account for, and excuse the tyranny of man, many ingenious arguments have been brought forward to prove, that the two sexes, in the acquirement of virtue, ought to aim at attaining a very different character: or, to speak explicitly, women are not allowed to have sufficient strength of mind to acquire what really deserves the name of virtue. Yet it should seem, allowing them to have souls, that there is but one way appointed by Providence to lead *mankind* to either virtue or happiness.

If then women are not a swarm of ephemeron triflers, why should they be kept in ignorance under the specious name of innocence? Men complain, and with reason, of the follies and caprices of our sex, when they do not keenly satirize our headstrong passions and groveling vices.—Behold, I should answer, the natural effect of ignorance! The mind will ever be unstable that has only prejudices to rest on, and the current will run with destructive fury when there are no barriers to break its force. Women are told from their infancy, and taught by the example of their mothers, that a little knowledge of human weakness, justly termed cunning, softness of temper, *outward* obedience, and a scrupulous attention to a puerile kind of propriety, will obtain for them the protection of man; and should they be beautiful, every thing else is needless, for, at least, twenty years of their lives.

Thus Milton describes our first frail mother; though when he tells us that

---

7 [MW's note.] Men of abilities scatter seeds that grow up and have a great influence on the forming opinion; and when once the public opinion preponderates, through the exertion of reason, the overthrow of arbitrary power is not very distant.

women are formed for softness and sweet attractive grace,[1] I cannot comprehend his meaning, unless, in the true Mahometan strain,[2] he meant to deprive us of souls, and insinuate that we were beings only designed by sweet attractive grace, and docile blind obedience, to gratify the senses of man when he can no longer soar on the wing of contemplation.

How grossly do they insult us who thus advise us only to render ourselves gentle, domestic brutes! For instance, the winning softness so warmly, and frequently, recommended, that governs by obeying. What childish expressions, and how insignificant is the being—can it be an immortal one? who will condescend to govern by such sinister methods! "Certainly," says Lord Bacon, "man is of kin to the beasts by his body; and if he be not of kin to God by his spirit, he is a base and ignoble creature!"[3] Men, indeed, appear to me to act in a very unphilosophical manner when they try to secure the good conduct of women by attempting to keep them always in a state of childhood. Rousseau was more consistent when he wished to stop the progress of reason in both sexes, for if men eat of the tree of knowledge, women will come in for a taste; but, from the imperfect cultivation which their understandings now receive, they only attain a knowledge of evil.

Children, I grant, should be innocent; but when the epithet is applied to men, or women, it is but a civil term for weakness. For if it be allowed that women were destined by Providence to acquire human virtues, and by the exercise of their understandings, that stability of character which is the firmest ground to rest our future hopes upon, they must be permitted to turn to the fountain of light, and not forced to shape their course by the twinkling of a mere satellite. Milton, I grant, was of a very different opinion; for he only bends to the indefeasible right of beauty, though it would be difficult to render two passages which I now mean to contrast, consistent. But into similar inconsistencies are great men often led by their senses.

> "To whom thus Eve with *perfect beauty* adorn'd.
> My Author and Disposer, what thou bidst
> *Unargued* I obey; so God ordains;
> God is *thy law, thou mine*: to know no more
> Is Woman's *happiest* knowledge and her *praise*."[4]

These are exactly the arguments that I have used to children; but I have added, your reason is now gaining strength, and, till it arrives at some degree of maturity, you must look up to me for advice—then you ought to *think*, and only rely on God. [. . .]

As a proof that education gives this appearance of weakness to females, we may

---

1   "Not equal, as their sex not equal seemed;/ For contemplation he and valor formed,/ For softness she and sweet attractive grace,/ He for God only, she for God in him" (Milton, *Paradise Lost* 4. 296–9).
2   Wollstonecraft voices a commonplace eighteenth-century assumption (see **p. 109**, note 1).
3   Francis Bacon, "On Atheisme," *The Essaies of Sir Francis Bacon* (London, 1612) 89.
4   Milton, *Paradise Lost* 4. 634–8; MW's italics.

instance the example of military men, who are, like them, sent into the world before their minds have been stored with knowledge or fortified by principles. The consequences are similar; soldiers acquire a little superficial knowledge, snatched from the muddy current of conversation, and, from continually mixing with society, they gain, what is termed a knowledge of the world; and this acquaintance with manners and customs has frequently been confounded with a knowledge of the human heart. But can the crude fruit of casual observation, never brought to the test of judgment, formed by comparing speculation and experience, deserve such a distinction? Soldiers, as well as women, practise the minor virtues with punctilious politeness. Where is then the sexual difference, when the education has been the same? All the difference that I can discern, arises from the superior advantage of liberty, which enables the former to see more of life.

It is wandering from my present subject, perhaps, to make a political remark; but, as it was produced naturally by the train of my reflections, I shall not pass it silently over.

Standing armies can never consist of resolute, robust men; they may be well disciplined machines, but they will seldom contain men under the influence of strong passions, or with very vigorous faculties. And as for any depth of understanding, I will venture to affirm, that it is as rarely to be found in the army as amongst women; and the cause, I maintain, is the same. It may be further observed, that officers are also particularly attentive to their persons, fond of dancing, crowded rooms, adventures, and ridicule.[5] Like the *fair* sex, the business of their lives is gallantry.—They were taught to please, and they only live to please. Yet they do not lose their rank in the distinction of sexes, for they are still reckoned superior to women, though in what their superiority consists, beyond what I have just mentioned, it is difficult to discover.

The great misfortune is this, that they both acquire manners before morals, and a knowledge of life before they have, from reflection, any acquaintance with the grand ideal outline of human nature. The consequence is natural; satisfied with common nature, they become a prey to prejudices, and taking all their opinions on credit, they blindly submit to authority. So that, if they have any sense, it is a kind of instinctive glance, that catches proportions, and decides with respect to manners; but fails when arguments are to be pursued below the surface, or opinions analyzed.

May not the same remark be applied to women? Nay, the argument may be carried still further, for they are both thrown out of a useful station by the unnatural distinctions established in civilized life. Riches and hereditary honours have made cyphers of women to give consequence to the numerical figure; and idleness has produced a mixture of gallantry and despotism into society; which leads the very men who are the slaves of their mistresses to tyrannize over their sisters, wives, and daughters. This is only keeping them in rank and file, it is true.

5   [MW's note.] Why should women be censured with petulant acrimony, because they seem to have a passion for a scarlet coat? Has not education placed them more on a level with soldiers than any other class of men?

Strengthen the female mind by enlarging it, and there will be an end to blind obedience; but, as blind obedience is ever sought for by power, tyrants and sensualists are in the right when they endeavour to keep women in the dark, because the former only want slaves, and the latter a play-thing. The sensualist, indeed, has been the most dangerous of tyrants, and women have been duped by their lovers, as princes by their ministers, whilst dreaming that they reigned over them.

I now principally allude to Rousseau, for his character of Sophia[6] is, undoubtedly, a captivating one, though it appears to me grossly unnatural; however it is not the superstructure, but the foundation of her character, the principles on which her education was built, that I mean to attack; nay, warmly as I admire the genius of that able writer, whose opinions I shall often have occasion to cite, indignation always takes place of admiration, and the rigid frown of insulted virtue effaces the smile of complacency, which his eloquent periods are wont to raise, when I read his voluptuous reveries. Is this the man, who, in his ardour for virtue, would banish all the soft arts of peace, and almost carry us back to Spartan discipline? Is this the man who delights to paint the useful struggles of passion, the triumphs of good dispositions, and the heroic flights which carry the glowing soul out of itself?—How are these mighty sentiments lowered when he describes the pretty foot and enticing airs of his little favourite! But, for the present, I wave the subject, and, instead of severely reprehending the transient effusions of overweening sensibility, I shall only observe, that whoever has cast a benevolent on society, must often have been gratified by the sight of humble mutual love, not dignified by sentiment, or strengthened by a union in intellectual pursuits. The domestic trifles of the day have afforded matters for cheerful converse, and innocent caresses have softened toils which did not require great exercise of mind or stretch of thought: yet, has not the sight of this moderate felicity excited more tenderness than respect? An emotion similar to what we feel when children are playing, or animals sporting,[7] whilst the contemplation of the noble struggles of suffering merit has raised admiration, and carried our thoughts to that world where sensation will give place to reason.

Women are, therefore, to be considered either as moral beings, or so weak that they must be entirely subjected to the superior faculties of men.

Let us examine this question. Rousseau declares that a woman should never, for a moment, feel herself independent, that she should be governed by fear to exercise her *natural* cunning, and made a coquetish slave in order to render her a more alluring object of desire, a *sweeter* companion to man, whenever he chooses to relax himself. He carries the arguments, which he pretends to draw from the indications of nature, still further, and insinuates that truth and fortitude, the

---

6   In book 5 of Rousseau's *Emile* he described his ideal woman, the submissive Sophie (excerpted in Contexts (**pp. 17–22**) and discussed in detail by Wollstonecraft in chapter 5.1).

7   [MW's note.] Similar feelings has Milton's pleasing picture of paradisiacal happiness ever raised in my mind; yet, instead of envying the lovely pair, I have, with conscious dignity, or Satanic pride, turned to hell for sublimer objects. In the same style, when viewing some noble monument of human art, I have traced the emanation of the Deity in the order I admired, till, descending from that giddy height, I have caught myself contemplating the grandest of all human sights;—for fancy quickly placed, in some solitary recess, an outcast of fortune, rising superior to passion and discontent.

corner stones of all human virtue, should be cultivated with certain restrictions, because, with respect to the female character, obedience is the grand lesson which ought to be impressed with unrelenting rigour.

What nonsense! when will a great man arise with sufficient strength of mind to puff away the fumes which pride and sensuality have thus spread over the subject! If women are by nature inferior to men, their virtues must be the same in quality, if not in degree, or virtue is a relative idea; consequently, their conduct should be founded on the same principles, and have the same aim. [. . .]

Besides, the woman who strengthens her body and exercises her mind will, by managing her family and practising various virtues, become the friend, and not the humble dependent of her husband; and if she, by possessing such substantial qualities, merit his regard, she will not find it necessary to conceal her affection, nor to pretend to an unnatural coldness of constitution to excite her husband's passions. In fact, if we revert to history, we shall find that the women who have distinguished themselves have neither been the most beautiful nor the most gentle of their sex.

Nature, or, to speak with strict propriety, God, has made all things right; but man has sought him out many inventions to mar the work. I now allude to that part of Dr. Gregory's treatise,[8] where he advises a wife never to let her husband know the extent of her sensibility or affection. Voluptuous precaution, and as ineffectual as absurd.—Love, from its very nature, must be transitory. To seek for a secret that would render it constant, would be as wild a search as for the philosopher's stone, or the grand panacea: and the discovery would be equally useless, or rather pernicious, to mankind. The most holy band of society is friendship. It has been well said, by a shrewd satirist, "that rare as true love is, true friendship is still rarer."[9]

This is an obvious truth, and the cause not lying deep, will not elude a slight glance of inquiry.

Love, the common passion, in which chance and sensation take place of choice and reason, is, in some degree, felt by the mass of mankind; for it is not necessary to speak, at present, of the emotions that rise above or sink below love. This passion, naturally increased by suspense and difficulties, draws the mind out of its accustomed state, and exalts the affections; but the security of marriage, allowing the fever of love to subside, a healthy temperature is thought insipid, only by those who have not sufficient intellect to substitute the calm tenderness of friendship, the confidence of respect, instead of blind admiration, and the sensual emotions of fondness.

This is, must be, the course of nature.—Friendship or indifference inevitably succeeds love.—And this constitution seems perfectly to harmonize with the system of government which prevails in the moral world. Passions are spurs to action, and open the mind; but they sink into mere appetites, become a personal and momentary gratification, when the object is gained, and the satisfied mind

---

8   John Gregory, *A Father's Legacy to his Daughters* (1774); Wollstonecraft critiques this influential conduct book in chapter 5.3 (**p. 142**).
9   La Rochefoucauld, *Maxims and Reflections* (1678) (Berwick, 1791) 53.

rests in enjoyment. The man who had some virtue whilst he was struggling for a crown, often becomes a voluptuous tyrant when it graces his brow; and, when the lover is not lost in the husband, the dotard, a prey to childish caprices, and fond jealousies, neglects the serious duties of life, and the caresses which should excite confidence in his children are lavished on the overgrown child, his wife.

In order to fulfil the duties of life, and to be able to pursue with vigour the various employments which form the moral character, a master and mistress of a family ought not to continue to love each other with passion. I mean to say, that they ought not to indulge those emotions which disturb the order of society, and engross the thoughts that should be otherwise employed. The mind that has never been engrossed by one object wants vigour—if it can long be so, it is weak.

A mistaken education, a narrow, uncultivated mind, and many sexual prejudices, tend to make women more constant than men; but, for the present, I shall not touch on this branch of the subject. I will go still further, and advance, without dreaming of a paradox, that an unhappy marriage is often very advantageous to a family, and that the neglected wife is, in general, the best mother. And this would almost always be the consequence if the female mind were more enlarged: for, it seems to be the common dispensation of Providence, that what we gain in present enjoyment should be deducted from the treasure of life, experience; and that when we are gathering the flowers of the day and revelling in pleasure, the solid fruit of toil and wisdom should not be caught at the same time. The way lies before us, we must turn to the right or left; and he who will pass life away in bounding from one pleasure to another, must not complain if he acquire neither wisdom nor respectability of character. [. . .]

Gentleness of manners, forbearance and long-suffering, are such amiable Godlike qualities, that in sublime poetic strains the Deity has been invested with them; and, perhaps, no representation of his goodness so strongly fastens on the human affections as those that represent him abundant in mercy and willing to pardon. Gentleness, considered in this point of view, bears on its front all the characteristics of grandeur, combined with the winning graces of condescension; but what a different aspect it assumes when it is the submissive demeanour of dependence, the support of weakness that loves, because it wants protection; and is forbearing, because it must silently endure injuries; smiling under the lash at which it dare not snarl. Abject as this picture appears, it is the portrait of an accomplished woman, according to the received opinion of female excellence, separated by specious reasoners from human excellence. Or, they[10] kindly restore the rib, and make one moral being of a man and woman; not forgetting to give her all the "submissive charms."[11]

How women are to exist in that state where there is to be neither marrying nor giving in marriage,[12] we are not told. For though moralists have agreed that the

---

10 [MW's note.] Vide Rousseau, and Swedenborg. [Ed.: Rousseau, *Emile* 377; Emmanuel Swedenborg (1688–1772), *On Marriages in Heaven; and On the Nature of Heavenly Conjugal Love* (1768). Wollstonecraft reviewed a 1789 edition of Swedenborg.]
11 Milton, *Paradise Lost* 4. 497–8: "he in delight/ Both of her beauty and submissive charms/ Smiled with superior love."
12 Matthew 22:30.

tenor of life seems to prove that *man* is prepared by various circumstances for a future state, they constantly concur in advising *woman* only to provide for the present. Gentleness, docility, and a spaniel-like affection are, on this ground, consistently recommended as the cardinal virtues of the sex; and, disregarding the arbitrary economy of nature, one writer has declared that it is masculine for a woman to be melancholy. She was created to be the toy of man, his rattle, and it must jingle in his ears whenever, dismissing reason, he chooses to be amused.

To recommend gentleness, indeed, on a broad basis is strictly philosophical. A frail being should labour to be gentle. But when forbearance confounds right and wrong, it ceases to be a virtue; and, however convenient it may be found in a companion—that companion will ever be considered as an inferior, and only inspire a vapid tenderness, which easily degenerates into contempt. Still, if advice could really make a being gentle, whose natural disposition admitted not of such a fine polish, something towards the advancement of order would be attained; but if, as might quickly be demonstrated, only affectation be produced by this indiscriminate counsel, which throws a stumbling-block in the way of gradual improvement, and true melioration of temper, the sex is not much benefited by sacrificing solid virtues to the attainment of superficial graces, though for a few years they may procure the individuals regal sway.

As a philosopher,[13] I read with indignation the plausible epithets which men use to soften their insults; and, as a moralist, I ask what is meant by such heterogeneous associations, as fair defects, amiable weaknesses, &c.? If there be but one criterion of morals, but one archetype for man, women appear to be suspended by destiny, according to the vulgar tale of Mahomet's coffin;[14] they have neither the unerring instinct of brutes, nor are allowed to fix the eye of reason on a perfect model. They were made to be loved, and must not aim at respect, lest they should be hunted out of society as masculine.

But to view the subject in another point of view. Do passive indolent women make the best wives? Confining our discussion to the present moment of existence, let us see how such weak creatures perform their part? Do the women who, by the attainment of a few superficial accomplishments, have strengthened the prevailing prejudice, merely contribute to the happiness of their husbands? Do they display their charms merely to amuse them? And have women, who have early imbibed notions of passive obedience, sufficient character to manage a family or educate children? So far from it, that, after surveying the history of woman, I cannot help, agreeing with the severest satirist, considering the sex as the weakest as well as the most oppressed half of the species. What does history disclose but marks of inferiority, and how few women have emancipated themselves from

---

13 Wollstonecraft's self-identification as philosopher is a bold gesture that asserts women's right to this historically masculine intellectual realm; conservative reviewers objected to such "female philosophers" on principle, and in modern criticism Wollstonecraft's authorial identity as Enlightenment philosopher (as opposed to "woman") has been seen as a significant indication of her intended audience and aim (see in particular Kelly (pp. 88–9), Poovey (pp. 75–6) and Johnson (pp. 79–80)).

14 A commonly held Western fallacy that Mohammed's coffin is in Mecca, suspended between heaven and earth.

the galling yoke of sovereign man?—So few, that the exceptions remind me of an ingenious conjecture respecting Newton: that he was probably a being of a superior order, accidentally caged in a human body. Following the same train of thinking, I have been led to imagine that the few extraordinary women who have rushed in eccentrical directions out of the orbit prescribed to their sex, were *male* spirits, confined by mistake in female frames. But if it be not philosophical to think of sex when the soul is mentioned, the inferiority must depend on the organs; or the heavenly fire, which is to ferment the clay, is not given in equal portions.

But avoiding, as I have hitherto done, any direct comparison of the two sexes collectively, or frankly acknowledging the inferiority of woman, according to the present appearance of things, I shall only insist that men have increased that inferiority till women are almost sunk below the standard of rational creatures. Let their faculties have room to unfold, and their virtues to gain strength, and then determine where the whole sex must stand in the intellectual scale. Yet let it be remembered, that for a small number of distinguished women I do not ask a place. [. . .]

These may be termed Utopian dreams.—Thanks to that Being who impressed them on my soul, and gave me sufficient strength of mind to dare to exert my own reason, till, becoming dependent only on him for the support of my virtue, I view, with indignation, the mistaken notions that enslave my sex.

I love man as my fellow; but his scepter, real, or usurped, extends not to me, unless the reason of an individual demands my homage; and even then the submission is to reason, and not to man. In fact, the conduct of an accountable being must be regulated by the operations of its own reason; or on what foundation rests the throne of God?

It appears to me necessary to dwell on these obvious truths, because females have been insulated, as it were; and, while they have been stripped of the virtues that should clothe humanity, they have been decked with artificial graces that enable them to exercise a short-lived tyranny. Love, in their bosoms, taking place of every nobler passion, their sole ambition is to be fair, to raise emotion instead of inspiring respect; and this ignoble desire, like the servility in absolute monarchies, destroys all strength of character. Liberty is the mother of virtue, and if women be, by their very constitution, slaves, and not allowed to breathe the sharp invigorating air of freedom, they must ever languish like exotics, and be reckoned beautiful flaws in nature.

As to the argument respecting the subjection in which the sex has ever been held, it retorts on man. The many have always been enthralled by the few; and monsters, who scarcely have shewn any discernment of human excellence, have tyrannized over thousands of their fellow-creatures. Why have men of superior endowments submitted to such degradation? For, is it not universally acknowledged that kings, viewed collectively, have ever been inferior, in abilities and virtue, to the same number of men taken from the common mass of mankind— yet, have they not, and are they not still treated with a degree of reverence that is an insult to reason? China is not the only country where a living man has been made a God. *Men* have submitted to superior strength to enjoy with impunity the pleasure of the moment—*women* have only done the same, and therefore till it is proved that the courtier, who servilely resigns the birthright of a man, is not a moral agent, it cannot be demonstrated that woman is essentially inferior to man because she has always been subjugated.

Brutal force has hitherto governed the world, and that the science of politics is in its infancy, is evident from philosophers scrupling to give the knowledge most useful to man that determinate distinction.

I shall not pursue this argument any further than to establish an obvious inference, that as sound politics diffuse liberty, mankind, including woman, will become more wise and virtuous.

CHAP. III.

THE SAME SUBJECT CONTINUED.

BODILY strength from being the distinction of heroes is now sunk into such unmerited contempt that men, as well as women, seem to think it unnecessary: the latter, as it takes from their feminine graces, and from that lovely weakness the source of their undue power; and the former, because it appears inimical to the character of a gentleman.[1]

That they have both by departing from one extreme run into another, may easily be proved; but first it may be proper to observe, that a vulgar error has obtained a degree of credit, which has given force to a false conclusion, in which an effect has been mistaken for a cause.

People of genius have, very frequently, impaired their constitutions by study or careless inattention to their health, and the violence of their passions bearing a proportion to the vigour of their intellects, the sword's destroying the scabbard has become almost proverbial, and superficial observers have inferred from thence, that men of genius have commonly weak, or, to use a more fashionable phrase, delicate constitutions. Yet the contrary, I believe, will appear to be the fact; for, on diligent inquiry, I find that strength of mind has, in most cases, been accompanied by superior strength of body,—natural soundness of constitution,— not that robust tone of nerves and vigour of muscles, which arise from bodily labour, when the mind is quiescent, or only directs the hands.

Dr. Priestley[2] has remarked, in the preface to his biographical chart, that the majority of great men have lived beyond forty-five. And, considering the thoughtless manner in which they have lavished their strength, when investigating a favourite science they have wasted the lamp of life, forgetful of the midnight hour; or, when, lost in poetic dreams, fancy has peopled the scene, and the soul has been disturbed, till it shook the constitution, by the passions that meditation had raised; whose objects, the baseless fabric of a vision, faded before the exhausted eye, they must have had iron frames. Shakspeare never grasped the airy dagger with a nerveless hand,[3] nor did Milton tremble when he led Satan

---

1   On the significance for Wollstonecraft of strength in men and in women, see Johnson (**pp. 79–80**) and Craciun (**pp. 82–4**), respectively.

2   Joseph Priestley, *A Description of a Chart of Biography* (1765).

3   Shakespeare, *Macbeth* 2.1.33–49.

far from the confines of his dreary prison.—These were not the ravings of imbe-
cility, the sickly effusions of distempered brains; but the exuberance of fancy,
that "in a fine phrenzy" wandering, was not continually reminded of its material
shackles.[4]

I am aware that this argument would carry me further than it may be supposed I wish to go; but I follow truth, and, still adhering to my first position, I
will allow that bodily strength seems to give man a natural superiority over
woman; and this is the only solid basis on which the superiority of the sex can
be built. But I still insist, that not only the virtue, but the *knowledge* of the
two sexes should be the same in nature, if not in degree, and that women,
considered not only as moral, but rational creatures, ought to endeavour to
acquire human virtues (or perfections) by the *same* means as men, instead of
being educated like a fanciful kind of *half* being—one of Rousseau's wild
chimeras.[5]

But, if strength of body be, with some shew of reason, the boast of men, why
are women so infatuated as to be proud of a defect? Rousseau has furnished them
with a plausible excuse, which could only have occurred to a man, whose imagination had been allowed to run wild, and refine on the impressions made by exquisite senses;—that they might, forsooth, have a pretext for yielding to a natural
appetite without violating a romantic species of modesty, which gratifies the pride
and libertinism of man.

Women, deluded by these sentiments, sometimes boast of their weakness, cun-
ningly obtaining power by playing on the *weakness* of men; and they may well
glory in their illicit sway, for, like Turkish bashaws,[6] they have more real power
than their masters: but virtue is sacrificed to temporary gratifications, and the
respectability of life to the triumph of an hour.

Women, as well as despots, have now, perhaps, more power than they would
have if the world, divided and subdivided into kingdoms and families, were governed by laws deduced from the exercise of reason; but in obtaining it, to carry on
the comparison, their character is degraded, and licentiousness spread through
the whole aggregate of society. The many become pedestal to the few. I, therefore,
will venture to assert, that till women are more rationally educated, the progress
of human virtue and improvement in knowledge must receive continual checks.
And if it be granted that woman was not created merely to gratify the appetite of

---

4   Shakespeare, *A Midsummer Night's Dream* 5.1.12; Wollstonecraft praises fancy and imagination
     more fully in "Hints" (**pp. 161–4**).
5   [MW's note.] [. . .] "Women have most wit, men have most genius; women observe, men reason:
     from the concurrence of both we derive the clearest light and the most perfect knowledge, which
     the human mind is, of itself, capable of attaining. In one word, from hence we acquire the most
     intimate acquaintance, both with ourselves and others, of which our nature is capable; and it is
     thus that art has a constant tendency to perfect those endowments which nature has bestowed. –
     The world is the book of women." *Rousseau's Emilius*. I hope my readers still remember the
     comparison, which I have brought forward, between women and officers. [Rousseau, *Emile* 387.]
6   Turkish pashas were symbolic of absolutist rule, particularly in feminist writings of this period
     which often used the figure of the harem to represent the nadir of women's oppression. Throughout
     Rights of Woman, Wollstonecraft complicates this association of women as the victims of sexual
     despotism by simultaneously seeing them as tyrants (similar to her comparison in chapter 2 of
     women and soldiers), the desired alternative to such power imbalances being republican equality.

man, or to be the upper servant, who provides his meals and takes care of his linen, it must follow, that the first care of those mothers or fathers, who really attend to the education of females, should be, if not to strengthen the body, at least, not to destroy the constitution by mistaken notions of beauty and female excellence; nor should girls ever be allowed to imbibe the pernicious notion that a defect can, by any chemical process of reasoning, become an excellence. In this respect, I am happy to find, that the author of one of the most instructive books, that our country has produced for children, coincides with me in opinion; I shall quote his pertinent remarks to give the force of his respectable authority to reason.[7]

But should it be proved that woman is naturally weaker than man, whence does it follow that it is natural for her to labour to become still weaker than nature intended her to be? Arguments of this cast are an insult to common sense, and savour of passion. The *divine right* of husbands, like the divine right of kings, may, it is to be hoped, in this enlightened age, be contested without danger, and, though conviction may not silence many boisterous disputants, yet, when any prevailing prejudice is attacked, the wise will consider, and leave the narrow-minded to rail with thoughtless vehemence at innovation.

The mother, who wishes to give true dignity of character to her daughter, must, regardless of the sneers of ignorance, proceed on a plan diametrically opposite to that which Rousseau has recommended with all the deluding charms of eloquence and philosophical sophistry: for his eloquence renders absurdities plausible, and his dogmatic conclusions puzzle, without convincing, those who have not ability to refute them.

Throughout the whole animal kingdom every young creature requires almost continual exercise, and the infancy of children, conformable to this intimation, should be passed in harmless gambols, that exercise the feet and hands, without requiring very minute direction from the head, or the constant attention of a nurse. In fact, the care necessary for self-preservation is the first natural exercise of the understanding, as little inventions to amuse the present moment unfold the imagination. But these wise designs of nature are counteracted by mistaken fondness or blind zeal. The child is not left a moment to its own direction, particularly a girl, and thus rendered dependent—dependence is called natural.

To preserve personal beauty, woman's glory! the limbs and faculties are cramped with worse than Chinese bands,[8] and the sedentary life which they are condemned to live, whilst boys frolic in the open air, weakens the muscles and relaxes the nerves. [. . .]

---

7 Wollstonecraft quotes in a footnote from Thomas Day's *The History of Sandford and Merton* (sixth edn, 1791), vol. 3, 207–9.
8 The Chinese practice of foot-binding was often used as an example of how women are oppressed (because made artificially weak) through social practices and education that enforce beauty at the expense of health. Macaulay writes: "A foot too small for the size of the body, is, in my eye, rather a deformity than a beauty. . . . Nature, if you do not restrain her, or turn her out of her course, is equal to the task both of fashioning the beauty of the person, and confirming the strength of the constitution" (*Letters on Education*, 43–4). Jean Baptiste de Boyer wrote in detail of how foot-binding was designed to physically prevent women from being able to leave the patriarchal home, *Chinese Letters* (London: Browne, 1741) Letter 2.

The baneful consequences which flow from inattention to health during infancy, and youth, extend further than is supposed—dependence of body naturally produces dependence of mind; and how can she be a good wife or mother, the greater part of whose time is employed to guard against or endure sickness? Nor can it be expected that a woman will resolutely endeavour to strengthen her constitution and abstain from enervating indulgencies, if artificial notions of beauty, and false descriptions of sensibility, have been early entangled with her motives of action. Most men are sometimes obliged to bear with bodily inconveniencies, and to endure, occasionally, the inclemency of the elements; but genteel women are, literally speaking, slaves to their bodies, and glory in their subjection.

I once knew a weak woman of fashion, who was more than commonly proud of her delicacy and sensibility. She thought a distinguishing taste and puny appetite the height of all human perfection, and acted accordingly.—I have seen this weak sophisticated being neglect all the duties of life, yet recline with self-complacency on a sofa, and boast of her want of appetite as a proof of delicacy that extended to, or, perhaps, arose from, her exquisite sensibility: for it is difficult to render intelligible such ridiculous jargon.—Yet, at the moment, I have seen her insult a worthy old gentlewoman, whom unexpected misfortunes had made dependent on her ostentatious bounty, and who, in better days, had claims on her gratitude. Is it possible that a human creature could have become such a weak and depraved being, if, like the Sybarites,[9] dissolved in luxury, every thing like virtue had not been worn away, or never impressed by precept, a poor substitute, it is true, for cultivation of mind, though it serves as a fence against vice?

Such a woman is not a more irrational monster than some of the Roman emperors, who were depraved by lawless power. Yet, since kings have been more under the restraint of law, and the curb, however weak, of honour, the records of history are not filled with such unnatural instances of folly and cruelty, nor does the despotism that kills virtue and genius in the bud, hover over Europe with that destructive blast which desolates Turkey, and renders the men, as well as the soil, unfruitful.

Women are every where in this deplorable state; for, in order to preserve their innocence, as ignorance is courteously termed, truth is hidden from them, and they are made to assume an artificial character before their faculties have acquired any strength. Taught from their infancy that beauty is woman's sceptre, the mind shapes itself to the body, and, roaming round its gilt cage, only seeks to adorn its prison. Men have various employments and pursuits which engage their attention, and give a character to the opening mind; but women, confined to one, and having their thoughts constantly directed to the most insignificant part of themselves, seldom extend their views beyond the triumph of the hour. But were their understanding once emancipated from the slavery to which the pride and sensuality of man and their short-sighted desire, like that of dominion in tyrants, of

9   The Greek colony of Sybaris in Italy was traditionally associated with hedonism.

present sway, has subjected them, we should probably read of their weaknesses with surprise. I must be allowed to pursue the argument a little farther. [. . .]

It is time to effect a revolution in female manners—time to restore to them their lost dignity—and make them, as a part of the human species, labour by reforming themselves to reform the world. It is time to separate unchangeable morals from local manners. – If men be demi-gods—why let us serve them! And if the dignity of the female soul be as disputable as that of animals—if their reason does not afford sufficient light to direct their conduct whilst unerring instinct is denied— they are surely of all creatures the most miserable! and, bent beneath the iron hand of destiny, must submit to be a *fair defect* in creation.[10] But to justify the ways of Providence[11] respecting them, by pointing out some irrefragable reason for thus making such a large portion of mankind accountable and not accountable, would puzzle the subtilest casuist.

The only solid foundation for morality appears to be the character of the supreme Being; the harmony of which arises from a balance of attributes;—and, to speak with reverence, one attribute seems to imply the *necessity* of another. He must be just, because he is wise, he must be good, because he is omnipotent. For to exalt one attribute at the expence of another equally noble and neces- sary, bears the stamp of the warped reason of man—the homage of passion. Man, accustomed to bow down to power in his savage state, can seldom divest himself of this barbarous prejudice, even when civilization determines how much superior mental is to bodily strength; and his reason is clouded by these crude opinions, even when he thinks of the Deity.—His omnipotence is made to swallow up, or preside over his other attributes, and those mortals are sup- posed to limit his power irreverently, who think that it must be regulated by his wisdom.

I disclaim that specious humility which, after investigating nature, stops at the author.—The High and Lofty One, who inhabiteth eternity, doubtless possesses many attributes of which we can form no conception; but reason tells me that they cannot clash with those I adore—and I am compelled to listen to her voice.[12] [. . .]

I wish to sum up what I have said in a few words, for I here throw down my gauntlet, and deny the existence of sexual virtues,[13] not excepting modesty. For man and woman, truth, if I understand the meaning of the word, must be the same; yet the fanciful female character, so prettily drawn by poets and novelists, demanding the sacrifice of truth and sincerity, virtue becomes a relative idea, having no other foundation than utility, and of that utility men pretend arbitrarily to judge, shaping it to their own convenience.

---

10 Milton, *Paradise Lost* 10. 888–92; Adam asks, "O why did God,/ Creator wise, that peopled highest heav'n,/ With Spirits masculine, create at last/ This novelty on earth, this fair defect/ Of nature," i.e., woman.
11 Milton, *Paradise Lost* 1. 25–6: "I may assert Eternal Providence,/ And justify the ways of God to men."
12 One of many statements by Wollstonecraft on the compatibility of reason and god; see Robinson (pp. 71–3).
13 Virtues that are based on one's sex and are not universal.

Women, I allow, may have different duties to fulfil; but they are *human* duties, and the principles that should regulate the discharge of them, I sturdily maintain, must be the same. [. . .]

CHAP. IV.

OBSERVATIONS ON THE STATE OF DEGRADATION TO WHICH WOMAN IS REDUCED BY VARIOUS CAUSES.

[. . .] The stamen of immortality, if I may be allowed the phrase, is the perfectibility of human reason; for, were man created perfect, or did a flood of knowledge break in upon him, when he arrived at maturity, that precluded error, I should doubt whether his existence would be continued after the dissolution of the body. But, in the present state of things, every difficulty in morals that escapes from human discussion, and equally baffles the investigation of profound thinking, and the lightning glance of genius, is an argument on which I build my belief of the immortality of the soul. Reason is, consequentially, the simple power of improvement; or, more properly speaking, of discerning truth. Every individual is in this respect a world in itself. More or less may be conspicuous in one being than another; but the nature of reason must be the same in all, if it be an emanation of divinity, the tie that connects the creature with the Creator; for, can that soul be stamped with the heavenly image, that is not perfected by the exercise of its own reason?[1] Yet outwardly ornamented with elaborate care, and so adorned to delight man, "that with honour he may love,"[2] the soul of woman is not allowed to have this distinction, and man, ever placed between her and reason, she is always represented as only created to see through a gross medium, and to take things on trust. But dismissing these fanciful theories, and considering woman as a whole, let it be what it will, instead of a part of man, the inquiry is whether she have reason or not. If she have, which, for a moment, I will take for granted, she was not created merely to be the solace of man, and the sexual should not destroy the human character.

Into this error men have, probably, been led by viewing education in a false light; not considering it as the first step to form a being advancing gradually towards perfection;[3] but only as a preparation for life. On this sensual error, for I must call it so, has the false system of female manners been reared, which robs the whole sex of its dignity, and classes the brown and fair with the smiling flowers

---

1   [MW's note.] "The brutes," says Lord Monboddo, "remain in the state in which nature has placed them, except in so far as their natural instinct is improved by the culture *we* bestow upon them". [Ed.: James Burnett, Lord Monboddo, *Of the Origin and Progress of Language* (Edinburgh: Kincaid and Creech, 1773) vol. 1, 124–39; Wollstonecraft's italics). As with Smellie (chapter 1, **p. 113**), Wollstonecraft emphasizes the differences between humans and other animals, and the impact of education on shaping abilities and progress; she simultaneously downplays Smellie's and Burnett's insistence on a continuum between species, for example, "For I deny, that in the natural state, and previous to any acquired habit, there is any difference with respect to mental faculties betwixt us and the brute, to whom I suppose those philosophers will not allow the privilege of consciousness" (Burnett, 144).]

2   [MW's note.] Vide Milton. [Ed.: *Paradise Lost* 8. 577–8.]

3   [MW's note.] This word is not strictly just, but I cannot find a better.

that only adorn the land. This has ever been the language of men, and the fear of departing from a supposed sexual character, has made even women of superiour sense adopt the same sentiments.[4] Thus understanding, strictly speaking, has been denied to woman; and instinct, sublimated into wit and cunning, for the purposes of life, has been substituted in its stead.

The power of generalizing ideas, of drawing comprehensive conclusions from individual observations, is the only acquirement, for an immortal being, that really deserves the name of knowledge. Merely to observe, without endeavouring to account for any thing, may (in a very incomplete manner) serve as the common sense of life; but where is the store laid up that is to clothe the soul when it leaves the body?

This power has not only been denied to women; but writers have insisted that it is inconsistent, with a few exceptions, with their sexual character. Let men prove this, and I shall grant that woman only exists for man. I must, however, previously remark, that the power of generalizing ideas, to any great extent, is not very common amongst men or women. But this exercise is the true cultivation of the understanding; and every thing conspires to render the cultivation of the understanding more difficult in the female than the male world. [. . .]

A wild wish has just flown from my heart to my head, and I will not stifle it though it may excite a horse-laugh.—I do earnestly wish to see the distinction of sex confounded in society, unless where love animates the behaviour. For this distinction is, I am firmly persuaded, the foundation of the weakness of character

---

4   [MW's note.] "Pleasure's the portion of th' *inferior* kind;/ But glory, virtue, Heaven for *man* design'd."
    After writing these lines, how could Mrs. Barbauld write the following ignoble comparison.

> *"To a Lady, with some painted flowers."*
> "Flowers to the fair: to you these flowers I bring,
> And strive to greet you with an earlier spring.
> *Flowers* SWEET, *and gay, and* DELICATE LIKE YOU
> *Emblems of innocence, and beauty too.*
> With flowers the Graces bind their yellow hair,
> And flowery wreaths consenting lovers wear.
> *Flowers, the sole luxury which nature knew,*
> In Eden's pure and guiltless garden grew.
> *To loftier forms are rougher tasks assign'd;*
> *The sheltering oak resists the stormy wind,*
> *The tougher yew repels invading foes,*
> *And the tall pine for future navies grows;*
> *But this soft family, to cares unknown,*
> *Were born for pleasure and delight* ALONE.
> Gay without toil, and lovely without art,
> *They spring to* CHEER *the sense, and* GLAD *the heart.*
> Nor blush, my fair, to own you copy these;
> *Your* BEST, *your* SWEETEST *empire is*—TO PLEASE."

So the men tell us; but virtue, says reason, must be acquired by *rough* toils, and useful struggles with worldly *cares*. [Ed.: Wollstonecraft quotes *Poems* (1773) by Anna Laetitia Barbauld (1743–1852), adding the italics. The first quotation is from "To Mrs. P[riestley], with some Drawings of Birds and Insects"; "inferior kind" refers to birds and insects, and "man" to humanity. The second poem is included in its entirety. Wollstonecraft had excerpted Barbauld in *The Female Reader*; for Barbauld's response, see her poem "The Rights of Woman" (pp. 41–2), and also Wollstonecraft's letter to Macaulay (pp. 23–4).]

ascribed to woman; is the cause why the understanding is neglected, whilst accomplishments are acquired with sedulous care: and the same cause accounts for their preferring the graceful before the heroic virtues.

Mankind, including every description, wish to be loved and respected by *something*; and the common herd will always take the nearest road to the completion of their wishes. The respect paid to wealth and beauty is the most certain, and unequivocal; and, of course, will always attract the vulgar eye of common minds. Abilities and virtues are absolutely necessary to raise men from the middle rank of life into notice; and the natural consequence is notorious, the middle rank contains most virtue and abilities. Men have thus, in one station, at least an opportunity of exerting themselves with dignity, and of rising by the exertions which really improve a rational creature; but the whole female sex are, till their character is formed, in the same condition as the rich: for they are born, I now speak of a state of civilization, with certain sexual privileges, and whilst they are gratuitously granted them, few will ever think of works of supererogation, to obtain the esteem of a small number of superiour people. [. . .]

In short, women, in general, as well as the rich of both sexes, have acquired all the follies and vices of civilization, and missed the useful fruit. It is not necessary for me always to premise, that I speak of the condition of the whole sex, leaving exceptions out of the question. Their senses are inflamed, and their understandings neglected, consequently they become the prey of their senses, delicately termed sensibility, and are blown about by every momentary gust of feeling. Civilized women are, therefore, so weakened by false refinement, that, respecting morals, their condition is much below what it would be were they left in a state nearer to nature.[5] Ever restless and anxious, their over exercised sensibility not only renders them uncomfortable themselves, but troublesome, to use a soft phrase, to others. All their thoughts turn on things calculated to excite emotion; and feeling, when they should reason, their conduct is unstable, and their opinions are wavering—not the wavering produced by deliberation or progressive views, but by contradictory emotions. By fits and starts they are warm in many pursuits; yet this warmth, never concentrated into perseverance, soon exhausts itself; exhaled by its own heat, or meeting with some other fleeting passion, to which reason has never given any specific gravity, neutrality ensues. Miserable, indeed, must be that being whose cultivation of mind has only tended to inflame its passions! A distinction should be made between inflaming and strengthening them. The passions thus pampered, whilst the judgment is left unformed, what can be expected to ensue?—Undoubtedly, a mixture of madness and folly!

This observation should not be confined to the *fair* sex; however, at present, I only mean to apply it to them.

Novels, music, poetry, and gallantry, all tend to make women the creatures of

---

5   "Civilized women . . . left": in the first edition, this phrase read instead as: "They are, therefore, in a much worse condition than they would be in were they."

sensation,[6] and their character is thus formed in the mould of folly during the time they are acquiring accomplishments, the only improvement they are excited, by their station in society, to acquire. This overstretched sensibility naturally relaxes the other powers of the mind, and prevents intellect from attaining that sovereignty which it ought to attain to render a rational creature useful to others, and content with its own station: for the exercise of the understanding, as life advances, is the only method pointed out by nature to calm the passions.

Satiety has a very different effect, and I have often been forcibly struck by an emphatical description of damnation:—when the spirit is represented as continually hovering with abortive eagerness round the defiled body, unable to enjoy any thing without the organs of sense. Yet, to their senses, are women made slaves, because it is by their sensibility that they obtain present power. [. . .]

I am fully persuaded that we should hear of none of these infantine airs, if girls were allowed to take sufficient exercise, and not confined in close rooms till their muscles are relaxed, and their powers of digestion destroyed. To carry the remark still further, if fear in girls, instead of being cherished, perhaps, created, were treated in the same manner as cowardice in boys, we should quickly see women with more dignified aspects. It is true, they could not then with equal propriety be termed the sweet flowers that smile in the walk of man; but they would be more respectable members of society, and discharge the important duties of life by the light of their own reason. "Educate women like men," says Rousseau, "and the more they resemble our sex the less power will they have over us."[7] This is the very point I aim at. I do not wish them to have power over men; but over themselves.

In the same strain have I heard men argue against instructing the poor; for many are the forms that aristocracy assumes. "Teach them to read and write," say they, "and you take them out of the station assigned them by nature." An eloquent Frenchman[8] has answered them, I will borrow his sentiments. But they know not, when they make man a brute, that they may expect every instant to see him transformed into a ferocious beast. Without knowledge there can be no morality!

Ignorance is a frail base for virtue! Yet, that it is the condition for which woman was organized, has been insisted upon by the writers who have most vehemently argued in favour of the superiority of man; a superiority not in degree, but essence; though, to soften the argument, they have laboured to prove, with chivalrous generosity, that the sexes ought not to be compared; man was made to reason, woman to feel: and that together, flesh and spirit, they make the most perfect whole, by blending happily reason and sensibility into one character.

6   One of many attacks on sensibility and its pernicious effects on women and society; Wollstonecraft goes into greater depth regarding the literature of sensibility in chapter 13.2. Yet it is important to note that she is not rejecting sensibility wholescale, but distinguishing between its destructive and beneficial aspects; see Whale (pp. 90–1), Barker-Benfield (pp. 67–9), and Myers (pp. 86–8) on her positive views on sensibility, and Poovey (pp. 75–6) and Kaplan (pp. 76–7) on her negative views.
7   Rousseau, Emile, 363.
8   Unidentified.

And what is sensibility? "Quickness of sensation; quickness of perception; delicacy." Thus is it defined by Dr. Johnson;[9] and the definition gives me no other idea than of the most exquisitely polished instinct. I discern not a trace of the image of God in either sensation or matter. Refined seventy times seven, they are still material; intellect dwells not there; nor will fire ever make lead gold!

I come round to my old argument; if woman be allowed to have an immortal soul, she must have, as the employment of life, an understanding to improve. And when, to render the present state more complete, though every thing proves it to be but a fraction of a mighty sum, she is incited by present gratification to forget her grand destination, nature is counteracted, or she was born only to procreate and rot. Or, granting brutes, of every description, a soul, though not a reasonable one, the exercise of instinct and sensibility may be the step, which they are to take, in this life, towards the attainment of reason in the next; so that through all eternity they will lag behind man, who, why we cannot tell, had the power given him of attaining reason in his first mode of existence. [. . .]

[Y]et when a man seduces a woman, it should, I think, be termed a *left-handed* marriage,[10] and the man should be *legally* obliged to maintain the woman and her children, unless adultery, a natural divorcement, abrogated the law. And this law should remain in force as long as the weakness of women caused the word seduction to be used as an excuse for their frailty and want of principle; nay, while they depend on man for a subsistence, instead of earning it by the exertion of their own hands or heads. But these women should not, in the full meaning of the relationship, be termed wives, or the very purpose of marriage would be subverted, and all those endearing charities that flow from personal fidelity, and give a sanctity to the tie, when neither love nor friendship unites the hearts, would melt into selfishness. The woman who is faithful to the father of her children demands respect, and should not be treated like a prostitute; though I readily grant that if it be necessary for a man and woman to live together in order to bring up their offspring, nature never intended that a man should have more than one wife.

Still, highly as I respect marriage, as the foundation of almost every social virtue, I cannot avoid feeling the most lively compassion for those unfortunate females who are broken off from society, and by one error torn from all those affections and relationships that improve the heart and mind. It does not frequently even deserve the name of error; for many innocent girls become the dupes of a sincere, affectionate heart, and still more are, as it may emphatically be termed, *ruined* before they know the difference between virtue and vice:—and thus prepared by their education for infamy, they become infamous. Asylums and

9 Johnson, *Dictionary* (1755); see Whale (**pp. 90–1**), Myers (**pp. 86–8**), and Barker-Benfield (**pp. 67–9**) on Wollstonecraft and sensibility.
10 A morganatic, or left-handed, marriage was one in which a man and woman of different ranks (typically a man of "exalted rank") married with the provision that the lower-ranked spouse remained in their lower station, and that any offspring not inherit the rank or property of the high-ranking parent (*OED*).

Magdalens[11] are not the proper remedies for these abuses. It is justice, not charity, that is wanting in the world!

A woman who has lost her honour, imagines that she cannot fall lower, and as for recovering her former station, it is impossible; no exertion can wash this stain away. Losing thus every spur, and having no other means of support, prostitution becomes her only refuge, and the character is quickly depraved by circumstances over which the poor wretch has little power, unless she possesses an uncommon portion of sense and loftiness of spirit. Necessity never makes prostitution the business of men's lives; though numberless are the women who are thus rendered systematically vicious. This, however, arises, in a great degree, from the state of idleness in which women are educated, who are always taught to look up to man for a maintenance, and to consider their persons as the proper return for his exertions to support them. Meretricious airs, and the whole science of wantonness, have then a more powerful stimulus than either appetite or vanity; and this remark gives force to the prevailing opinion, that with chastity all is lost that is respectable in woman. Her character depends on the observance of one virtue, though the only passion fostered in her heart—is love. Nay, the honour of a woman is not made even to depend on her will.

When Richardson[12] makes Clarissa tell Lovelace that he had robbed her of her honour, he must have had strange notions of honour and virtue. For, miserable beyond all names of misery is the condition of a being, who could be degraded without its own consent! This excess of strictness I have heard vindicated as a salutary error. I shall answer in the words of Leibnitz—"Errors are often useful; but it is commonly to remedy other errors."[13]

Most of the evils of life arise from a desire of present enjoyment that outruns itself. The obedience required of women in the marriage state comes under this description; the mind, naturally weakened by depending on authority, never exerts its own powers, and the obedient wife is thus rendered a weak indolent mother. Or, supposing that this is not always the consequence, a future state of existence is scarcely taken into the reckoning when only negative virtues are cultivated. For, in treating of morals, particularly when women are alluded to, writers have too often considered virtue in a very limited sense, and made the foundation of it *solely* worldly utility; nay, a still more fragile base has been given to this stupendous fabric, and the wayward fluctuating feelings of men have been

---

11 The Magdalen Hospital in London was founded in 1758, one of many such institutions designed to reform prostitutes (see Markman Ellis, *The Politics of Sensibility* (Cambridge: Cambridge University Press, 1996) 160–89). Wollstonecraft's unfinished novel *The Wrongs of Woman* focuses on an alliance between a working-class former prostitute and a middle-class mother, making extensive use of the marriage/prostitution connection she develops in *Rights of Woman*.

12 [MW's note.] Dr. Young supports the same opinion, in his plays, when he talks of the misfortune that shunned the light of day. [Ed.: Samuel Richardson (1689–1761), *Clarissa* (1747–8), in which Lovelace rapes Clarissa; Edward Young (1683–1765), *Busiris, King of Egypt* (1715) i.i.]

13 German philosopher G.W. Leibnitz (1646–1716) is known for his optimist doctrine that we live in the best of all possible worlds, critiqued in Voltaire's *Candide*; Wollstonecraft quotes from the Preface to Leibnitz's *Theodicy* (1710). For Wollstonecraft's changing ideas on theodicy and justice, see Robinson (pp. 71–3).

made the standard of virtue. Yes, virtue as well as religion, has been subjected to the decisions of taste.

It would almost provoke a smile of contempt, if the vain absurdities of man did not strike us on all sides, to observe, how eager men are to degrade the sex from whom they pretend to receive the chief pleasure of life; and I have frequently with full conviction retorted Pope's[14] sarcasm on them; or, to speak explicitly, it has appeared to me applicable to the whole human race. A love of pleasure or sway seems to divide mankind, and the husband who lords it in his little haram thinks only of his pleasure or his convenience. To such lengths, indeed, does an intemperate love of pleasure carry some prudent men, or worn out libertines, who marry to have a safe bed-fellow, that they seduce their own wives.—Hymen[15] banishes modesty, and chaste love takes its flight.

Love, considered as an animal appetite, cannot long feed on itself without expiring. And this extinction in its own flame, may be termed the violent death of love. But the wife who has thus been rendered licentious, will probably endeavour to fill the void left by the loss of her husband's attentions; for she cannot contentedly become merely an upper servant after having been treated like a goddess. She is still handsome, and, instead of transferring her fondness to her children, she only dreams of enjoying the sunshine of life. Besides, there are many husbands so devoid of sense and parental affection, that during the first effervescence of voluptuous fondness they refuse to let their wives suckle their children.[16] They are only to dress and live to please them: and love—even innocent love, soon sinks into lasciviousness when the exercise of a duty is sacrificed to its indulgence.

Personal attachment is a very happy foundation for friendship; yet, when even two virtuous young people marry, it would, perhaps, be happy if some circumstances checked their passion; if the recollection of some prior attachment, or disappointed affection, made it on one side, at least, rather a match founded on esteem. In that case they would look beyond the present moment, and try to render the whole of life respectable, by forming a plan to regulate a friendship which only death ought to dissolve.

Friendship is a serious affection; the most sublime of all affections, because it is founded on principle, and cemented by time. The very reverse may be said of love. In a great degree, love and friendship cannot subsist in the same bosom; even when inspired by different objects they weaken or destroy each other, and for the same object can only be felt in succession. The vain fears and fond jealousies, the winds which fan the flame of love, when judiciously or artfully tempered, are both incompatible with the tender confidence and sincere respect of friendship.

---

14 Alexander Pope, "Epistle to a Lady. Of the Characters of Women" (ll. 207–10): "In Men, we various Ruling Passions find,/ In Women, two almost divide the kind;/ Those, only fix'd, they first or last obey,/ The Love of Pleasure, and the Love of Sway."
15 The god of marriage.
16 Breast-feeding was passionately advocated by those, like Rousseau and Wollstonecraft, who saw (middle-class) motherhood as central to the health of civic society (an ideal sometimes called "republican motherhood"); see Pateman (pp. 62–3) and Colley (pp. 65–7) on the private/public-sphere debate.

Love, such as the glowing pen of genius has traced, exists not on earth, or only resides in those exalted, fervid imaginations that have sketched such dangerous pictures. Dangerous, because they not only afford a plausible excuse, to the voluptuary who disguises sheer sensuality under a sentimental veil; but as they spread affectation, and take from the dignity of virtue. Virtue, as the very word imports, should have an appearance of seriousness, if not of austerity; and to endeavour to trick her out in the garb of pleasure, because the epithet has been used as another name for beauty, is to exalt her on a quicksand; a most insidious attempt to hasten her fall by apparent respect. Virtue and pleasure are not, in fact, so nearly allied in this life as some eloquent writers have laboured to prove. Pleasure prepares the fading wreath, and mixes the intoxicating cup; but the fruit which virtue gives, is the recompence of toil: and, gradually seen as it ripens, only affords calm satisfaction; nay, appearing to be the result of the natural tendency of things, it is scarcely observed. Bread, the common food of life, seldom thought of as a blessing, supports the constitution and preserves health; still feasts delight the heart of man, though disease and even death lurk in the cup or dainty that elevates the spirits or tickles the palate. The lively heated imagination likewise, to apply the comparison, draws the picture of love, as it draws every other picture, with those glowing colours, which the daring hand will steal from the rainbow that is directed by a mind, condemned in a world like this, to prove its noble origin by panting after unattainable perfection; ever pursuing what it acknowledges to be a fleeting dream. An imagination of this vigorous cast can give existence to insubstantial forms, and stability to the shadowy reveries which the mind naturally falls into when realities are found vapid. It can then depict love with celestial charms, and dote on the grand ideal object—it can imagine a degree of mutual affection that shall refine the soul, and not expire when it has served as a "scale to heavenly;"[17] and, like devotion, make it absorb every meaner affection and desire. In each others arms, as in a temple, with its summit lost in the clouds, the world is to be shut out, and every thought and wish, that do not nurture pure affection and permanent virtue.—Permanent virtue! alas! Rousseau, respectable visionary! thy paradise would soon be violated by the entrance of some unexpected guest. Like Milton's it would only contain angels, or men sunk below the dignity of rational creatures. Happiness is not material, it cannot be seen or felt! Yet the eager pursuit of the good which every one shapes to his own fancy, proclaims man the lord of this lower world, and to be an intelligential creature, who is not to receive, but acquire happiness. They, therefore, who complain of the delusions of passion, do not recollect that they are exclaiming against a strong proof of the immortality of the soul.

But leaving superior minds to correct themselves, and pay dearly for their experience, it is necessary to observe, that it is not against strong, persevering passions; but romantic wavering feelings that I wish to guard the female heart by exercising the understanding: for these paradisiacal reveries are oftener the effect of idleness than of a lively fancy. [. . .]

17 Milton, *Paradise Lost* 8. 591–2.

In tracing the causes that, in my opinion, have degraded woman, I have confined my observations to such as universally act upon the morals and manners of the whole sex, and to me it appears clear that they all spring from want of understanding. Whether this arise from a physical or accidental weakness of faculties, time alone can determine; for I shall not lay any great stress on the example of a few women[18] who, from having received a masculine education, have acquired courage and resolution; I only contend that the men who have been placed in similar situations, have acquired a similar character—I speak of bodies of men, and that men of genius and talents have started out of a class, in which women have never yet been placed.

CHAP. V.

ANIMADVERSIONS ON SOME OF THE WRITERS WHO HAVE RENDERED WOMEN OBJECTS OF PITY, BORDERING ON CONTEMPT.

[. . .]

SECT. I.

I SHALL begin with Rousseau, and give a sketch of his character of woman, in his own words, interspersing comments and reflections. My comments, it is true, will all spring from a few simple principles, and might have been deduced from what I have already said; but the artificial structure has been raised with so much ingenuity, that it seems necessary to attack it in a more circumstantial manner, and make the application myself.

Sophia, says Rousseau, should be as perfect a woman as Emilius is a man, and to render her so, it is necessary to examine the character which nature has given to the sex.[1]

He then proceeds to prove that woman ought to be weak and passive, because she has less bodily strength than man; and hence infers, that she was formed to please and to be subject to him; and that it is her duty to render herself *agreeable* to her master—this being the grand end of her existence.[2] Still, however, to give a little mock dignity to lust, he insists that man should not exert his strength, but depend on the will of the woman, when he seeks for pleasure with her. [. . .]

This is certainly only an education of the body; but Rousseau is not the only man who has indirectly said that merely the person of a *young* woman, without

---

18   [MW's note.] Sappho, Eloisa, Mrs. Macaulay, the Empress of Russia, Madame d'Eon, &c. These, and many more, may be reckoned exceptions; and, are not all heroes, as well as heroines, exceptions to general rules? I wish to see women neither heroines nor brutes; but reasonable creatures. [Sappho (*c.*600 BC) of Lesbos was a leading lyric poet; Heloise (*c.*1101–64), was a French scholar secretly married to Abelard, and their correspondence inspired Pope's "Eloisa to Abelard" (1717) and Rousseau's *Julie, or the New Héloise*; Catharine Macaulay (1731–91) was a feminist and historian admired by Wollstonecraft (see **p. 23**); Catharine II (1729–96) was Empress of Russia; Charles de Beaumont, Chevalier d'Eon (1728–1810) was French diplomat and swordsman who masqueraded as a woman.]

1   Wollstonecraft's critique of Rousseau here and throughout the *Rights of Woman* is the heart of her argument; see the excerpt from and headnote for Rousseau's *Emile* (**p. 17**) and Sapiro (**pp. 63–5**).

2   Wollstonecraft here refers to a previously quoted passage from Rousseau (excerpted **p. 18**).

any mind, unless animal spirits come under that description, is very pleasing. To render it weak, and what some may call beautiful, the understanding is neglected, and girls forced to sit still, play with dolls and listen to foolish conversations;—the effect of habit is insisted upon as an undoubted indication of nature. I know it was Rousseau's opinion that the first years of youth should be employed to form the body, though in educating Emilius he deviates from this plan; yet, the difference between strengthening the body, on which strength of mind in a great measure depends, and only giving it an easy motion, is very wide.

Rousseau's observations, it is proper to remark, were made in a country where the art of pleasing was refined only to extract the grossness of vice. He did not go back to nature, or his ruling appetite disturbed the operations of reason, else he would not have drawn these crude inferences.

In France[3] boys and girls, particularly the latter, are only educated to please, to manage their persons, and regulate their exterior behaviour; and their minds are corrupted, at a very early age, by the worldly and pious cautions they receive to guard them against immodesty. I speak of past times. The very confessions which mere children were obliged to make, and the questions asked by the holy men, I assert these facts on good authority, were sufficient to impress a sexual character; and the education of society was a school of coquetry and art. At the age of ten or eleven; nay, often much sooner, girls began to coquet, and talked, unreproved, of establishing themselves in the world by marriage.

In short, they were treated like women, almost from their very birth, and compliments were listened to instead of instruction. These, weakening the mind, Nature was supposed to have acted like a stepmother, when she formed this after-thought of creation.

Not allowing them understanding, however, it was but consistent to subject them to authority independent of reason; and to prepare them for this subjection, he gives the following advice:

"Girls ought to be active and diligent; nor is that all; they should also be early subjected to restraint. This misfortune, if it really be one, is inseparable from their sex; nor do they ever throw it off but to suffer more cruel evils. They must be subject, all their lives, to the most constant and severe restraint, which is that of decorum: it is, therefore, necessary to accustom them early to such confinement, that it may not afterwards cost them too dear; and to the suppression of their caprices, that they may the more readily submit to the will of others. If, indeed, they be fond of being always at work, they should be sometimes compelled to lay it aside. Dissipation, levity, and inconstancy, are faults that readily spring up from their first propensities, when corrupted or perverted by too much indulgence. To prevent this abuse, we should teach them, above all things, to lay a due restraint on themselves. The life of a modest woman is reduced, by our absurd institutions, to a perpetual conflict with herself: not but it is just that this sex should partake of the sufferings which arise from those evils it hath caused us."[4]

---

3   On Wollstonecraft's changing conceptions of French national character, see Wellington (**pp. 73–4**).
4   Rousseau, *Emile* 369; Bloom translates the first line as "Girls ought to be vigilant and industrious."

And why is the life of a modest woman a perpetual conflict? I should answer, that this very system of education makes it so. Modesty, temperance, and self-denial, are the sober offspring of reason; but when sensibility is nurtured at the expence of the understanding, such weak beings must be restrained by arbitrary means, and be subjected to continual conflicts; but give their activity of mind a wider range, and nobler passions and motives will govern their appetites and sentiments.

"The common attachment and regard of a mother, nay, mere habit, will make her beloved by her children, if she do nothing to incur their hate. Even the constraint she lays them under, if well directed, will increase their affection, instead of lessening it; because a state of dependence being natural to the sex, they perceive themselves formed for obedience."[5]

This is begging the question; for servitude not only debases the individual, but its effects seem to be transmitted to posterity. Considering the length of time that women have been dependent, is it surprising that some of them hug their chains, and fawn like the spaniel? "These dogs," observes a naturalist, "at first kept their ears erect; but custom has superseded nature, and a token of fear is become a beauty."[6]

"For the same reason," adds Rousseau, "women have, or ought to have, but little liberty; they are apt to indulge themselves excessively in what is allowed them. Addicted in every thing to extremes, they are even more transported at their diversions than boys."[7]

The answer to this is very simple. Slaves[8] and mobs have always indulged themselves in the same excesses, when once they broke loose from authority.— The bent bow recoils with violence, when the hand is suddenly relaxed that forcibly held it; and sensibility, the play-thing of outward circumstances, must be subjected to authority, or moderated by reason. [. . .]

"The superiority of address, peculiar to the female sex, is a very equitable indemnification for their inferiority in point of strength: without this, woman would not be the companion of man; but his slave: it is by her superiour art and ingenuity that she preserves her equality, and governs him while she affects to obey. Woman has every thing against her, as well our faults, as her own timidity and weakness; she has nothing in her favour, but her subtilty and her beauty. Is it not very reasonable, therefore, she should cultivate both?"[9] Greatness of mind can never dwell with cunning, or address; for I shall not boggle about words, when their direct signification is insincerity and falsehood, but content myself with observing, that if any class of mankind be so created that it must necessarily be educated by rules not strictly deducible from truth, virtue is an affair of convention. How could Rousseau dare to assert, after giving this advice, that in the grand end of existence the object of both sexes should be the same, when he

---

5   Rousseau, *Emile* 369–70.
6   Smellie, *The Philosophy of Natural History* (1790) 1: 462.
7   Rousseau, *Emile* 370.
8   Wollstonecraft may be alluding to the 1791 St. Domingo slave revolution; see Ferguson (**p. 70**).
9   Rousseau, *Emile* 371.

well knew that the mind, formed by its pursuits, is expanded by great views swallowing up little ones, or that it becomes itself little?

Men have superior strength of body; but were it not for mistaken notions of beauty, women would acquire sufficient to enable them to earn their own subsistence, the true definition of independence; and to bear those bodily inconveniencies and exertions that are requisite to strengthen the mind.

Let us then, by being allowed to take the same exercise as boys,[10] not only during infancy, but youth, arrive at perfection of body, that we may know how far the natural superiority of man extends. For what reason or virtue can be expected from a creature when the seed-time of life is neglected? None—did not the winds of heaven casually scatter many useful seeds in the fallow ground. [. . .]

SECT. II.

DR. FORDYCE's sermons[11] have long made a part of a young woman's library. . . . Dr. Fordyce may have had a very laudable end in view; but these discourses are written in such an affected style, that were it only on that account, and had I nothing to object against his *mellifluous* precepts, I should not allow girls to peruse them, unless I designed to hunt every spark of nature out of their composition, melting every human quality into female meekness and artificial grace. I say artificial, for true grace arises from some kind of independence of mind. [. . .]

Even recommending piety he uses the following argument. "Never, perhaps, does a fine woman strike more deeply, than when, composed into pious recollection, and possessed with the noblest considerations, she assumes, without knowing it, superior dignity and new graces; so that the beauties of holiness seem to radiate about her, and the by-standers are almost induced to fancy her already worshipping amongst her kindred angels!" Why are women to be thus bred up with a desire of conquest? the very word, used in this sense, gives me a sickly qualm! Do religion and virtue offer no stronger motives, no brighter reward? Must they always be debased by being made to consider the sex of their companions? Must they be taught always to be pleasing? And when levelling their small artillery at the heart of man, is it necessary to tell them that a little sense is sufficient to render their attention *incredibly soothing*? "As a small degree of knowledge entertains in a woman, so from a woman, though for a different reason, a small expression of kindness delights, particularly if she have beauty!" I should have supposed for the same reason.

Why are girls to be told that they resemble angels; but to sink them below women? Or, that a gentle innocent female is an object that comes nearer to the

---

10 Wollstonecraft's conservative contemporaries objected in particular to this suggestion. For example, Benjamin Silliman wrote that "As a necessary preparative for the support of bodily fatigue, the female philosopher recommends an early initiation of females into the athletic sports, and gymnastic exercises of boys and young men. She would have them run, leap, box, wrestle, fence and fight, that the united exertion of bodily and mental energy may produce, by mysterious cooperation, that amazing force of character, of which she supposes her sex to be capable" (*Letters of Shahcoolen* (Boston, 1802) 26–7); see also Polwhele (**pp. 44–6**).
11 James Fordyce (1720–96), *Sermons to Young Women* (London, 1765); see Kelly (**pp. 88–9**) on Wollstonecraft's reading of conduct books like Fordyce's and Gregory's (in the upcoming section).

idea which we have formed of angels than any other. Yet they are told, at the same time, that they are only like angels when they are young and beautiful; consequently, it is their persons, not their virtues, that procure them this homage. [. . .]

SECT. III.

SUCH paternal solicitude pervades Dr. Gregory's Legacy to his Daughters,[12] that I enter on the task of criticism with affectionate respect. [. . .]

A cultivated understanding, and an affectionate heart, will never want starched rules of decorum—something more substantial than seemliness will be the result; and, without understanding the behaviour here recommended, would be rank affectation. Decorum, indeed, is the one thing needful!—decorum is to supplant nature, and banish all simplicity and variety of character out of the female world. Yet what good end can all this superficial counsel produce? It is, however, much easier to point out this or that mode of behaviour, than to set the reason to work; but, when the mind has been stored with useful knowledge, and strengthened by being employed, the regulation of the behaviour may safely be left to its guidance.

Why, for instance, should the following caution be given when art of every kind must contaminate the mind; and why entangle the grand motives of action, which reason and religion equally combine to enforce, with pitiful worldly shifts and slight of hand tricks to gain the applause of gaping tasteless fools? "Be even cautious in displaying your good sense.[13] It will be thought you assume a superiority over the rest of the company—But if you happen to have any learning, keep it a profound secret, especially from the men who generally look with a jealous and malignant eye on a woman of great parts, and a cultivated understanding."[14] If men of real merit, as he afterwards observes, be superior to this meanness, where is the necessity that the behaviour of the whole sex should be modulated to please fools, or men, who having little claim to respect as individuals, choose to keep close in their phalanx. [. . .]

SECT. IV.

[. . .] Mrs. Chapone's Letters[15] are written with such good sense, and unaffected humility, and contain so many useful observations, that I only mention them to pay the worthy writer this tribute of respect. I cannot, it is true, always coincide in opinion with her; but I always respect her.

The very word respect brings Mrs. Macaulay to my remembrance. The woman of the greatest abilities, undoubtedly, that this country has ever produced.—And

12 John Gregory, *A Father's Legacy to His Daughters* (1774).
13 [MW's note.] Let women once acquire good sense—and if it deserve the name, it will teach them; or, of what use will it be? how to employ it.
14 Gregory, *Legacy* 31–2; see also Fordyce, *Sermons* 1: 296–300.
15 Hester Chapone (1727–1801) was a leading Bluestocking, author of *Letters on the Improvement of the Mind: Addressed to a Lady* (1773). Wollstonecraft earlier in this section had attacked women writers who, like Anna Laetitia Barbauld in chapter 3, "argue in the same track as men": Hester Lynch Piozzi (1741–1821), who was a close friend of Samuel Johnson, and Madame de Staël (author of *Corinne* (1807)) because of her praise of Sophie in Rousseau's *Emile*.

yet this woman has been suffered to die without sufficient respect being paid to her memory.[16]

Posterity, however, will be more just; and remember that Catharine Macaulay was an example of intellectual acquirements supposed to be incompatible with the weakness of her sex. In her style of writing, indeed, no sex appears, for it is like the sense it conveys, strong and clear.

I will not call hers a masculine understanding, because I admit not of such an arrogant assumption of reason; but I contend that it was a sound one, and that her judgment, the matured fruit of profound thinking, was a proof that a woman can acquire judgment, in the full extent of the word. Possessing more penetration than sagacity, more understanding than fancy, she writes with sober energy and argumentative closeness; yet sympathy and benevolence give an interest to her sentiments, and that vital heat to arguments, which forces the reader to weigh them.[17]

When I first thought of writing these strictures I anticipated Mrs. Macaulay's approbation, with a little of that sanguine ardour, which it has been the business of my life to depress; but soon heard with the sickly qualm of disappointed hope; and the still seriousness of regret—that she was no more! [. . .]

CHAP. VI.

THE EFFECT WHICH AN EARLY ASSOCIATION OF IDEAS HAS UPON THE CHARACTER.

[. . .] Education thus only supplies the man of genius with knowledge to give variety and contrast to his associations; but there is an habitual association of ideas,[1] that grows "with our growth,"[2] which has a great effect on the moral character of mankind; and by which a turn is given to the mind that commonly remains throughout life. So ductile is the understanding, and yet so stubborn, that the associations which depend on adventitious circumstances, during the period that the body takes to arrive at maturity, can seldom be disentangled by reason. One idea calls up another, its old associate, and memory, faithful to the first impressions, particularly when the intellectual powers are not employed to cool our sensations, retraces them with mechanical exactness.

This habitual slavery, to first impressions, has a more baneful effect on the female than the male character, because business and other dry employments of the understanding, tend to deaden the feelings and break associations that do

---

16 Catharine Macaulay died 22 June 1791; see Wollstonecraft's letter to her (**pp. 22–3**).
17 [MW's note.] Coinciding in opinion with Mrs. Macaulay relative to many branches of education, I refer to her valuable work, instead of quoting her sentiments to support my own. [Ed.: Macaulay's *Letters on Education* had inspired the *Rights of Woman* and, like Wollstonecraft, Macaulay had suffered social ostracism because of her unconventional relationship (she married a man twenty-six years younger than her).]

---

1 Associationism was a central tenet of eighteenth-century sensationalist psychology and physiology, emphasizing the importance of experience and "impressions" (not innate ideas) in shaping character. Associationism built on Locke's theory of the *tabula rasa* and was closely associated with David Hartley (1705–57), especially as popularized by Joseph Priestley in his *Hartley's Theory of the Human Mind* (1775).
2 Alexander Pope, *An Essay on Man* (1733–4) 2. 136.

violence to reason. But females, who are made women of when they are mere children, and brought back to childhood when they ought to leave the go-cart for ever, have not sufficient strength of mind to efface the superinductions of art that have smothered nature.

Every thing that they see or hear serves to fix impressions, call forth emotions, and associate ideas, that give a sexual character to the mind. False notions of beauty and delicacy stop the growth of their limbs and produce a sickly soreness, rather than delicacy of organs; and thus weakened by being employed in unfolding instead of examining the first associations, forced on them by every surrounding object, how can they attain the vigour necessary to enable them to throw off their factitious character?—where find strength to recur to reason and rise superiour to a system of oppression, that blasts the fair promises of spring? This cruel association of ideas, which every thing conspires to twist into all their habits of thinking, or, to speak with more precision, of feeling, receives new force when they begin to act a little for themselves; for they then perceive that it is only through their address to excite emotions in men, that pleasure and power are to be obtained. Besides, the books professedly written for their instruction, which make the first impression on their minds, all inculcate the same opinions. [. . .]

CHAP. VII.

MODESTY.—COMPREHENSIVELY CONSIDERED, AND NOT AS A SEXUAL VIRTUE.

[. . .] Modesty must be equally cultivated by both sexes, or it will ever remain a sickly hot-house plant, whilst the affectation of it, the fig leaf borrowed by wantonness, may give a zest to voluptuous enjoyments.

Men will probably still insist that woman ought to have more modesty than man; but it is not dispassionate reasoners who will most earnestly oppose my opinion. No, they are the men of fancy, the favourites of the sex, who outwardly respect and inwardly despise the weak creatures whom they thus sport with. They cannot submit to resign the highest sensual gratification, nor even to relish the epicurism of virtue—self-denial.

To take another view of the subject, confining my remarks to women.

The ridiculous falsities[1] which are told to children, from mistaken notions of modesty, tend very early to inflame their imaginations and set their little minds to

---

1   [MW's note.] Children very early see cats with their kittens, birds with their young ones, &c. Why then are they not to be told that their mothers carry and nourish them in the same way? As there would then be no appearance of mystery they would never think of the subject more. Truth may always be told to children, if it be told gravely; but it is the immodesty of affected modesty, that does all the mischief; and this smoke heats the imagination by vainly endeavouring to obscure certain objects. If, indeed, children could be kept entirely from improper company, we should never allude to any such subjects; but as this is impossible, it is best to tell them the truth, especially as such information, not interesting them, will make no impression on their imagination. [Ed.: contemporary conservatives like Thomas Taylor and Richard Polwhele objected to Wollstonecraft's call for frankness with children regarding sexuality. In Wollstonecraft's translation of *Elements for Morality* (1790), Salzmann had elaborated that "the most efficacious method to root out this dreadful evil [of sexual impurity], which poisons the source of human happiness, would be speak to children of the organs of generation as freely as we speak of the other parts of the body, and explain to them the noble use which they were designed for, and how they may be injured" (*Works* 2: 9; this quote

work, respecting subjects, which nature never intended they should think of till the body arrived at some degree of maturity; then the passions naturally begin to take place of the senses, as instruments to unfold the understanding, and form the moral character.

In nurseries, and boarding-schools, I fear, girls are first spoiled; particularly in the latter. A number of girls sleep in the same room, and wash together. And, though I should be sorry to contaminate an innocent creature's mind by instilling false delicacy, or those indecent prudish notions, which early cautions respecting the other sex naturally engender, I should be very anxious to prevent their acquiring nasty, or immodest habits; and as many girls have learned very nasty tricks, from ignorant servants, the mixing them thus indiscriminately together, is very improper.

To say the truth women are, in general, too familiar with each other, which leads to that gross degree of familiarity that so frequently renders the marriage state unhappy. Why in the name of decency are sisters, female intimates, or ladies and their waiting-women, to be so grossly familiar as to forget the respect which one human creature owes to another? That squeamish delicacy which shrinks from the most disgusting offices when affection[2] or humanity lead us to watch at a sick pillow, is despicable. But, why women in health should be more familiar with each other than men are, when they boast of their superior delicacy, is a solecism in manners which I could never solve.

In order to preserve health and beauty, I should earnestly recommend frequent ablutions, to dignify my advice that it may not offend the fastidious ear; and, by example, girls ought to be taught to wash and dress alone, without any distinction of rank; and if custom should make them require some little assistance, let them not require it till that part of the business is over which ought never to be done before a fellow-creature; because it is an insult to the majesty of human nature. Not on the score of modesty, but decency; for the care which some modest women take, making at the same time a display of that care, not to let their legs be seen, is as childish as immodest.[3] [. . .]

It may be thought that I lay too great a stress on personal reserve; but it is ever the handmaid of modesty. So that were I to name the graces that ought to adorn beauty, I should instantly exclaim, cleanliness, neatness, and personal reserve. It is obvious, I suppose, that the reserve I mean, has nothing sexual in it, and that I think it *equally* necessary in both sexes. So necessary, indeed, is that reserve and cleanliness which indolent women too often neglect, that I will venture to affirm that when two or three women live in the same house, the one will be most

---

was misrepresented as Wollstonecraft's by Taylor in *Rights of Brutes*). Wollstonecraft's call for sexual education became linked to the sensationalized accounts of her life that portrayed her as a source of sexual corruption (see Bisset, Beloe and Polwhele (**pp. 46–7, 53, 44–6**), in contrast to twentieth-century critics like Mary Poovey and Cora Kaplan.]

2 [MW's note.] Affection would rather make one choose to perform these offices, to spare the delicacy of a friend, by still keeping a veil over them, for the personal helplessness, produced by sickness, is of an humbling nature.

3 [MW's note.] I remember to have met with a sentence, in a book of education, that made me smile. "It would be needless to caution you against putting your hand, by chance, under your neck handkerchief; for a modest woman never did so!" [untraced]

respected by the male part of the family, who reside with them, leaving love entirely out of the question, who pays this kind of habitual respect to her person. [. . .]

After the foregoing remarks, it is almost superfluous to add, that I consider all those feminine airs of maturity, which succeed bashfulness, to which truth is sacrificed, to secure the heart of a husband, or rather to force him to be still a lover when nature would, had she not been interrupted in her operations, have made love give place to friendship, as immodest. The tenderness which a man will feel for the mother of his children is an excellent substitute for the ardour of unsatisfied passion; but to prolong that ardour it is indelicate, not to say immodest, for women to feign an unnatural coldness of constitution. Women as well as men ought to have the common appetites and passions of their nature, they are only brutal when unchecked by reason: but the obligation to check them is the duty of mankind, not a sexual duty. Nature, in these respects, may safely be left to herself; let women only acquire knowledge and humanity, and love will teach them modesty.[4] There is no need of falsehoods, disgusting as futile, for studied rules of behaviour only impose on shallow observers; a man of sense soon sees through, and despises the affectation. [. . .]

CHAP. VIII.

MORALITY UNDERMINED BY SEXUAL NOTIONS OF THE IMPORTANCE OF A GOOD REPUTATION.

[. . .] Men are certainly more under the influence of their appetites than women; and their appetites are more depraved by unbridled indulgence and the fastidious contrivances of satiety.[1] Luxury has introduced a refinement in eating, that destroys the constitution; and, a degree of gluttony which is so beastly, that a perception of seemliness of behaviour must be worn out before one being could eat immoderately in the presence of another, and afterwards complain of the oppression that his intemperance naturally produced. Some women, particularly French women, have also lost a sense of decency in this respect; for they will talk very calmly of an indigestion. It were to be wished that idleness was not allowed to generate, on the rank soil of wealth, those swarms of summer insects that feed on putrefaction, we should not then be disgusted by the sight of such brutal excesses.

There is one rule relative to behaviour that, I think, ought to regulate every other; and it is simply to cherish such an habitual respect for mankind as may prevent us from disgusting a fellow-creature for the sake of a present indulgence. The shameful indolence of many married women, and others a little advanced in

---

4 [MW's note.] The behaviour of many newly married women has often disgusted me. They seem anxious never to let their husbands forget the privilege of marriage; and to find no pleasure in his society unless he is acting the lover. Short, indeed, must be the reign of love, when the flame is thus constantly blown up, without its receiving any solid fewel!

1 Appetite has multiple associations at this time, combining anxieties over food, sex, and luxury; see Guest (pp. 77–9) on Wollstonecraft's anti-luxury and anti-commercialism rhetoric and Poovey (pp. 75–6) on sexual appetite. On appetite and anorexia see Ewa Badowska, "The Anorexic Body of Liberal Feminism: Mary Wollstonecraft's *Vindication of the Rights of Woman*," *Tulsa Studies in Women's Literature* 17 (1998) 283–304.

life, frequently leads them to sin against delicacy. For, though convinced that the person is the band of union between the sexes, yet, how often do they from sheer indolence, or, to enjoy some trifling indulgence, disgust?

The depravity of the appetite which brings the sexes together, has had a still more fatal effect. Nature must ever be the standard of taste, the gauge of appetite—yet how grossly is nature insulted by the voluptuary. Leaving the refinements of love out of the question; nature, by making the gratification of an appetite, in this respect, as well as every other, a natural and imperious law to preserve the species, exalts the appetite, and mixes a little mind and affection with a sensual gust. The feelings of a parent mingling with an instinct merely animal, give it dignity; and the man and woman often meeting on account of the child, a mutual interest and affection is excited by the exercise of a common sympathy. Women then having necessarily some duty to fulfil, more noble than to adorn their persons, would not contentedly be the slaves of casual lust; which is now the situation of a very considerable number who are, literally speaking, standing dishes to which every glutton may have access.

I may be told that great as this enormity is, it only affects a devoted part of the sex—devoted for the salvation of the rest. But, false as every assertion might easily be proved, that recommends the sanctioning a small evil to produce a greater good; the mischief does not stop here, for the moral character, and peace of mind, of the chaster part of the sex, is undermined by the conduct of the very women to whom they allow no refuge from guilt: whom they inexorably consign to the exercise of arts that lure their husbands from them, debauch their sons, and force them, let not modest women start, to assume, in some degree, the same character themselves. For I will venture to assert, that all the causes of female weakness, as well as depravity, which I have already enlarged on, branch out of one grand cause—want of chastity in men.[2]

This intemperance, so prevalent, depraves the appetite to such a degree, that a wanton stimulus is necessary to rouse it; but the parental design of nature is forgotten, and the mere person, and that for a moment, alone engrosses the thoughts. So voluptuous, indeed, often grows the lustful prowler, that he refines on female softness. Something more soft than woman is then sought for; till, in Italy and Portugal, men attend the levees of equivocal beings, to sigh for more than female languor.[3]

To satisfy this genus of men, women are made systematically voluptuous, and though they may not all carry their libertinism to the same height, yet this heartless intercourse with the sex, which they allow themselves, depraves both sexes, because the taste of men is vitiated; and women, of all classes, naturally square their behaviour to gratify the taste by which they obtain pleasure and power. Women becoming, consequently, weaker, in mind and body, than they ought to be, were one of the grand ends of their being taken into the account, that of bearing and nursing children, have not sufficient strength to discharge the first

2   See Poovey (**pp. 75–6**) and Poston (**pp. 80–2**).
3   On Wollstonecraft's fear of a breakdown in sexual distinctions (and of homosexuality) see Johnson (**pp. 79–80**).

duty of a mother; and sacrificing to lasciviousness the parental affection, that ennobles instinct, either destroy the embryo in the womb,[4] or cast it off when born. Nature in every thing demands respect, and those who violate her laws seldom violate them with impunity. The weak enervated women who particularly catch the attention of libertines, are unfit to be mothers, though they may conceive; so that the rich sensualist, who has rioted among women, spreading depravity and misery, when he wishes to perpetuate his name, receives from his wife only an half-formed being that inherits both its father's and mother's weakness. [. . .]

CHAP. IX.

OF THE PERNICIOUS EFFECTS WHICH ARISE FROM THE UNNATURAL DISTINCTIONS ESTABLISHED IN SOCIETY.

[. . .] The preposterous distinctions of rank, which render civilization a curse, by dividing the world between voluptuous tyrants, and cunning envious dependents, corrupt, almost equally, every class of people, because respectability is not attached to the discharge of the relative duties of life, but to the station, and when the duties are not fulfilled the affections cannot gain sufficient strength to fortify the virtue of which they are the natural reward. Still there are some loop-holes out of which a man may creep, and dare to think and act for himself; but for a woman it is an herculean task, because she has difficulties peculiar to her sex to overcome, which require almost super-human powers.

A truly benevolent legislator always endeavours to make it the interest of each individual to be virtuous; and thus private virtue becoming the cement of public happiness, an orderly whole is consolidated by the tendency of all the parts towards a common centre. But, the private or public virtue of woman is very problematical; for Rousseau, and a numerous list of male writers, insist that she should all her life be subjected to a severe restraint, that of propriety. Why subject her to propriety—blind propriety, if she be capable of acting from a nobler spring, if she be an heir of immortality? Is sugar always to be produced by vital blood?[1] Is one half of the human species, like the poor African slaves, to be subject to prejudices that brutalize them, when principles would be a surer guard, only to sweeten the cup of man? Is not this indirectly to deny woman reason? for a gift is a mockery, if it be unfit for use.

Women are, in common with men, rendered weak and luxurious by the relaxing pleasures which wealth procures; but added to this they are made slaves to their persons, and must render them alluring that man may lend them his reason

---

4   Abortion was criminalized by Lord Ellenborough's Crime Bill in 1803: "the act made abortion after quickening murder by statutory law and abortion (or willful 'miscarriage') prior to quickening a felony" (John Riddle, *Eve's Herbs: A History of Contraception and Abortion in the West* (Cambridge: Harvard University Press, 1997) 207). In 1792, abortion before quickening was not considered a crime, and although "By the late eighteenth century, anything explicitly causing an abortion was dropped from the official publications" in medicine and botany, such substances (for example, pennyroyal, wormwood, juniper) remained easily available and known to induce abortion (Riddle, 202).

1   By 1800 over 200,000 tons of slave-produced sugar were imported annually by Britain; the abolition movement conducted a boycott of sugar which many women supported.

to guide their tottering steps aright. Or should they be ambitious, they must govern their tyrants by sinister tricks, for without rights there cannot be any incumbent duties. The laws respecting woman, which I mean to discuss in a future part,[2] make an absurd unit of a man and his wife; and then, by the easy transition of only considering him as responsible, she is reduced to a mere cypher.

The being who discharges the duties of its station is independent; and, speaking of women at large, their first duty is to themselves as rational creatures, and the next, in point of importance, as citizens, is that, which includes so many, of a mother. The rank in life which dispenses with their fulfilling this duty, necessarily degrades them by making them mere dolls. Or, should they turn to something more important than merely fitting drapery upon a smooth block, their minds are only occupied by some soft platonic attachment; or, the actual management of an intrigue may keep their thoughts in motion; for when they neglect domestic duties, they have it not in their power to take the field and march and counter-march like soldiers, or wrangle in the senate to keep their faculties from rusting. [. . .]

But fair and softly, gentle reader, male or female, do not alarm thyself, for though I have compared the character of a modern soldier with that of a civilized woman, I am not going to advise them to turn their distaff into a musket, though I sincerely wish to see the bayonet converted into a pruning-hook. I only recreated an imagination, fatigued by contemplating the vices and follies which all proceed from a feculent stream of wealth that has muddied the pure rills of natural affection, by supposing that society will some time or other be so constituted, that man must necessarily fulfil the duties of a citizen, or be despised, and that while he was employed in any of the departments of civil life, his wife, also an active citizen, should be equally intent to manage her family, educate her children, and assist her neighbours.

But, to render her really virtuous and useful, she must not, if she discharge her civil duties, want, individually, the protection of civil laws; she must not be dependent on her husband's bounty for her subsistence during his life, or support after his death—for how can a being be generous who has nothing of its own? or, virtuous, who is not free? The wife, in the present state of things, who is faithful to her husband, and neither suckles nor educates her children, scarcely deserves the name of a wife, and has no right to that of a citizen. But take away natural rights, and duties become null. [. . .]

Besides, when poverty is more disgraceful than even vice, is not morality cut to the quick? Still to avoid misconstruction, though I consider that women in the common walks of life are called to fulfil the duties of wives and mothers, by religion and reason, I cannot help lamenting that women of a superiour cast have not a road open by which they can pursue more extensive plans of usefulness and independence. I may excite laughter, by dropping an hint, which I mean to pursue, some future time, for I really think that women ought to have representatives,

---

2   Part 2 of the *Rights of Woman* was never written, but Wollstonecraft did focus on legal injustices in her unfinished novel, *The Wrongs of Woman, or Maria*; see also "Hints" (**pp. 161–4**).

instead of being arbitrarily governed without having any direct share allowed them in the deliberations of government.[3]

But, as the whole system of representation is now, in this country, only a convenient handle for despotism, they need not complain, for they are as well represented as a numerous class of hard working mechanics, who pay for the support of royalty when they can scarcely stop their children's mouths with bread. How are they represented whose very sweat supports the splendid stud of an heir apparent, or varnishes the chariot of some female favourite who looks down on shame? Taxes on the very necessaries of life, enable an endless tribe of idle princes and princesses to pass with stupid pomp before a gaping crowd, who almost worship the very parade which costs them so dear. This is mere gothic grandeur, something like the barbarous useless parade of having sentinels on horseback at Whitehall, which I could never view without a mixture of contempt and indignation. [. . .]

But what have women to do in society? I may be asked, but to loiter with easy grace; surely you would not condemn them all to suckle fools and chronicle small beer! No. Women might certainly study the art of healing, and be physicians as well as nurses. And midwifery, decency seems to allot to them, though I am afraid the word midwife, in our dictionaries, will soon give place to *accoucheur*,[4] and one proof of the former delicacy of the sex be effaced from the language.

They might, also, study politics,[5] and settle their benevolence on the broadest basis; for the reading of history will scarcely be more useful than the perusal of romances, if read as mere biography; if the character of the times, the political improvements, arts, &c. be not observed. In short, if it be not considered as the history of man; and not of particular men, who filled a niche in the temple of fame, and dropped into the black rolling stream of time, that silently sweeps all before it, into the shapeless void called—eternity.—For shape, can it be called, "that shape hath none?"[6]

Business of various kinds, they might likewise pursue, if they were educated in a more orderly manner, which might save many from common and legal prostitution.[7] Women would not then marry for a support, as men accept of places under government, and neglect the implied duties; nor would an attempt to earn their own subsistence, a most laudable one! sink them almost to the level of those poor abandoned creatures who live by prostitution. For are not milliners and

---

3   In 1792 only a small minority of British men could vote, and British women did not get the vote until 1928 (on Wollstonecraft's idea of good government, see Virginia Sapiro, *A Vindication of Political Virtue* (Chicago: University of Chicago Press, 1992) 230–7).

4   Wollstonecraft's awareness of the displacement of midwives by man-midwives, or *accoucheurs*, in the eighteenth century inspired her own choice of a female midwife for the birth of her second child; see Ornella Moscucci, *The Science of Woman* (Cambridge: Cambridge University Press, 1990) 42–74.

5   Women who wrote overtly on politics were consistently denounced by moralists (women included) and conduct book writers. James Fordyce (critiqued **p. 141**) is representative: "war, commerce, politics, exercises of strength and dexterity, abstract philosophy, and all the abstruser sciences, are most properly the province of men" (*Sermons* 1: 272); see also *Emile* 386–7.

6   Referring to death, in Milton, *Paradise Lost* 2. 667.

7   "Legal prostitution" refers to marriage, a connection that Wollstonecraft elaborated on in her unfinished novel, *The Wrongs of Woman, or Maria*.

mantua-makers reckoned the next class? The few employments open to women, so far from being liberal, are menial; and when a superiour education enables them to take charge of the education of children as governesses, they are not treated like the tutors of sons, though even clerical tutors are not always treated in a manner calculated to render them respectable in the eyes of their pupils, to say nothing of the private comfort of the individual. But as women educated like gentlewomen, are never designed for the humiliating situation which necessity sometimes forces them to fill; these situations are considered in the light of a degradation; and they know little of the human heart, who need to be told, that nothing so painfully sharpens sensibility as such a fall in life.

Some of these women might be restrained from marrying by a proper spirit or delicacy, and others may not have had it in their power to escape in this pitiful way from servitude; is not that government then very defective, and very unmindful of the happiness of one half of its members, that does not provide for honest, independent women, by encouraging them to fill respectable stations? But in order to render their private virtue a public benefit, they must have a civil existence in the State, married or single; else we shall continually see some worthy woman, whose sensibility has been rendered painfully acute by undeserved contempt, droop like "the lily broken down by a plow-share."[8]

It is a melancholy truth; yet such is the blessed effect of civilization! the most respectable women are the most oppressed; and, unless they have understandings far superiour to the common run of understandings, taking in both sexes, they must, from being treated like contemptible beings, become contemptible. How many women thus waste life away the prey of discontent, who might have practised as physicians, regulated a farm, managed a shop, and stood erect, supported by their own industry, instead of hanging their heads surcharged with the dew of sensibility, that consumes the beauty to which it at first gave lustre; nay, I doubt whether pity and love are so near akin as poets feign, for I have seldom seen much compassion excited by the helplessness of females, unless they were fair; then, perhaps, pity was the soft handmaid of love, or the harbinger of lust.

How much more respectable is the woman who earns her own bread by fulfilling any duty, than the most accomplished beauty!—beauty did I say?—so sensible am I of the beauty of moral loveliness, or the harmonious propriety that attunes the passions of a well-regulated mind, that I blush at making the comparison; yet I sigh to think how few women aim at attaining this respectability by withdrawing from the giddy whirl of pleasure, or the indolent calm that stupifies the good sort of women it sucks in. [. . .]

Would men but generously snap our chains, and be content with rational fellowship instead of slavish obedience, they would find us more observant daughters, more affectionate sisters, more faithful wives, more reasonable mothers—in a word, better citizens.[9] We should then love them with true affection, because we should learn to respect ourselves; and the peace of mind of a worthy man

8   Fenelon, *Adventures of Telemachus* (London, 1699) 1: 152.
9   On citizenship and women, see Pateman (**pp. 62–3**) and Colley (**pp. 65–7**).

would not be interrupted by the idle vanity of his wife, nor the babes sent to nestle in a strange bosom, having never found a home in their mother's.

CHAP. X.
PARENTAL AFFECTION.
PARENTAL affection is, perhaps, the blindest modification of perverse self-love; for we have not, like the French,[1] two terms to distinguish the pursuit of a natural and reasonable desire, from the ignorant calculations of weakness. Parents often love their children in the most brutal manner, and sacrifice every relative duty to promote their advancement in the world.—To promote, such is the perversity of unprincipled prejudices, the future welfare of the very beings whose present existence they imbitter by the most despotic stretch of power. Power, in fact, is ever true to its vital principle, for in every shape it would reign without controul or inquiry. Its throne is built across a dark abyss, which no eye must dare to explore, lest the baseless fabric should totter under investigation. Obedience, unconditional obedience, is the catch-word of tyrants of every description, and to render "assurance doubly sure,"[2] one kind of despotism supports another. [. . .]

CHAP. XI.
DUTY TO PARENTS.
[. . .] But, respect for parents is, generally speaking, a much more debasing principle; it is only a selfish respect for property. The father who is blindly obeyed, is obeyed from sheer weakness, or from motives that degrade the human character.

A great proportion of the misery that wanders, in hideous forms, around the world, is allowed to rise from the negligence of parents; and still these are the people who are most tenacious of what they term a natural right, though it be subversive of the birth-right of man, the right of acting according to the direction of his own reason. [. . .]

CHAP. XII.
ON NATIONAL EDUCATION.
[. . .] It is not for the benefit of society that a few brilliant men should be brought forward at the expence of the multitude. It is true, that great men seem to start up, as great revolutions occur, at proper intervals, to restore order, and to blow aside the clouds that thicken over the face of truth; but let more reason and virtue prevail in society, and these strong winds would not be necessary. Public education, of every denomination, should be directed to form citizens; but if you wish to make good citizens, you must first exercise the affections of a son and a brother. This is the only way to expand the heart; for public affections, as well as public virtues, must ever grow out of the private character, or they are merely meteors

---

1   [MW's note.] *L'amour propre. L'amour de soi même.* [Ed.: Rousseau defines the former as self-love (leading to selfish conflict) and the latter as self-esteem (leading to virtue) in the *Discourse on the Origin and Foundations of Inequality* (in *Rousseau's Political Writings*, ed. Alan Ritter and Julia Conaway Bondanella (New York: Norton, 1988) 27–8) and in *Emile*, 92, 213–14).]
2   Shakespeare, *Macbeth* 4.1.83.

that shoot athwart a dark sky, and disappear as they are gazed at and admired. [. . .]

When, therefore, I call women slaves, I mean in a political and civil sense; for, indirectly they obtain too much power, and are debased by their exertions to obtain illicit sway.

Let an enlightened nation[1] then try what effect reason would have to bring them back to nature, and their duty; and allowing them to share the advantages of education and government with man, see whether they will become better, as they grow wiser and become free. They cannot be injured by the experiment; for it is not in the power of man to render them more insignificant than they are at present.

To render this practicable, day schools, for particular ages, should be established by government, in which boys and girls might be educated together.[2] The school for the younger children, from five to nine years of age, ought to be absolutely free and open to all classes.[3] A sufficient number of masters should also be chosen by a select committee, in each parish, to whom any complaint of negligence, &c. might be made, if signed by six of the children's parents.

Ushers[4] would then be unnecessary; for I believe experience will ever prove that this kind of subordinate authority is particularly injurious to the morals of youth. What, indeed, can tend to deprave the character more than outward submission and inward contempt? Yet how can boys be expected to treat an usher with respect, when the master seems to consider him in the light of a servant, and almost to countenance the ridicule which becomes the chief amusement of the boys during the play hours?

But nothing of this kind could occur in an elementary day-school, where boys and girls, the rich and poor, should meet together. And to prevent any of the distinctions of vanity, they should be dressed alike, and all obliged to submit to the same discipline, or leave the school. The school-room ought to be surrounded by a large piece of ground, in which the children might be usefully exercised, for at this age they should not be confined to any sedentary employment for more than an hour at a time. But these relaxations might all be rendered a part of

---

1   [MW's note.] France.
2   Wollstonecraft's call for co-education of boys and girls (like that for children's independence in chapters 11 and 12) was seen by conservatives to lead to promiscuity and rebellion, especially after the scandalous details of her own life were known after 1798. The parodic *Sketch of the Rights of Boys and Girls* (London: J. Bew, 1792), by "Launcelot Light and Laetitia Lookabout," joked that "it would be better to bring up boys and girls promiscuously together" (p. 34). Jane West's didactic *Letters Addressed to a Young Man* (London: Strahan, 1801) saw in co-education a dangerous "contempt for prescription, parental authority, experience" (3: 364).
3   [MW's note.] Treating this part of the subject, I have borrowed some hints from a very sensible pamphlet, written by the late bishop of Autun on Public Education. [Ed.: the *Rights of Woman* is dedicated to Talleyrand, Bishop of Autun, whose 1791 *Rapport sur l'instruction publique* argued for universal public education until age eight, when women "should confine themselves in the paternal home" because "The paternal home is better for the education of women; they have less need to learn to deal with the interests of others, than to accustom themselves to a calm and secluded life. Destined to domestic cares, it is in the bosom of their family that they should receive their first lessons and their first examples" (Appendix B.1 in Wollstonecraft's *The Vindications*, ed. Macdonald and Scherf, 399, 398).]
4   Assistant teachers.

elementary education, for many things improve and amuse the senses, when introduced as a kind of show, to the principles of which, dryly laid down, children would turn a deaf ear. For instance, botany, mechanics, and astronomy. Reading, writing, arithmetic, natural history, and some simple experiments in natural philosophy, might fill up the day; but these pursuits should never encroach on gymnastic plays in the open air. The elements of religion, history, the history of man, and politics, might also be taught by conversations, in the socratic form.

After the age of nine, girls and boys, intended for domestic employments, or mechanical trades, ought to be removed to other schools, and receive instruction, in some measure appropriated to the destination of each individual, the two sexes being still together in the morning; but in the afternoon, the girls should attend a school, where plain-work, mantua-making, millinery, &c. would be their employment.[5]

The young people of superior abilities, or fortune, might now be taught, in another school, the dead and living languages, the elements of science, and continue the study of history and politics, on a more extensive scale, which would not exclude polite literature. [. . .]

Humanity to animals should be particularly inculcated as a part of national education, for it is not at present one of our national virtues.[6] Tenderness for their humble dumb domestics, amongst the lower class, is oftener to be found in a savage than a civilized state. For civilization prevents that intercourse which creates affection in the rude hut, or mud hovel, and leads uncultivated minds who are only depraved by the refinements which prevail in the society, where they are trodden under foot by the rich, to domineer over them to revenge the insults that they are obliged to bear from their superiors.

This habitual cruelty is first caught at school, where it is one of the rare sports of the boys to torment the miserable brutes that fall in their way. The transition, as they grow up, from barbarity to brutes to domestic tyranny over wives, children, and servants, is very easy. Justice, or even benevolence, will not be a powerful spring of action unless it extend to the whole creation; nay, I believe that it may be delivered as an axiom, that those who can see pain, unmoved, will soon learn to inflict it. [. . .]

The want of natural affection, in many women, who are drawn from their duty by the admiration of men, and the ignorance of others, render the infancy of man a much more perilous state than that of brutes; yet men are unwilling to place women in situations proper to enable them to acquire sufficient understanding to know how even to nurse their babes.

---

5   Despite Wollstonecraft's focus here on traditionally female labor, she departs sharply from Talleyrand's proposal that after age eight girls return to the "paternal home" (see pp. 95 and 102).

6   Cruelty to animals and cruelty to women was a connection made by feminists throughout the eighteenth and nineteenth centuries, borne out in the links between the anti–vivisection and feminist movements in the nineteenth and twentieth centuries (Taylor parodied this connection in A Vindication of the Rights of Brutes (pp. 40–1). Catharine Macaulay in Letters on Education included eating animal flesh as part of this cruelty that would "denature" human sympathy (Letters 38–39), an idea in step with eighteenth-century theories of sentimentality (see Barker-Benfield, Culture of Sensibility 231–6, and Wollstonecraft, Works 2: 151–4).

So forcibly does this truth strike me, that I would rest the whole tendency of my reasoning upon it, for whatever tends to incapacitate the maternal character, takes woman out of her sphere.

But it is vain to expect the present race of weak mothers either to take that reasonable care of a child's body, which is necessary to lay the foundation of a good constitution, supposing that it do not suffer for the sins of its fathers; or, to manage its temper so judiciously that the child will not have, as it grows up, to throw off all that its mother, its first instructor, directly or indirectly taught; and unless the mind have uncommon vigour, womanish follies will stick to the character throughout life. The weakness of the mother will be visited on the children! And whilst women are educated to rely on their husbands for judgment, this must ever be the consequence, for there is no improving an understanding by halves, nor can any being act wisely from imitation, because in every circumstance of life there is a kind of individuality, which requires an exertion of judgment to modify general rules. The being who can think justly in one track, will soon extend its intellectual empire; and she who has sufficient judgment to manage her children, will not submit, right or wrong, to her husband, or patiently to the social laws which make a nonentity of a wife.

In public schools women, to guard against the errors of ignorance, should be taught the elements of anatomy and medicine, not only to enable them to take proper care of their own health, but to make them rational nurses of their infants, parents, and husbands; for the bills of mortality are swelled by the blunders of self-willed old women, who give nostrums of their own without knowing any thing of the human frame.[7] It is likewise proper only in a domestic view, to make women acquainted with the anatomy of the mind, by allowing the sexes to associate together in every pursuit; and by leading them to observe the progress of the human understanding in the improvement of the sciences and arts; never forgetting the science of morality; or the study of the political history of mankind.

A man has been termed a microcosm; and every family might also be called a state. States, it is true, have mostly been governed by arts that disgrace the character of man; and the want of a just constitution, and equal laws, have so perplexed the notions of the worldly wise, that they more than question the reasonableness of contending for the rights of humanity. Thus morality; polluted in the national reservoir, sends off streams of vice to corrupt the constituent parts of the body politic; but should more noble, or rather, more just principles regulate the laws, which ought to be the government of society, and not those who execute them, duty might become the rule of private conduct.

---

7 This powerful cultural taboo against women's knowledge of the human body was central to contemporary resistance against women's training in medicine, midwifery, and even painting (it was considered improper for women to attend life drawing classes); on man-midwifery see Moscucci, *Science of Woman* 42–74). Wollstonecraft's incorporation of medicine and anatomy within women's scope of knowledge marks an important departure from contemporary definitions of modesty, leading to conservative charges that her educational plan would corrupt girls; see chapter 7 (**p. 144**) for her distinction between true modesty and affectation, and for her controversial call for sexual education; for objections, see Bisset, Beloe and Polwhele (**pp. 46–7, 53, 44–6**). See also Mary Hays's similar argument in *Appeal to the Men of Great Britain* (New York: Garland, 1974) 196–9.

Besides, by the exercise of their bodies and minds women would acquire that mental activity so necessary in the maternal character, united with the fortitude that distinguishes steadiness of conduct from the obstinate perverseness of weakness. For it is dangerous to advise the indolent to be steady, because they instantly become rigorous, and to save themselves trouble, punish with severity faults that the patient fortitude of reason might have prevented.

But fortitude presupposes strength of mind; and is strength of mind to be acquired by indolent acquiescence? by asking advice instead of exerting the judgment? by obeying through fear, instead of practising the forbearance, which we all stand in need of ourselves?—The conclusion which I wish to draw, is obvious; make women rational creatures, and free citizens, and they will quickly become good wives, and mothers; that is—if men do not neglect the duties of husbands and fathers. [. . .]

CHAP. XIII.

SOME INSTANCES OF THE FOLLY WHICH THE IGNORANCE OF WOMEN GENERATES; WITH CONCLUDING REFLECTIONS ON THE MORAL IMPROVEMENT THAT A REVOLUTION IN FEMALE MANNERS MIGHT NATURALLY BE EXPECTED TO PRODUCE.

[. . .]

SECT. II.

ANOTHER instance of that feminine weakness of character, often produced by a confined education, is a romantic twist of the mind, which has been very properly termed *sentimental*.

Women subjected by ignorance to their sensations, and only taught to look for happiness in love, refine on sensual feelings, and adopt metaphysical notions respecting that passion, which lead them shamefully to neglect the duties of life, and frequently in the midst of these sublime refinements they plump into actual vice.

These are the women who are amused by the reveries of the stupid novelists,[1] who, knowing little of human nature, work up stale tales, and describe meretricious scenes, all retailed in a sentimental jargon, which equally tend to corrupt the taste, and draw the heart aside from its daily duties. I do not mention the understanding, because never having been exercised, its slumbering energies rest inactive, like the lurking particles of fire which are supposed universally to pervade matter.

Females, in fact, denied all political privileges, and not allowed, as married women, excepting in criminal cases, a civil existence, have their attention naturally drawn from the interest of the whole community to that of the minute parts, though the private duty of any member of society must be very imperfectly performed when not connected with the general good. The mighty business of female

1   Wollstonecraft's dispute here is both with conservative conduct book writers who argued that women's reading of novels corrupted them, and with popular fiction itself which she saw as an insufficient source of education; see Myers (**pp. 86–8**) and Whale (**pp. 90–1**).

life is to please,[2] and restrained from entering into more important concerns by political and civil oppression, sentiments become events, and reflection deepens what it should, and would have effaced, if the understanding had been allowed to take a wider range.

But, confined to trifling employments, they naturally imbibe opinions which the only kind of reading calculated to interest an innocent frivolous mind, inspires. Unable to grasp any thing great, is it surprising that they find the reading of history a very dry task, and disquisitions addressed to the understanding intolerably tedious, and almost unintelligible? Thus are they necessarily dependent on the novelist for amusement. Yet, when I exclaim against novels, I mean when contrasted with those works which exercise the understanding and regulate the imagination.—For any kind of reading I think better than leaving a blank still a blank, because the mind must receive a degree of enlargement and obtain a little strength by a slight exertion of its thinking powers; besides, even the productions that are only addressed to the imagination, raise the reader a little above the gross gratification of appetites, to which the mind has not given a shade of delicacy. [. . .]

When, therefore, I advise my sex not to read such flimsy works, it is to induce them to read something superiour; for I coincide in opinion with a sagacious man, who, having a daughter and niece under his care, pursued a very different plan with each.

The niece, who had considerable abilities, had, before she was left to his guardianship, been indulged in desultory reading. Her he endeavoured to lead, and did lead to history and moral essays; but his daughter, whom a fond weak mother had indulged, and who consequently was averse to every thing like application, he allowed to read novels: and used to justify his conduct by saying, that if she ever attained a relish for reading them, he should have some foundation to work upon; and that erroneous opinions were better than none at all.

In fact the female mind has been so totally neglected, that knowledge was only to be acquired from this muddy source, till from reading novels some women of superiour talents learned to despise them.

The best method, I believe, that can be adopted to correct a fondness for novels is to ridicule them: not indiscriminately, for then it would have little effect; but, if a judicious person, with some turn for humour, would read several to a young girl, and point out both by tones, and apt comparisons with pathetic incidents and heroic characters in history, how foolishly and ridiculously they caricatured human nature, just opinions might be substituted instead of romantic sentiments.

In one respect, however, the majority of both sexes resemble, and equally shew a want of taste and modesty. Ignorant women, forced to be chaste to preserve their reputation, allow their imagination to revel in the unnatural and meretricious scenes sketched by the novel writers of the day, slighting as insipid the sober

2   See the excerpts from Rousseau's *Emile* (**pp. 17–22**), Barbauld (**pp. 41–2**), and Barrett Browning (**pp. 54–5**).

dignity, and matron graces of history,[3] whilst men carry the same vitiated taste into life, and fly for amusement to the wanton, from the unsophisticated charms of virtue, and the grave respectability of sense.

Besides, the reading of novels makes women, and particularly ladies of fashion, very fond of using strong expressions and superlatives in conversation; and, though the dissipated artificial life which they lead prevents their cherishing any strong legitimate passion, the language of passion in affected tones slips for ever from their glib tongues, and every trifle produces those phosphoric bursts which only mimick in the dark the flame of passion. [...]

SECT. VI.

[...] To render women truly useful members of society, I argue that they should be led, by having their understandings cultivated on a large scale, to acquire a rational affection for their country, founded on knowledge, because it is obvious that we are little interested about what we do not understand. And to render this general knowledge of due importance, I have endeavoured to shew that private duties are never properly fulfilled unless the understanding enlarges the heart; and that public virtue is only an aggregate of private. But, the distinctions established in society undermine both, by beating out the solid gold of virtue, till it becomes only the tinsel-covering of vice; for whilst wealth renders a man more respectable than virtue, wealth be sought before virtue; and, whilst women's persons are caressed, when a childish simper shews an absence of mind—the mind will lie fallow. Yet, true voluptuousness must proceed from the mind—for what can equal the sensations produced by mutual affection, supported by mutual respect? What are the cold, or feverish caresses of appetite, but sin embracing death,[4] compared with the modest overflowings of a pure heart and exalted imagination? Yes, let me tell the libertine of fancy when he despises understanding in woman— that the mind, which he disregards, gives life to the enthusiastic affection from which rapture, short-lived as it is, alone can flow! And, that, without virtue, a sexual attachment must expire, like a tallow candle in the socket, creating intolerable disgust. To prove this, I need only observe, that men who have wasted great part of their lives with women, and with whom they have sought for pleasure with eager thirst, entertain the meanest opinion of the sex.—Virtue, true refiner of joy!—if foolish men were to fright thee from earth, in order to give loose to all their appetites without a check—some sensual wight of taste would scale the heavens to invite thee back, to give a zest to pleasure!

That women at present are by ignorance rendered foolish or vicious, is, I think, not to be disputed; and, that the most salutary effects tending to improve mankind might be expected from a REVOLUTION in female manners, appears, at least, with a face of probability, to rise out of the observation. For as marriage has been

---

3   [MW's note.] I am not now alluding to that superiority of mind which tragi-comedy leads to the creation of ideal beauty, when [life], surveyed with a penetrating eye, appears a tragi-comedy, in which little can be seen to satisfy the heart without the help of fancy. [Ed.: the second edition has "he" in place of "life."]

4   In Milton's *Paradise Lost* (2. 790–809), Death (the son of Satan and Sin) rapes his mother Sin, but Wollstonecraft transforms Sin into the active agent.

termed the parent of those endearing charities which draw man from the brutal herd, the corrupting intercourse that wealth, idleness, and folly, produce between the sexes, is more universally injurious to morality than all the other vices of mankind collectively considered. To adulterous lust the most sacred duties are sacrificed, because before marriage, men, by a promiscuous intimacy with women, learned to consider love as a selfish gratification—learned to separate it not only from esteem, but from the affection merely built on habit, which mixes a little humanity with it. Justice and friendship are also set at defiance, and that purity of taste is vitiated which would naturally lead a man to relish an artless display of affection rather than affected airs. But that noble simplicity of affection, which dares to appear unadorned, has few attractions for the libertine, though it be the charm, which by cementing the matrimonial tie, secures to the pledges of a warmer passion the necessary parental attention; for children will never be properly educated till friendship subsists between parents.[5] Virtue flies from a house divided against itself—and a whole legion of devils take up their residence there.[6]

The affection of husbands and wives cannot be pure when they have so few sentiments in common, and when so little confidence is established at home, as must be the case when their pursuits are so different. That intimacy from which tenderness should flow, will not, cannot subsist between the vicious.

Contending, therefore, that the sexual distinction which men have so warmly insisted upon, is arbitrary, I have dwelt on an observation, that several sensible men, with whom I have conversed on the subject, allowed to be well founded; and it is simply this, that the little chastity to be found amongst men, and consequent disregard of modesty, tend to degrade both sexes; and further, that the modesty of women, characterized as such, will often be only the artful veil of wantonness instead of being the natural reflection of purity, till modesty be universally respected.

From the tyranny of man, I firmly believe, the greater number of female follies proceed; and the cunning, which I allow makes at present a part of their character, I likewise have repeatedly endeavoured to prove, is produced by oppression. [. . .]

Asserting the rights which women in common with men ought to contend for, I have not attempted to extenuate their faults; but to prove them to be the natural consequence of their education and station in society. If so, it is reasonable to suppose that they will change their character, and correct their vices and follies, when they are allowed to be free in a physical, moral, and civil sense.[7]

Let woman share the rights and she will emulate the virtues of man; for she must grow more perfect when emancipated, or justify the authority that chains such a weak being to her duty.—If the latter, it will be expedient to open a fresh

---

5 Wollstonecraft writes on friendship, not passion, as the basis of marriage in chapter 4.
6 Matthew 12:25; Mark 3:25, 5:9; Luke 8:30, 11:17.
7 [MW's note.] I had further enlarged on the advantages which might reasonably be expected to result from an improvement in female manners, towards the general reformation of society; but it appeared to me that such reflections would more properly close the last volume. [Ed.: part 2 of the *Rights of Woman* was never written, but Wollstonecraft did focus on legal injustices in her unfinished novel, *The Wrongs of Woman, or Maria*; see also the "Hints" (pp. 161–4).]

trade with Russia for whips; a present which a father should always make to his son-in-law on his wedding day, that a husband may keep his whole family in order by the same means; and without any violation of justice reign, wielding this sceptre, sole master of his house, because he is the only being in it who has reason:—the divine, indefeasible earthly sovereignty breathed into man by the Master of the universe. Allowing this position, women have not any inherent rights to claim; and, by the same rule, their duties vanish, for rights and duties are inseparable.

Be just then, O ye men of understanding! and mark not more severely what women do amiss, than the vicious tricks of the horse or the ass for whom ye provide provender—and allow her the privileges of ignorance, to whom ye deny the rights of reason, or ye will be worse than Egyptian task-masters, expecting virtue where nature has not given understanding!

END OF THE FIRST VOLUME.

Hints

Chiefly designed to have been incorporated in the Second Part of the Vindication of the Rights of Woman.[1]

1. INDOLENCE is the source of nervous complaints, and a whole host of cares. This devil might say that his name was legion.

2. It should be one of the employments of women of fortune, to visit hospitals, and superintend the conduct of inferiors.

3. It is generally supposed, that the imagination of women is particularly active, and leads them astray. Why then do we seek by education only to exercise their imagination and feeling, till the understanding, grown rigid by disuse, is unable to exercise itself—and the superfluous nourishment the imagination and feeling have received, renders the former romantic, and the latter weak?

4. Few men have risen to any great eminence in learning, who have not received something like a regular education. Why are women expected to surmount difficulties that men are not equal to?

5. Nothing can be more absurd than the ridicule of the critic, that the heroine of his mock-tragedy was in love with the very man whom she ought least to have loved; he could not have given a better reason. How can passion gain strength any other way? In Otaheite,[2] love cannot be known, where the obstacles to irritate an indiscriminate appetite, and sublimate the simple sensations of desire till they mount to passion, are never known. There a man or woman cannot love the very person they ought not to have loved—nor does jealousy ever fan the flame.

6. It has frequently been observed, that, when women have an object in view, they pursue it with more steadiness than men, particularly love. This is not a compliment. Passion pursues with more heat than reason, and with most ardour during the absence of reason.

---

1   The "Hints" were published by Godwin in volume 4 of the *Posthumous Works of the Author of the Vindication of the Rights of Woman* (London: Joseph Johnson, 1798).
2   Tahiti.

7. Men are more subject to the physical love than women.[3] The confined education of women makes them more subject to jealousy.

8. Simplicity seems, in general, the consequence of ignorance, as I have observed in the characters of women and sailors—the being confined to one track of impressions.

9. I know of no other way of preserving the chastity of mankind, than that of rendering women rather objects of love than desire. The difference is great. Yet, while women are encouraged to ornament their persons at the expence of their minds, while indolence renders them helpless and lascivious (for what other name can be given to the common intercourse between the sexes?) they will be, generally speaking, only objects of desire; and, to such women, men cannot be constant. Men, accustomed only to have their senses moved, merely seek for a selfish gratification in the society of women, and their sexual instinct, being neither supported by the understanding nor the heart, must be excited by variety.

10. We ought to respect old opinions; though prejudices, blindly adopted, lead to error, and preclude all exercise of the reason. The emulation which often makes a boy mischievous, is a generous spur; and the old remark, that unlucky, turbulent boys, make the wisest and best men, is true, spite of Mr. Knox's arguments.[4] It has been observed, that the most adventurous horses, when tamed or domesticated, are the most mild and tractable.

11. The children who start up suddenly at twelve or fourteen, and fall into decays, in consequence, as it is termed, of outgrowing their strength, are in general, I believe, those children, who have been bred up with mistaken tenderness, and not allowed to sport and take exercise in the open air. This is analogous to plants: for it is found that they run up sickly, long stalks, when confined.

12. Children should be taught to feel deference, not to practise submission.

13. It is always a proof of false refinement, when a fastidious taste overpowers sympathy.

14. Lust appears to be the most natural companion of wild ambition; and love of human praise, of that dominion erected by cunning.

15. "Genius decays as judgment increases."[5] Of course, those who have the least genius, have the earliest appearance of wisdom.

16. A knowledge of the fine arts, is seldom subservient to the promotion of either religion or virtue. Elegance is often indecency; witness our prints.

17. There does not appear to be any evil in the world, but what is necessary. The doctrine of rewards and punishments, not considered as a means of reformation, appears to me an infamous libel on divine goodness.

18. Whether virtue is founded on reason or revelation, virtue is wisdom, and vice is folly. Why are positive punishments?

19. Few can walk alone. The staff of Christianity is the necessary support of human weakness. But an acquaintance with the nature of man and virtue, with

---

3   Mary Robinson similarly sexualizes men, in direct opposition to Rousseau: "the passions of men originate in sensuality: those of women, in sentiment: man loves corporeally, woman mentally: which is the nobler creature?" (*Letter to the Women of England* (1799) 10).
4   Vicesimus Knox, *Essays, Moral and Literary* (1782) 2.
5   Immanuel Kant (1724–1804), *The Critique of Judgment* (1790) 1.1.50.

just sentiments on the attributes, would be sufficient, without a voice from heaven, to lead some to virtue, but not the mob.

20. I only expect the natural reward of virtue, whatever it may be. I rely not on a positive reward. The justice of God can be vindicated by a belief in a future state—but a continuation of being vindicates it as clearly, as the positive system of rewards and punishments—by evil educing good for the individual, and not for an imaginary whole. The happiness of the whole must arise from the happiness of the constituent parts, or this world is not a state of trial, but a school.

21. The vices acquired by Augustus[6] to retain his power, must have tainted his soul, and prevented that increase of happiness a good man expects in the next stage of existence. This was a natural punishment.

22. The lover is ever most deeply enamoured, when it is with he knows not what—and the devotion of a mystic has a rude Gothic grandeur in it, which the respectful adoration of a philosopher will never reach. I may be thought fanciful; but it has continually occurred to me, that, though, I allow, reason in this world is the mother of wisdom—yet some flights of the imagination seem to reach what wisdom cannot teach—and, while they delude us here, afford a glorious hope, if not a foretaste, of what we may expect hereafter. He that created us, did not mean to mark us with ideal images of grandeur, the *baseless fabric of a vision*[7]—No— that perfection we follow with hopeless ardour when the whisperings of reason are heard, may be found, when not incompatible with our state, in the round of eternity. Perfection indeed must, even then, be a comparative idea—but the wisdom, the happiness of a superior state, has been supposed to be intuitive, and the happiest effusions of human genius have seemed like inspiration—the deductions of reason destroy sublimity.

23. I am more and more convinced, that poetry is the first effervescence of the imagination, and the forerunner of civilization.

24. When the Arabs had no trace of literature or science, they composed beautiful verses on the subjects of love and war. The flights of the imagination, and the laboured deductions of reason, appear almost incompatible.

25. Poetry certainly flourishes most in the first rude state of society. The passions speak most eloquently, when they are not shackled by reason. The sublime expression, which has been so often quoted, [Genesis, 1:3.] is perhaps a barbarous flight; or rather the grand conception of an uncultivated mind; for it is contrary to nature and experience, to suppose that this account is founded on facts—It is doubtless a sublime allegory. But a cultivated mind would not thus have described the creation—for, arguing from analogy, it appears that creation must have been a comprehensive plan, and that the Supreme Being always uses second causes, slowly and silently to fulfil his purpose. This is, in reality, a more sublime view of that power which wisdom supports: but it is not the sublimity that would strike the impassioned mind, in which the imagination took place of intellect. Tell a being, whose affections and passions have been more exercised

---

6 Rousseau also used Augustus (63 BC–14 CE), who gained power through assasinations and civil war, as an example of ambition bringing misery (*Emile* 242–3).
7 Shakespeare, *The Tempest*, 4.1.151.

than his reason, that God said, *Let there be light! and there was light*; and he would prostrate himself before the Being who could thus call things out of nothing, as if they were: but a man in whom reason had taken place of passion, would not adore, till wisdom was conspicuous as well as power, for his admiration must be founded on principle.

26. Individuality is ever conspicuous in those enthusiastic flights of fancy, in which reason is left behind, without being lost sight of.

27. The mind has been too often brought to the test of enquiries which only reach to matter—put into the crucible, though the magnetic and electric fluid escapes from the experimental philosopher.

28. Mr. Kant has observed, that the understanding is sublime, the imagination beautiful—yet it is evident, that poets, and men who undoubtedly possess the liveliest imagination, are most touched by the sublime, while men who have cold, enquiring minds, have not this exquisite feeling in any great degree, and indeed seem to lose it as they cultivate their reason.[8]

29. The Grecian buildings are graceful—they fill the mind with all those pleasing emotions, which elegance and beauty never fail to excite in a cultivated mind—utility and grace strike us in unison—the mind is satisfied—things appear just what they ought to be: a calm satisfaction is felt, but the imagination has nothing to do—no obscurity darkens the gloom—like reasonable content, we can say why we are pleased—and this kind of pleasure may be lasting, but it is never great.[9]

30. When we say that a person is an original, it is only to say in other words that he thinks. "The less a man has cultivated his rational faculties, the more powerful is the principle of imitation, over his actions, and his habits of thinking. Most women, of course, are more influenced by the behaviour, the fashions, and the opinions of those with whom they associate, than men." (Smellie.)[10]

When we read a book which supports our favourite opinions, how eagerly do we suck in the doctrines, and suffer our minds placidly to reflect the images which illustrate the tenets we have embraced? We indolently or quietly acquiesce in the conclusion, and our spirit animates and connects the various subjects. But, on the contrary, when we peruse a skilful writer, who does not coincide in opinion with us, how is the mind on the watch to detect fallacy? And this coolness often prevents our being carried away by a stream of eloquence, which the prejudiced mind terms declamation—a pomp of words.—We never allow ourselves to be warmed; and, after contending with the writer, are more confirmed in our own

---

8 Kant, *Observations on the Feeling of the Beautiful and Sublime* (1764) and "The Analytic of the Sublime" in *The Critique of Judgment* (1790); see also Whale (p. 90–1) and Myers (p. 86–8).

9 Wollstonecraft's distinction in the "Hints" between the sublime and the beautiful continues her debate with the aesthetic theory of Edmund Burke (and also Kant; see previous footnote), whose *A Philosophical Enquiry into the Origin of Our Ideas of the Sublime and Beautiful* (1759) famously delineated a gendered distinction between the masculine sublime and feminine beautiful. Qualities Burke associated with the sublime (and with masculinity) included power, terror, obscurity, vastness, loudness, and roughness; Wollstonecraft's sustained critique of Burke's gendering of the sublime and beautiful may be found in her *Vindication of the Rights of Men* (*Works* 5: 1–78).

10 Smellie, *The Philosophy of Natural History* (1790) 1: 469.

opinion, as much perhaps from a spirit of contradiction as from reason.—Such is the strength of man!

31. It is the individual manner of seeing and feeling, pourtrayed by a strong imagination in bold images that have struck the senses, which creates all the charms of poetry. A great reader is always quoting the description of another's emotions; a strong imagination delights to paint its own. A writer of genius makes us feel; an inferior author reason.

32. Some principle prior to self-love must have existed: the feeling which produced the pleasure, must have existed before the experience.

THE END

4

Further Reading

Further Reading

Recommended Editions of Wollstonecraft

Collected Letters of Mary Wollstonecraft, ed. Ralph Wardle (Ithaca: Cornell University Press, 1979).

Wollstonecraft's letters offer an invaluable, often contrary, insight into her published writings; edited by Wardle, whose biography *Mary Wollstonecraft* (Lincoln: University of Nebraska Press, 1951) was the first modern biography to fully explore the political and intellectual significance of her writings.

A Critical Edition of Mary Wollstonecraft's A Vindication of the Rights of Woman, ed. Ulrich Hardt (Troy, NY: Whitston, 1982).

A valuable research tool for close comparison of the textual variations between Wollstonecraft's various editions.

Mary, A Fiction, and The Wrongs of Woman, or Maria, ed. Gary Kelly (Oxford: Oxford University Press, 1976).

Wollstonecraft's two novels nicely encapsulate her ongoing political transformation from pre-revolutionary proponent of sensibility to a much more critical and conflicted perspective on sensibility and romance. As its title suggests, Wollstonecraft's last novel, *The Wrongs of Woman* (unfinished and posthumously published), is in many respects the counterpart of *The Rights of Woman*, illustrating the oppression women endured due to their lack of rights.

A Short Residence in Sweden, Norway and Denmark, ed. Richard Holmes (Harmondsworth: Penguin, 1987).

Wollstonecraft's beautifully written travel writings, with their reflections on the sublime and beautiful landscape and on the social and political surroundings, influenced the younger Romantics and reveal the new aesthetic and political directions Wollstonecraft was taking before she died.

The Vindications: A Vindication of the Rights of Men and A Vindication of the Rights of Woman, ed. D.L. Macdonald and Kathleen Scherf (Peterborough: Broadview Press, 1997).

The best paperback edition available, with ample annotations and an excellent selection of contemporary political documents and responses to both *Vindications*, emphasizing their origins in the "revolutionary moment" of the early 1790s.

The Works of Mary Wollstonecraft, 7 vols., ed. Janet Todd and Marilyn Butler (London: William Pickering, 1989).

The complete works, including her translations, with thorough annotations and useful documentation regarding the attribution of anonymous reviews in the *Analytical Review*.

Recommended Book-Length Studies of Wollstonecraft

Conger, Syndy, *Mary Wollstonecraft and the Language of Sensibility* (London: Associated University Presses, 1994).

An in-depth exploration of Wollstonecraft's writings in the context of eighteenth-century sensibility.

Falco, Maria, ed., *Feminist Interpretations of Mary Wollstonecraft* (Pennsylvania: Penn State University Press, 1996).

Wide-ranging collection that examines Wollstonecraft's significance across disciplines.

Godwin, William, *Memoirs of the Author of a Vindication of "The Rights of Woman,"* ed. Pamela Clemit and Gina Luria Walker (Peterborough: Broadview, 2001).

An exemplary edition of Godwin's controversial account of Wollstonecraft's life, including numerous reviews, important contextual sources, and nineteenth-century reception.

Jump, Harriet, ed., *Lives of the Great Romantics III: Godwin, Wollstonecraft, and Mary Shelley by their Contemporaries*. Volume 2: Wollstonecraft (London: Pickering & Chatto, 1999).

Valuable resource that reprints nineteenth-century responses to Wollstonecraft in facsimile form.

Kelly, Gary, *Revolutionary Feminism: The Mind and Career of Mary Wollstonecraft* (London: Macmillan, 1992).

Biographically grounded critical overview of Wollstonecraft's works that places her arguments in their political context, emphasizing her role as bourgeois professional.

Lorch, Jennifer, *Mary Wollstonecraft: The Making of a Radical Feminist* (New York: St. Martin's Press, 1990).

Recuperation of Wollstonecraft as a radical writer, as opposed to a liberal bourgeois one.

Sapiro, Virginia, *A Vindication of Political Virtue: The Political Theory of Mary Wollstonecraft* (Chicago: University of Chicago Press, 1992).
A subtly argued, detailed investigation of Wollstonecraft's contributions to Western political theory, organized thematically.

Todd, Janet and Moira Ferguson, Twayne English Author Series, *Mary Wollstonecraft* (Boston: Twayne, 1984).
Useful and accessible general overview of Wollstonecraft's career and political arguments; a good place to begin intitial inquiries.

Tomalin, Claire, *The Life and Death of Mary Wollstonecraft* (1974; revised edn, Harmondsworth: Penguin, 1992).
Remains the most lucid and influential biography. Janet Todd's recent *Mary Wollstonecraft: A Revolutionary Life* (London: Weidenfeld & Nicolson, 2000) is longer and focuses on what Wollstonecraft's letters reveal about her life.

Further Reading

All of the essays and books excerpted in the Interpretations section are recommended for further reading, and full citations are given in the respective headnotes. The works below are also recommended for further reading.

Ackland, Michael. "The Embattled Sexes: Blake's Debt to Wollstonecraft in the Four Zoas," *Blake* 16 (Winter 1982–3) 172–83.
Badowska, Eva. "The Anorexic Body of Liberal Feminism: Mary Wollstonecraft's *Vindication of the Rights of Woman*," *Tulsa Studies in Women's Literature* 17.2 (Fall 1998) 283–304.
Burdett, Carolyn. "A Difficult Vindication: Olive Schreiner's Wollstonecraft Introduction," published with Schreiner's "Introduction to the Life of Mary Wollstonecraft and the Rights of Woman," *History Workshop Journal* 37 (1994) 177–93.
Caine, Barbara. *Victorian Feminists*, Oxford: Oxford University Press, 1993.
Ellis, Markman. *The Politics of Sensibility*, Cambridge: Cambridge University Press, 1996.
Fordyce, James. *Sermons to Young Women* (1765), reprinted in facsimile with John Gregory's *A Father's Legacy to his Daughters* (1774) as Vol. 1 of *Female Education in the Age of Enlightenment*, with introduction by Janet Todd, London: Pickering, 1996.
Gatens, Moira. *Feminism and Philosophy*, Cambridge: Polity, 1991.
Gregory, John. *A Father's Legacy to his Daughters* (1774), reprinted with Fordyce, above.

Hays, Mary. *Appeal to the Men of Great Britain in Behalf of Women*, facsimile edition with introduction by Gina Luria, New York: Garland, 1974.

Jones, Vivien. "The Death of Mary Wollstonecraft," *British Journal for Eighteenth-Century Studies* 20 (1997) 187–205.

Jump, Harriet Devine. *Mary Wollstonecraft, Writer*, Hemel Hempstead: Harvester Wheatsheaf, 1994.

Kegan Paul, Charles "Mary Wollstonecraft: A Vindication," *Frasers Magazine*, n.s. 17 (June 1878) 748–62.

McCarthy, William. " 'We Hoped the *Woman* Was Going to Appear': Repression, Desire, and Gender in Anna Letitia Barbauld's Early Poems," in *Romantic Women Writers: Voices and Countervoices*, ed. Paula Feldman and Theresa Kelley, Hanover: University Press of New England, 1995 (113–37).

McCrystal, John. "Revolting Women: The Use of Revolutionary Discourse in Mary Astell and Mary Wollstonecraft Compared," *History of Political Thought* 14.2 (Summer 1993) 189–203.

McGann, Jerome. *The Poetics of Sensibility: A Revolution in Literary Style*, Oxford: Clarendon, 1996.

Mackenzie, Catriona. "Reason and Sensibility: The Ideal of Women's Self-Governance in the Writings of Mary Wollstonecraft," *Hypatia: A Journal of Feminist Philosophy* 8: 4 (Fall 1993) 35–55.

Mellor, Anne. *Mothers of the Nation: Women's Political Writing in England, 1780–1830*, Bloomington: Indiana University Press, 2000.

Moore, Jane. *Mary Wollstonecraft*, Plymouth: Northcote House, 1999.

Myers, Mitzi, "Reform or Ruin: A 'Revolution in Female Manners'," *Studies in Eighteenth-Century Culture* 11 (1982) 199–216.

Opie, Amelia. *Adeline Mowbray*, ed. Shelley King and John Pierce, Oxford: Oxford University Press, 1999.

Rousseau, Jean-Jacques. *Discourse on the Origin and Foundations of Inequality Among Men* (1755), in *Rousseau's Political Writings*, ed. Alan Ritter and Julia Conaway Bondanella, trans. Julia Conaway Bonadella, New York: Norton, 1988 (3–57).

Schiebinger, Londa. *Nature's Body: Gender in the Making of Modern Science*, Boston: Beacon, 1993.

St Clair, William. *The Godwins and the Shelleys: The Biography of a Family*, London: Faber & Faber, 1989.

Taylor, Anya. "Coleridge, Wollstonecraft and the Rights of Woman," in *Coleridge's Visionary Languages*, ed. Tim Fulford, Rochester, NY: Brewer, 1993 (83–98).

Taylor, Barbara. "For the Love of God: Religion and the Erotic Imagination in Wollstonecraft's Feminism" in Yeo, ed., *Mary Wollstonecraft and 200 Years of Feminisms* (15–35).

—— "Mary Wollstonecraft and the Wild Wish of Early Feminism," *History Workshop Journal* 33 (1992) 197–219.

Thiébaux, Marcelle. "Mary Wollstonecraft in Federalist America, 1791–1802," in *The Evidence of the Imagination*, ed. Donald Reiman, Michael Jaye, and Betty Bennett, New York: New York University Press, 1978 (195–235).

Trott, Nicola. "Sexing the Critic: Mary Wollstonecraft at the Turn of the

Century," in *1798: The Year of the Lyrical Ballads*, ed. Richard Cronin, London: Macmillan, 1998 (32–67).

Wang, Orrin. *Fantastic Modernity: Dialectical Readings in Romanticism*, Baltimore: Johns Hopkins Press, 1996.

Weiss, Penny. "Wollstonecraft and Rousseau: The Gendered Fate of Political Theorists," in *Feminist Interpretations of Mary Wollstonecraft*, ed. Maria Falco, Pennsylvania: Penn State University Press, 1996.

Windle, John. *Mary Wollstonecraft Godwin, 1759–1797: a bibliography of the first and early editions, with briefer notes on later editions and translations*, 2nd edn, New Castle, Delaware: Oak Knoll, 2000.

Wu, Duncan, ed. *Romanticism: An Anthology*, 2nd edn, Oxford: Blackwell, 2000.

Yeo, Eileen Janes, ed. *Mary Wollstonecraft and 200 Years of Feminisms*, London: Rivers Oram, 1997.

Index

NOTE: Page numbers in bold indicate an extract by an author or from a particular work; page numbers followed by *n* indicate information is found only in a footnote. MW = Mary Wollstonecraft.

abandonment of children 148
abolition movement 69, 70
abortion 148
abuse *see* physical abuse; sexual abuse
accoucheurs 150
adultery 85, 134; *see also* infidelity
Aeschylus 26*n*, 114*n*
aesthetics 37, 86–8, 90, 99
alcoholism 81
Alderson, Amelia *see* Opie, Amelia Alderson
amour-propre/amour de soi même 18–19, 152*n*; *see also* self-love, self-esteem
Analytical Review 9, 14, 33, 84–5, 86*n*; MW as reviewer for 13, 68, 84, 86–8
anarchist feminism 59
anatomy: argument for carnivorousness 115*n*; women's ignorance of own 155
androgynous discourse 88–9
angels: MW as 51; women as 40, 141–2
animals 131*n*, 133, 140, 118, 120; and souls 129, 134; and reason 113*n*, 130*n*; rights of 40; and sex education 144–5*n*; teaching of humanity to 154
Anna Comnena 55
Anonymous: *Defence of the Character and Conduct of the Late Mary Wollstonecraft Godwin* 1, **52–3**
anorexia 146*n*
Anthony, Susan B. 36
anti-commercialism 77–9

Anti-Jacobin Review **46–7**, 86, 97
appetites 27, 105, 121–2, 126–7, 146–8, 158, 161; *see also* passions; sexuality
Arab poetry 163
architecture of Greece 164
Arden, Jane 7, 8, 81
aristocracy: dissipated sensibility of 10, 114; maintain ignorance of poor 133; MW in employment of 8; role in civilization 116; women compared to 132; *see also* leisured classes
Aristotle 40–1
army culture 116, 119
artificial taste 87, 110–11; in French 102–3
arts 162
associationism 143–4
Astell, Mary 71, 78, 96
atheism attributed to MW 33, 71
Augustus, Caesar 163
Austen, Jane 88
authoritarianism 116
autonomous individualism 63–5, 75–6

Bacon, Francis 118
Barbauld, Anna Laetitia **41–2**, 48, 131*n*, 142*n*
Barker-Benfield, G.J. 37–8, **67–9**
beauty 117, 118, 127, 141–2, 151, 164*n*
Bellamy, Thomas 86*n*
Beloe, William 2, 33, **53**
Berry, Mary 33, 34

Betham, (Mary) Matilda 86
Bible 72n; MW quotes from 40, 48
Bishop, Meredith 8, 13
Bisset, Robert 33, 46–7, 96
Blake, William 37, 112n; illustrates MW's books 10, 14, 50; "Mary" poem 3, 10, 50–2
Blind, Mathilde 57–8, 98
Blood, Fanny (later Skeys) 7–8, 12, 13, 43
blushing 44n, 51
body: discourse of 37, 75–84; importance of bodily strength 82–4, 125–6; modesty regarding 77, 144–6; women's ignorance of 155; see also physical strength; sexuality; weakness of women
Boyer, Jean-Baptiste de 127n
breastfeeding 136
British Critic 46, 53, 86n
Browning, Elizabeth Barrett 2, 33, 35, 54–5; "Aurora Leigh" 54
Browning, Robert 54
Burke, Edmund 9, 22, 84, 111n, 164n
Burney, Fanny 97
business see commerce/commercialism

Cambridge University: admission of women 58
carnivorousness 115n
Catherine the Great 138n
chain of being theory 113n
Chalmers, Alexander 86n
Chapone, Hester 142–3
character: effect of profession on 116; importance for female identity 111; national and sexual construction of 10, 73–4, 102–3, 139
chastity 103, 135, 157, 162; wanting in men 147–8, 159
childbearing: Rousseau on 21
children: born of depravity 147–8; equality for 46; health and fitness of 127–8, 153–4, 162; mothers' influence on 66; rights of 40; sex education for 144–5; women likened to 118, 122
China 124; footbinding practice 127
citizenship: equality versus difference dilemma 62–3; revolutionary call for equality in 96; role of mothers in 98, 103; Rousseau's autonomous male citizen ideal 63, 64–5, 66; women as citizens

62–3, 66, 96, 98, 148–52; see also public sphere
civilization 109, 116–17, 129; poetry and 163; result for women 132, 151; Rousseau's state of nature 64–5, 114–15, 117
cleanliness 145
clergy 116–17
co-education 9, 22–3, 77, 153n
cohabitation 10, 134
Coleridge, Samuel Taylor 1, 27
Coll, John Henry 33
Colley, Linda 37–8, 65–7, 98
colonialism 69, 70
commerce/commercialism: anti-commercialism 77–9; as career for women 150–1; Imlay's career 25, 26, 68
"Commonwealthman" ideal 68
Condorcet, Marquis de 96, 102n
conduct books 9, 17, 109, 141–2, 144, 150n, 156n; Rights of Woman as 89
conservatives condemn MW 33–4, 42, 44–7, 98
constancy see infidelity
consumerism 67–8, 78–9
coquetry 22, 105, 120, 139
Corday, Charlotte 97
corruption: feminine 78–9, 127; through power 117
Craciun, Adriana 82–4
Critical Review 85, 86n
cruelty 154
cunning as female trait 105, 112, 117, 120, 126, 159

Dacier, Anne 55
Davies, Emily 58n
Day, Thomas 127n
decorum 142; see also modesty
Defence of the Character and Conduct of the Late Mary Wollstonecraft Godwin (Anon.) 1, 52–3
Delilah (Biblical figure) 20
democracy 79–80
Denmark: engaged couples 74
dependency: encouraged in girls 127–8; engineered by men 76, 77; see also weakness of women
despotism 116, 117, 119, 126, 150, 152
disgusting behaviour of women 145, 146–7

Dissenters 41, 71–2
domestic duties 39, 68, 104; empowering
    role 121; MW's emphasis on 35, 58, 59;
    role for citizenship 63, 66, 98; Rousseau
    on 20–1; Talleyrand recommends 95;
    see also private sphere
domestic violence 57n, 80–2, 122, 154;
    MW's experience of 7, 81
dualism 40–1
duties and rights 58, 98, 102, 104, 113–14,
    149, 159–60; see also domestic duties

economic independence for women 8, 97–8
Edgeworth, Maria 88
education: calls for co-education 9, 22–3,
    77, 153n; equal access to education 98,
    103, 109, 133, 152–4, 161; lack of
    subordinates and enfeebles women 96,
    109, 111–12, 130–1, 133, 161; limited
    prospects for women after 151; and
    motherhood 66, 98, 103, 111; MW
    establishes schools 8, 13; MW's criteria
    for elementary day schools 153–4;
    resistance to education for women 85n,
    95, 102n, 154; Rights of Woman viewed
    as treatise on female education 33, 34,
    39, 40, 58, 59, 95; Rousseau on 9–10,
    17–22, 95, 102n, 133, 139; sex education
    144–5; Talleyrand on female education
    95, 102n, 153n; vocational classes 154
effeminacy: in French character 73, 74,
    102–3; undesirable trait in men 77, 79,
    80; see also femininity
Eisenstein, Zillah 64
elegance 162
Eliot, George 35
Ellis, Havelock 35
emotions 27, 91; see also passions;
    sensibility
empiricism 163–4
English Republic 34, 55–6
English Review 85
Enlightenment 72; see also reason
envy 51–2
Eon, Charles de Beaumont, Chevalier de
    138n
equality issues: equality versus difference
    62–3; inequality fosters tyranny 104;
    mental and spiritual equality 47, 48–9,
    89, 96, 112, 155, 156; MW on 37, 83–4,

102–5, 109–10; parodied 40–1, 46,
    153n; in revolutionary France 96, 102,
    103–5; Rousseau on 18–22, 138–41
European Magazine 85
Eve 23n, 117–18
evil 72, 114–15, 118, 162
exercise: for children 127–8, 153–4, 162;
    for female physical strength 58–9, 84, 98,
    133, 141
experience 95–6, 113
extra-marital relationships 134–5

fallen women 134–5
familiarity between women 145
family: MW on woman's role 66; Rousseau
    on woman's role 20–1
fancy see imagination
fashion: for feminine weakness 128;
    feminine weakness for 78–9, 164
fatherhood: MW on 105, 152; Rousseau on
    20–1
Fawcett, Millicent Garrett 35, 58–9
feelings see emotions; passions; sensibility
femininity: corrupted by commercial desires
    78–9; encouraged by men as form of
    subordination 110–12; in equal society
    105; in French character 73, 74, 102–3;
    gendered discourse of Rights of Woman
    88–9, 95, 123; imagination as trait of 37,
    161; immodesty between women 77,
    145; MW's condemnation of 36–7, 77,
    78–9, 83, 110–12; MW's perceived
    exaltation of 59; and private sphere 65;
    Rousseau on female nature 20, 22, 65,
    66, 120–1, 126, 138–41; see also
    effeminacy; weakness of women; women
feminism/feminist movement: attacks on
    44–6, 55; on cruelty 154n; equality
    versus difference dilemma 62–3; influence
    of MW on development of 34–7, 56–7,
    59–60, 76; of MW 3, 88–9, 96; responses
    to Rights of Woman 62–5, 75–7, 88–9,
    98; sexual impropriety associated with
    33–4, 56–7; view of women in Islam
    109n
Feminist Studies 59–60
Ferguson, Moira 69–71
fiction: MW on 68, 86–8, 111, 156–8, 161
flower imagery 24, 41, 109, 130–1, 133
footbinding in China 127

Fordyce, James 9, 17, 79, 96, 141–2, 150*n*
France: Constitution (1791) 103–4, 105; national character 10, 73–4, 102–3, 139; sexual mores in 103, 139, 146; *see also* French Revolution
freedom: Aristotelian view 40–1
French feminism 36–7, 62
French Revolution 10, 60, 70, 74, 85, 89; women of 96–7
friendship: in marriage 121, 136, 146, 159; MW's friendship with Fanny Blood 7–8, 12
Fuller, Margaret 35
Fuseli, Henry 8, 10, 42, 43, 45–6, 47, 54, 82

Gatens, Moira 36
gender: and character 73–4; and education 9–10, 23; equality versus difference dilemma 62–3; gendered discourse of *Rights of Woman* 88–9, 95, 123; Macaulay on nature of women 22–3; Rousseau on balance of power in sexes 18–22, 138–41; *see also* separate spheres ideology; sex differences
General Magazine 84–5, 86*n*
genius: Grant on 48–9; of MW 49–50, 60, 86*n*; MW on 90–1, 114, 125–6, 162, 164; Rousseau on 48; as standard for MW 87
genres in women's writing 89
Gentleman's Magazine 85, 86*n*
gentleness in women 122–3
Georgiana, Duchess of Devonshire 66
"Girl of the Period" critique 34–5, 55
gluttony 146
go-away-closer phenomenon 82
God: and evil 72, 114–15, 121, 162–3; gentleness of 122; MW's religious faith 71–3, 96, 129, 162–3
Godwin, William 1, 2, 16, 24; *Memoirs of the Author* 11, 15, 33, 42–4, 71, 84; *Memoirs* reviewed 46–7, 85–6; MW's letter to 28–9; MW's relationship with and marriage to 10–11, 28, 29–30, 61; posthumous publication of MW's work 10, 15, 42, 44*n*, 85, 98
Goethe, Johann Wolfgang von: *Sorrows of Young Werther* 7–8, 42, 43, 86*n*
Goldman, Emma 34, 59–60
Gouges, Olympe de 96, 97, 102*n*

governesses 151; MW's career as 8
government: representation for women 35, 39, 97, 149–50
Graham, Catharine Macaulay *see* Macaulay Graham, Catharine
Grant, Anne MacVicar 2, 37, **48–9**, 97
Greek architecture 164
Gregory, John 9, 17, 79, 96, 121, 142
Guest, Harriet **77–9**

happiness 90–1, 137, 162–3; *see also* pleasure
harem discourse 71, 109*n*, 126*n*, 136
Hartley, David 143*n*
Hays, Mary 11, 78; on female weakness 45; "Memoirs of Emma Courtney" 49; "Memoirs of Mary Wollstonecraft" 1, **49–50**; MW on vain humility of 25; MW's letter to **24–5**
Héloïse 138*n*
Hercules 20
Hesiod 26*n*, 114*n*
historicism in feminism 37
Homer 39*n*
hospital visiting as occupation 161
human nature 113–17
human rights: discourse on 9, 96; for men 103–4
Hymen 136

ignorance 117, 128, 133, 155, 162
imagination 25, 26, 27, 90–1, 99; as feminine trait 37, 161; on MW's 46; romanticizes love 137; and sensibility 87–8, 91; and sublime 164; of women 161
Imlay, Fanny 10, 15, 25, 26, 28, 85
Imlay, Gilbert 8; MW's letters to **25–8**, 68–9, 82, 86*n*, 90; MW's relationship with 10, 11, 14–15, 25–8, 29, 74, 85; MW's relationship with: commentary on 42–4, 52–3, 60–1, 82
immortality 61, 130, 131, 134, 137
improvement: on nature 115; reason empowers 130
Inchbald, Elizabeth 29
indecency 162; *see also* modesty
independence for women 8, 97–8, 102, 149, 150–1
individualism 63–5, 75–6

indolence 117, 146–7, 156, 161
infidelity: MW on 104, 105, 122, 162; Rousseau on 20–1; *see also* adultery
innocence 117, 118, 128
Islam 109, 118, 123
Islington school 8, 13

Janes, Regina M. **84–6**
jealousy 162
Johnson, Claudia 38, **79–80**
Johnson, Joseph 10, 24, 41, 50, 84; publishes MW's early works 8–9, 14, 29; publishes *Rights of Woman* 2; *see also* *Analytical Review*
Johnson, Samuel 25, 134

Kant, Immanuel 164
Kaplan, Cora 3, 36, 75, **76–7**, 83
Kelly, Gary **88–9**, 95
Kingsborough, Lord and Lady 8
knowledge: civilizing effects 133; corruption through 118; equality in 126; from reading 156; little goes a long way for women 141, 142
Knowles, John 54
Knox, Vicesimus 162

language of passion in fiction 158
"left-handed" marriage 134
Leibnitz, Gottfried Wilhelm 135
leisured classes 8, 55, 78–9, 98, 110; employment for women of 161; language of 158; *see also* aristocracy; middle classes
liberal democracy 79–80
liberal individualism 63–5, 75–6
libertinism 91, 147–8; *see also* lust; sexuality
liberty: dangers of 70, 114, 140; mother of virtue 124; in state of nature 64
Linton, Eliza Lynn 34, **55–6**
Linton, William 55
literacy 67–8
Literary Magazine 33, 84–5
literary tradition: *Rights of Woman* in 84–91
Littelton, Lord 25
Locke, John 95, 143*n*
London University: admission of women 58
Lorch, Jennifer 3

love 121–2, 136–7, 146, 161–2; MW on her own and Imlay's 27–8; women as objects of 161
lust 102, 138, 146–8, 158–9, 161, 162; *see also* sexuality
luxury 78, 117, 128, 146

Macaulay Graham, Catharine 2, 9, 71, 96, 138*n*; on footbinding 127*n*; *Letters on Education* 9, **22–3**, 70, 115*n*, 154*n*; MW on merits of 142–3; MW's letter to **23–4**
McGann, Jerome 37
Magdalen Hospital, London 135
man-midwifery 150, 155*n*
manners 119, 122, 158–9; of French 102–3
marriage 135–6, 158–9; in equal and unequal society 104–5, 111–12; inappropriateness of passion in 121–2, 136, 146, 159; indolence in 146–7, 156; left-handed marriage 134; MW accepts necessity of 10–11, 14–15, 29–30; MW perceived emphasis on 59; MW's early impressions of 7, 8; MW's rejection of 1–2, 10, 40, 53; as prostitution 97–8, 135*n*, 150*n*; Rousseau on fidelity in 20–1; *see also* adultery; cohabitation; infidelity
Martineau, Harriet 35, **56–7**, 58
Marxist feminism 3, 36
masculinity: Burke's discourse of 164*n*; gendered discourse of *Rights of Woman* 88–9, 95, 123; MW's admiration of 22–3, 37, 77, 79, 80, 83, 110, 112; and public sphere 65, 80; as quality in MW's writing 49, 50, 86*n*, 111*n*; superior physical strength of male 83–4; women discouraged from aspiring to 123
masturbation 145
medicine: role of women in 150; women's need for knowledge of 155
mental equality 47, 48–9, 112, 155, 156
middle classes 8, 98; critiques of 55, 78–9, 110; sensibility in 67, 69
midwifery 150, 155
militarism 116, 119
Mill, John Stuart 35, 57
Milton, John 72*n*, 117–18, 120*n*, 122, 125–6, 129, 137, 158*n*
mind/body dualism 40–1
Mirabeau, Comte de 85*n*
misogyny of MW 76, 77, 78, 98

modesty: of equal wife 105; immodesty between women 77, 144–6; lacking in France 103, 139, 146; MW on 159; Rousseau on conflict in women 139–40

monarchy 114, 116–17, 124–5; ostentation of 150; role of females 66; subjugation through feminization 80

Monboddo, James Burnett, Lord 130*n*

Monthly Magazine 85

Monthly Mirror 86*n*

Monthly Review 33, 39–40, 84–5

morality: of armed forces 116; condemnation of MW's conduct 10–11, 29, 33, 36, 42, 44–7, 51–2, 53, 85–6, 145*n*; engaged couples in Denmark 74; immodesty between women 77, 144–6; immorality of feminine nature 77, 132; liberal atmosphere in France 74, 102–3, 139, 146; marriage and extra-marital relationships 134–5; MW's moral thesis 90–1, 104, 116, 155; and reading habits 157–8; Rousseau on sex differences 18, 20–1; women writing on politics denounced 150*n*; *see also* modesty; sexuality

More, Hannah 55, 67; MW compared to 34, 44, 77–8

morganatic marriage 134*n*

motherhood: and citizenship 98, 103; compromises equality 49; and education 66, 98, 103, 111, 154, 155; effect of infidelity on 122; effect of lasciviousness on 147–8; in equal society 105; MW's emphasis on 35, 59, 98, 105, 146, 151–2; political role 66; "republican motherhood" 98, 103*n*, 136*n*; Rousseau on mother's role 20–1, 140

Mott, Lucretia 35–6

Myers, Mitzi 77, **86–8**, 90

Napoleonic wars 66–7

nationalism: and character 73–4; *see also* patriotism

nature: MW on superiority of male in 83–4; natural hierarchies 41*n*; Rousseau on balance of sexual power in 18–22, 138–41; Rousseau on natural man 64–5, 114, 115; Rousseau on natural woman 20, 22, 65, 66, 120–1, 126, 138–41;

Rousseau's state of nature 64–5, 114–15, 117

needlework 39

nervous complaints 23, 161

New Annual Register 33, 85

New Quarterly Magazine **57–8**

New York Magazine 84–5

Newington Green school 8, 13, 71

Newton, Sir Isaac 124

Norton, Caroline 57*n*

novels: MW on 68, 86–8, 111, 156–8, 161

obedience of women 117, 118, 120, 135, 140, 151

Odysseus 39*n*

Oliphant, Margaret 35, 36

Omphale 20

Opie, Amelia Alderson 11, 15; MW's letter to **29–30**

Opie, John: portrait of MW ii *illus*, 55

Otaheite (Tahiti) 161

Ovid 53*n*

Owen, Robert 36

Oxford University: admission of women 58

Paine, Thomas 2, 9, 40, 46, 96

Pandora 26*n*, 114

parental affection 152; *see also* fatherhood; motherhood

parliament: representation for women 35, 39, 97, 149–50

passions: fickleness of women's 132–3; of genius 49–50; inappropriate in marriage 121–2, 136, 146, 159; language of romantic fiction 158; MW and 49–50, 56, 83; and reason 161; *see also* sensibility; sexuality

passivity of women 75–6, 81, 123–4

Pateman, Carole 37, 38, **62–3**, 98

patriarchal society: citizenship in 62–3; *Rights of Woman* discourse in 89

patriotism 66–7, 68, 103, 114; *see also* nationalism

Paul, Charles Kegan 36

Penelope 39*n*

Pennell, Elizabeth 36

perfection 163

personal hygiene 145

philosophy: *Rights of Woman* as philosophical work 89, 123; women and 46, 49

physical abuse of women 57*n*, 80–2, 122, 154; MW's experience of 7, 81

physical strength: exercise for children 127–8, 153–4, 162; exercise for women 58–9, 84, 98, 133, 141; of genius 125–6; importance of 82–4, 125–6; *see also* weakness of women

piety 141

Piozzi, Hester Lynch 142*n*

pleasure 91, 136, 137; *see also* happiness

poetry: MW on 87, 163

political activity of women: in France 103*n*; motherhood as obstacle to 49; parliamentary representation 35, 39, 97, 149–50; resistance to 34, 39, 48; separate-spheres ideology 66–7; study of politics 150; women as passive bystanders 75; *see also* citizenship; public sphere

political theory of MW 62–74, 79–80, 97, 112–17, 149–50

Polwhele, Richard 33, 144*n*; *The Unsex'd Females* 2, 34, **44–6**

polygamy 134

poor: education for 133

Poovey, Mary 3, 36, 38, **75–6**, 83

Pope, Alexander 23, 72*n*, 136

Poston, Carol **80–2**

Price, Rev. Richard 8, 14, 71–2

Priestley, Joseph 25, 41, 125, 143*n*

primogeniture 7

private sphere 64, 65–6, 96, 104, 158; *see also* domestic duties

professions: education for 154; effect on moral character 57, 116; and independence for women 97, 150–1

Prometheus myth 26*n*, 90, 114*n*

promiscuity: associated with early feminism 33–4; and co-education 153*n*

prostitution 105, 134–5, 150–1; marriage as 97–8, 135*n*, 150*n*

providence 23, 71, 72

public sphere 34, 64, 66–7, 68, 77, 158; *see also* citizenship; political activity of women

publishing: sexual dynamics of 24

punishments and rewards 162

radicalism 34, 84

rape: Rousseau on 19

rationalism *see* reason

reading: and opinion 165; women's fiction 68, 86–8, 111, 156–8

reason 3, 104, 124; in conflict with sensibility 67–9, 76, 91, 133, 140; distinguishes human from nonhuman 113, 115, 129, 130; incompatibility with imagination 163–4; as masculine property 37, 77, 133, 134, 160; and passions 161; as property of woman 130–1; Rousseau denies to women 139; as spiritual guide 71–2, 96

religion 71–3, 96, 141, 162–3; MW on clergy 116

representation for women 35, 39, 97, 149–50

"republican motherhood" 98, 103*n*, 136*n*

republicanism/republican theories 79–80, 95, 98, 126*n*

resistance 18, 69, 70, 81

rewards and punishments 162

Richardson, Samuel 135

rights: of animals 40; of children 40; and duties 58, 98, 102, 104, 113–14, 149, 159–60; of man 103–4; voting rights 150*n*

Robinson, Daniel **71–3**

Robinson, Mary 11, **47**, 49, 53, 83, 97, 162*n*

Roland, Madame 97

romantic fiction 68, 86, 87–8, 111, 156–8, 161

Romanticism: and imagination 26*n*, 27, 37, 90–1, 99; literature of 1; and Prometheus myth 114*n*; reception of *Rights of Woman* 39–53; spirit of 3

Roscoe, William 9, 14

Rousseau, Jean-Jacques 2, 79, 137; *amour-propre/amour de soi même* 18–19, 152*n*; autonomous male citizen ideal 63, 64–5, 66; on education 9–10, 17–22, 95, 102*n*, 133, 139; *Emile, or On Education* 9–10, **17–22**, 48, 72, 120, 138–41; as father 20*n*; on genius 48; on liberty 70; MW critiques 10, 17, 72, 73, 89, 138–41; MW's affinity with 9–10, 17, 26, 120; on nature and role of women 18–22, 45*n*, 66, 76, 118, 120–1, 126, 138–41, 148;

and separate spheres ideology 95, 97, 98;
on sex differences 18–22, 76, 96, 138–41
Rowan, Archibald Hamilton 52

sailors 162
Samson 20
San Domingo Revolution 70, 96
Sapiro, Virginia 38, 63–5, 98
Sappho 53, 138*n*
Schreiner, Olive 35
seduction 134–5
self: woman's duty to 98
self-control 75–6
self-denial 139–40, 144
self-esteem (*amour de soi-même*) 18–19,
152*n*
self-love (*amour propre*) 18–19, 114, 152,
165
sense *see* reason
sensibility 67–9; of MW 28–9, 43, 46,
49–50, 68–9; MW on 37, 76, 87–8, 91,
127, 132–4, 140
sensualists 120, 148; *see also* sexuality
sentimentality 68, 79, 80, 154*n*; MW on
women's fiction 68, 86, 87–8, 111,
156–8, 161
separate-spheres ideology 64, 65–7, 95, 97,
98
Seward, Anna 33
sex differences 39–40, 79–80, 117–30,
130–1; dilemma for equality 62–3;
imagination and reason 37, 77, 133, 134,
160, 161; Macaulay on 22–3, 70; in
physical strength 45*n*, 82–4, 96, 109–12,
121; Rousseau on 18–22, 76–7, 96,
138–41; *see also* equality issues;
femininity; masculinity
sexual abuse 69, 81
sexuality 3, 27, 59, 76–84, 113; depravity
146–8; engaged couples in Denmark 74;
Hays on 49; immodesty between women
77, 144–6; liberal approach in France 74,
102–3, 139, 146; male appetites 76, 77,
105, 146–8, 159, 162; MW in France 74;
MW's ambivalence towards 82, 83;
MW's reputation 10–11, 29, 36, 42,
44–5, 46–7, 51–2, 53, 84, 85–6, 145*n*;
politics of 3; promiscuity associated with
early feminism 33–4; Rousseau critiqued
on 138, 139; Rousseau on 18–20; sex

education for children 144–5; social
mores regarding marriage and extra-
marital relationships 134–5; and virtue
126, 135–6, 158; voluptuousness 102,
146–8, 158; as woman's strength 126; *see
also* infidelity; love; marriage; passions
Shakespeare, William 125
Shelley, Mary (*née* Wollstonecraft Godwin):
birth 2, 3, 11; *Frankenstein* 1, 26, 114*n*
Shelley, Percy Bysshe 3, 26, 27, 114*n*
Silliman, Benjamin 97, 141*n*
Sketch of the Rights of Boys and Girls
(parody) 153*n*
Skeys, Fanny *see* Blood, Fanny
Skeys, Hugh 13
slavery: Aristotelian view 40; MW's
discourse of 69–71, 96, 104, 114, 116,
120, 124, 128, 133, 140, 148, 153; San
Domingo Revolution 70, 96; as woman's
lot 23
Smellie, William 113*n*, 130*n*, 164
snobbery 114
social class 110, 148; implications of *Rights
of Woman* 95; snobbery 114; *see also*
aristocracy; middle classes
social contract theory 62
society: MW on 113–17
soldiers: knowledge of 119; women
compared with 68, 119, 149
solitude 114
Somerset, James 70
Sophie (*Emile* character) 18–22, 120,
138–41
souls of women 117, 118, 124, 129, 134
Southey, Robert 1
spirituality 71–3, 96
Staël, Madame de 55
state of nature (Rousseau) 64–5, 114–15,
117
Stone, John Hurford 10
strength *see* physical strength
strong women 83
style, literary 111
sublime 164
subordination of women 109–10; Barrett
Browning on 54–5; Fawcett on 58–9;
Macaulay on 22–3, 96; MW on weakness
of women 122–9, 130–2, 138–9; Mary
Robinson on mental subordination 47;
Rousseau on 18–19, 65, 96, 138–9;

slavery discourse 69–71, 96, 104, 114, 116, 120, 124, 128, 140, 148, 153; *see also* weakness of women
suffrage movement 58, 59–60; MW's influence on 36, 97
sugar 148
Sybarites 127

tabula rasa 95, 143*n*
Tahiti (Otaheite) 161
Talleyrand-Périgord, Charles Maurice de, Bishop of Autun 14, 98; on female education 85*n*, 95, 102*n*, 153*n*; MW's dedication to 73, **102–5**
taste 87, 102–3, 110–11, 162
Taylor, Thomas **40–1**, 96, 144*n*, 154*n*
theodicy 71–3, 114–15, 162
Tomalin, Claire 72
Town and Country 97
trade *see* commercialism
Trimmer, Sarah 33
trust in victims of abuse 81–2
Turkish bashaws (pashas) 126
Twiss, Francis and Frances 29
tyranny: in effeminized society 80; of parenthood 152; and physical abuse 81–2; slaves overthrow 70; in unequal society 104, 117, 119–20, 124, 148–9, 159–60; voluptuous tyrant 122

United States: MW's influence on feminism in 35–6
university education for women 58

vanity 22, 110; in Mary Hays writing 25; reasons for 105, 111
vegetarianism 115*n*, 154*n*
Vindication of the Rights of Woman, A 1, 14, **101–60**; on body and sexuality 75–84, 144–6; critiques Rousseau 10, 17, 138–41; dedication to Talleyrand **102–5**; editions 2, 36, 58, 80; as education treatise 33, 34, 39, 40, 58, 59, 95; as feminist discourse 3, 88–9, 95; "Hints" for part two 37, 87, 90, 99, 107*n*, **161–5**; inspiration for 23–4; intention of 9; language and form of 88–9; in literary tradition 84–91; parodies of 40–1, 153*n*; as philosophical work 89, 123; political and social argument in 62–74, 79–80, 97,

112–17, 149–50; as religious work 72, 96; response on publication 33–6, 39–61, 84–6, 95, 98; 20C responses to 36–8, 59–91, 98; Victorian responses to 54–9, 98
virtue 102–3, 113, 148, 162; among leisured classes 110; Dissenter view of 71–2; experience as source of 95–6; as female aspiration 21, 112, 117, 129, 148; and pleasure 137; Rousseau on 21; and sexuality 126, 135–6, 158
vocational education 154
voluptuousness 102, 146–8, 158; *see also* sexuality
voting rights 150*n*; *see also* suffrage movement

weakness of women 45*n*, 82–4, 96, 109–12, 121; encouraged by men 22, 54–5, 76, 77, 117–18, 122–4, 126, 127–9, 130–2, 138–9; as weapon 18–20, 22; *see also* physical strength; subordination of women
Wellington, Jan 10, **73–4**
Werther (Goethe hero): MW likened to 7–8, 42, 43, 86*n*
West, Jane 153*n*
Whale, John 86, **90–1**
Wheatley, Phillis 70
whips 160
Williams, Helen Maria 10
Wollstonecraft, Edward John (father) 7, 13, 42–3, 69, 81
Wollstonecraft, Eliza (sister) 8, 13, 43
Wollstonecraft, Elizabeth (*née* Dixon, mother) 7, 8, 43, 81, 82
Wollstonecraft, Everina (sister) 7, 8, 13, 43
Wollstonecraft, Mary: affectionate nature 42–4, 68–9; ahead of her time 1, 3, 34, 35, 37, 56; biographies: general 36, 71; biographies: Godwin's *Memoirs* 11, 15, 33, **42–4**, 46–7, 71, 84, 85–6; birth and family life 7, 8, 42–3, 81–2; birth of Fanny 10; birth of Mary 2, 3, 11, 15; career in education 8; career as woman of letters 8–9, 28–9, 68, 84, 86–8; death after birth of Mary 2, 3, 11, 15, 85; experimental nature 1–2, 50, 60–1; influence of life on work 7; letters 2, 10, **23–30**, 44*n*, 68–9, 81, 82, 86*n*; marriage

opportunities 29–30; marriage registered with Imlay 14–15, 29; marriage to Godwin and its significance 10–11, 15, 29–30; moral perspective and sexuality 1–2, 10, 36, 42–3, 46–7, 85–6, 145*n*; obituaries for 85; ostracision for perceived impropriety 10–11, 29, 33, 42, 51–2; passionate friendships 7–8, 12; portraits ii *illus*, xvi *illus*, 9, 34–5, 55, 86*n*; posthumous reputation 2, 11, 42, 49–50, 51–2, 84, 85–6; relationships *see* Fuseli; Godwin; Imlay; religious beliefs 33, 71–3, 96, 162–3; reputation defended 49–53; as revolutionary 39, 60, 75, 85, 95; sexuality 74, 82; suicidal thoughts 28, 82; suicide attempts 10, 11, 15, 27, 42, 43*n*, 53, 85; tragedy of life 59–60; translations 14; WORKS: *The Female Reader* 14, 41, 89; *An Historical and Moral View of the origin and progress of the French Revolution* 15, 25; *Letters Written During a Short Residence in Norway, Denmark and Sweden* 10, 15, 27, 37, 73, 74, 90; *Maria see The Wrongs of Woman below*; *Mary, A Fiction* 14, 91; "On Poetry" 37, 87; *Original Stories from Real Life* 14, 50; *Posthumous Works* 10, 15, 42, 44*n*, 85, 98; *Thoughts on the Education of Daughters* 8, 13; *A Vindication of the Rights of Men* 1, 9, 14, 23–4, 60, 69, 72, 85, 95; *The Wrongs of Woman, or Maria* 10, 15, 85, 87, 88, 97–8, 99, 107*n*, 135*n*; *see also Vindication of the Rights of Woman*

Wollstonecraft, Ned (Edward, brother) 7

Wollstonecraft Godwin, Mary *see* Shelley, Mary

"Wollstonecraft's dilemma" 62–3

women: as citizens 62–3, 66, 96, 98, 148–52; nature formed by men 117–18; passivity of 75–6, 81, 123–4; Rousseau on role in relation to men 18–22, 76, 96, 138–41; slavery discourse on 69–71, 96, 104, 120, 124, 128, 140, 148, 153; *see also* femininity; subordination of women; weakness of women

women's movement: influence of MW on 34–7, 59–60, 97–8; *see also* feminism

Woolf, Virginia 2, 35, **60–1**

Wordsworth, William 1, 27

working classes: dangers of liberty for 70; education for 133; role of women in 149

Wright, Frances 35–6

Young, Edward 135*n*

Zeus 26*n*, 114*n*